Acclaim for **JESSICA MITFORD**'s

The American Way of Death Revisited

"*The American Way of Death Revisited* has lost none of the original work's power to shock, appall, and—despite the grim subject matter—jolt the funny bone."
—*Business Week*

"Jessica Mitford was *sui generis*. . . . Even in death, Mitford continues to serve as the scourge of those who would profit obscenely from dying."
—*Portland Oregonian*

"No less startling, or entertaining, than the original."
—*The New York Times Book Review*

"The 'value added' of this edition is considerable. . . . Nobody will ever bring to [the battle against the funeral industry] the combination of irony, brio, grit and vitriol that stamped the Mitford style."
—*Los Angeles Times*

"Excellent. . . . Her revealing interviews allow unscrupulous funeral-industry honchos to dig, as it were, their own graves." —*Entertainment Weekly*

"Even in death, Jessica Mitford continues to serve as the scourge of those who would profit obscenely from the dead." —*St. Louis Post-Dispatch*

JESSICA MITFORD

The American Way of Death Revisited

Jessica Mitford—of the notorious Mitford clan—was one of the most celebrated muckraking journalists of our time. Among her books are *Daughters and Rebels*, *The Trial of Dr. Spock*, and *Poison Penmanship: The Gentle Art of Muckraking*. Until her death in 1996, she lived in Oakland, California, with her husband, the labor lawyer Robert Treuhaft.

Also by JESSICA MITFORD

Daughters and Rebels

The American Way of Death

The Trial of Dr. Spock

Kind and Usual Punishment: The Prison Business

A Fine Old Conflict

Poison Penmanship: The Gentle Art of Muckraking

Faces of Philip: A Memoir of Philip Toynbee

Grace Had an English Heart

The American Way of Birth

The American Way of Death Revisited

The American Way of Death Revisited

JESSICA MITFORD

Vintage Books

A Division of Random House, Inc.

New York

FIRST VINTAGE BOOKS EDITION, JANUARY 2000

The Library of Congress has cataloged the Knopf edition as follows:
Mitford, Jessica, 1917–1996
The American way of death revisited / by Jessica Mitford. — 1st ed.
p. cm.
ISBN 0-679-45037-8
1. Undertakers and undertaking—United States. 2. Funeral rites and
ceremonies—Economic aspects—United States.
3. Mitford, Jessica, 1917–1996, The American Way of Death.
I. Title.
HD9999.U53U554   1998
338.4'736375'0973—dc21   97-49349
CIP

Vintage ISBN: 0-679-77186-7

www.vintagebooks.com

Printed in the United States of America
10 9 8 7 6 5 4

Dedicated to Karen Leonard, Lisa Carlson,
and Father Henry Wasielewski,
who, each and all, have inherited the mantle of
Scourge of the Undertaking Industry

CONTENTS

Contents

EDITOR'S NOTE

A t a happy lunch with me early in 1995, Jessica Mitford—
"Decca" to everyone who knew her—agreed to prepare an
updated version of her classic work *The American Way of
Death*. (As she reports in her introduction to this volume, we had
worked on that book together in the early sixties, and had remained
close friends both through a number of other publishing ventures and
after our professional relationship came to an end.) A lot had
changed in the funeral trade since the first edition was published, in
1963, and not many of the changes were for the better. The plan was
to retain from the original everything that still applied and to add
new chapters as needed, such as the report on the Tiburon conference
("Not Selling"), an investigation of the new international funeral
giants ("A Global Village of the Dead"), and an account of the fail-
ures of the Federal Trade Commission in the wake of new legislation
that was written largely in reaction to the first edition of the book.
Certain material—for instance, most of the chapter on floral tributes
("The Menace of P.O.")—was excised as no longer relevant,
although I suspect that the floral deluge that followed Princess
Diana's death would have evoked some new commentary on this
subject. And, of course, a great deal of updating—particularly of
prices—was needed.

Most of this work—including the new chapters mentioned above,
as well as the introduction and the final chapter, "New Hope for the
Dead"—Decca finished before her unexpected (and mercifully swift)
death from cancer, in 1996. What remained to be done was accomplished by three people. First, there was her brilliant research and
investigative assistant, Karen Leonard, who took on increasing
responsibilities and, indeed, soon found herself drawn into the
funeral reform movement. The second crucial person was Lisa Carlson, probably the most influential figure in that movement, who
made many generous contributions to the book, not the least of
which was her extensive help with the penultimate chapter, "Pay
Now—Die Poorer," which sets out the complex realities—and booby

traps—inherent in pay-in-advance funerals. Finally, Decca's husband, Robert Treuhaft, had made a promise to her just before she died: the distinguished labor- and civil-rights lawyer, who had worked with her on many of her books, would retire from his practice and see this book through to completion. This he heroically did.

Almost until her final week, Decca was reveling in the job, bombarding me and other pals with faxes that gleefully skewered the more fatuous and/or hypocritical high jinks of the industry. She could be ruthless—savage, even—when she was on the warpath, but she never stopped laughing, which is probably why *The American Way of Death* was not only welcomed as a necessary corrective in 1963 but was so enjoyed as a piece of writing. And why it still reads so well today.

The American Way of Death Revisited is being published exactly thirty-five years after the original edition. Unfortunately, the corrective is as necessary today as it was then. Fortunately, it is being applied.

ROBERT GOTTLIEB

FOREWORD

This would normally be the place to say (as critics of the American funeral trade invariably do), "I am not, of course, speaking of the vast majority of ethical undertakers." But the vast majority of ethical undertakers is precisely the subject of this book. To be "ethical" merely means to adhere to a prevailing code of morality, in this case one devised over the years by the undertakers themselves for their own purposes. The outlook of the average undertaker, who does adhere to the code of his calling, is to me more significant than that of his shadier colleagues, who are merely small-time crooks such as may be found in any sphere of business. Scandals, although they frequently erupt (misuse by undertakers of the coroner's office to secure business, bribery of hospital personnel to "steer" cases, the illegal reuse of coffins, fraudulent double charges in welfare cases), are not typical of the trade as a whole, and therefore are not part of the subject matter of this book.

Another point often made by critics of the modern American funeral is that if there are excesses in funerary matters, the public is to blame. I am unwilling on the basis of present evidence to find the public guilty; this defendant has only recently begun to present his case.

I have not included the atypical funerals: quaint death customs still practiced by certain Indian tribes, the rites accorded Gypsy kings and queens, the New Orleans jazz funerals, the great movie and gangland funerals which had their heyday in the thirties and still occur from time to time. I have regretfully avoided these byways, intriguing though they are, for the main highway—the "average," "typical" American funerary practices, surely fully as curious as any of the customs derived from ancient folklore or modern variants.

INTRODUCTION

To trace the origins of this book: my husband, Bob Treuhaft, got fired up on the subject of the funeral industry in the mid-to-late 1950s. A labor lawyer, he represented a number of trade unions. To his annoyance, he began to notice that when the breadwinner of a union family died, the hard-fought-for death benefit, achieved often through bitter struggle and intended for the benefit of the surviving spouse and children, would end up in the pockets of an undertaker. "These people seem to know exactly how much a warehouse worker gets, and how much an office secretary," he would complain, "and they set the price of the funeral accordingly."

Bob's idea of a solution was to organize a nonprofit group which through contract with a local undertaker would obtain simple, cheap funerals for its members at a fraction of the going rate. Thus was born the Bay Area Funeral Society (BAFS), its membership running heavily to Unitarians, co-op members, university professors and other eggheads. I am sorry to say I rather mocked these good folks, calling them the Necrophilists and teasing them about their Layaway Plan. Why pick on the wretched undertakers? I asked Bob. Are we not robbed ten times more by the pharmaceutical industry, the car manufacturers, the landlord?

After reading some of the trade magazines he brought home, I saw the point. Their very names were captivating: *Casket & Sunnyside, Mortuary Management,* and my favorite, *Concept: The Journal of Creative Ideas for Cemeteries.* Once hooked, I found them to be compulsive reading, revealing a fantasy world I never knew existed: "Futurama, the casket styled for the future . . ." "The True Companion Crypt, where husband and wife may be truly together forever. . . ." Spotting an ad for "The Practical Burial Footwear Company of Columbus, Ohio," I sent for samples and was rewarded with a package containing the "Fit-a-Fut Oxford." As a leaflet explains, these oxfords were specially designed, after two years of research, to fit the deceased foot after rigor mortis sets in. They are "fit-a-fut" because they lace up at the back as well as in the front, and the soles slope downwards. (Unfortunately, our son Benji, then in high school, wore them around the house, and they soon fell apart.)

Bob suggested that I write an article about the Bay Area Funeral Society, drawing on the trade magazines and their flights of rhetoric against the BAFS, the clergy, and anybody else who favored a return to simpler funerals. I did so, in a piece entitled "St. Peter, Don't You Call Me," which was rejected by every major magazine on the ground that it was too distasteful a subject.

It eventually found a home in *Frontier,* an obscure liberal monthly published in Los Angeles, circulation 2,000, in its issue of November 1958.

Prodded by Bob, the funeral society ordered 10,000 reprints and distributed these far and wide. An immediate consequence was an invitation for me to appear on Caspar Weinberger's weekly television program, "Profile, Bay Area," in a debate on the Bay Area Funeral Society featuring a Unitarian minister and myself versus two undertakers, who proved to be wildly comic adversaries.

Developments now came thick and fast. Terrence O'Flaherty, television columnist for the *San Francisco Chronicle,* reported that the program had generated more mail to his column than any public event since *The Bad Seed* was performed at a local junior high school. Roul Tunley, a staff writer on the *Saturday Evening Post,* read O'Flaherty's column and decided that the funeral society would be a good subject for the *Post.* His article, entitled "Can You Afford to Die?," came out in June 1961. Although I was actually sadly inactive in the funeral society, Tunley depicted me as "an Oakland housewife leading the shock troops of the rebellion to undermine the funeral directors, or 'bier barons,' and topple the high cost of dying."

The public reaction was absolutely astonishing. The *Post* editor reported that more mail had come in about Tunley's piece than about any other in the magazine's history, and observed that it "seemed to have touched a sensitive nerve." Bob got a call from the Oakland postmaster: "We have hundreds of letters here addressed simply 'Jessica Treuhaft, Oakland,' giving no street or number." (They were eventually delivered. One envelope bore the stark direction "Jessica Treuhaft, Cheap Funerals, Oakland.")

Surely this spate of letters showed enough public interest in the subject to warrant consideration of a book? I wrote to Roul Tunley, urging him to expand his piece into a book. He replied that he was too busy with other assignments. "Why don't you write it?" he suggested.

Bob and I discussed this possibility. I said I would consider it only if he would help and work with me on it full time. And so it was settled.

Aside from the usual difficulties that inevitably occur (at least in my experience) in the course of writing, a crisis of huge proportions threatened to sink the whole endeavor when the book was about half finished. At the outset, I had obtained contracts from the two publishers who had taken my first book, *Hons and Rebels* (in America, *Daughters and Rebels*), published in 1960: Victor Gollancz in England, and Houghton Mifflin in the U.S., with whom I was on the friendliest terms. They had both been pleased with the outline and first chapter of the funeral book. At some point I sent them more chapters, including a detailed account of exactly what happens in the funeral director's inner sanctum, the embalming room, which is strictly off-limits to the public, and especially to the family of the deceased. Hoping to infuse this admittedly revolting subject with a touch of macabre humor, I cast the whole description in mortuary jargon (see chapter 5, "The Story of Service").

To my extreme dismay, Victor Gollancz and the editor at Houghton Mifflin with one accord demanded the excision of this passage.

From Houghton Mifflin: "We think that you make your book harder to sell by going at too much length and in too gooey detail into the process of embalming." From Gollancz: "The joke, such as it is, surely is going on far too long. I cannot imagine any publisher here wanting it."

This was devastating news. As embalming is the ultimate fate of almost all Americans, the economic base of the funeral industry, and as practiced on a mass scale a uniquely American practice, to omit a description of it was unthinkable. We considered finishing the book and reproducing it for self-publication. At this point, my brilliant agent, Candida Donadio, stepped in. She found a publisher, Robert Gottlieb of Simon & Schuster.

Thenceforward, all was plain sailing. Gottlieb, at the age of thirty something of a prodigy in the publishing world, loved the embalming chapter and made an inestimable contribution to the book as a whole.

Months before *The American Way of Death* was published, the funeral industry became aware of the work in progress, and it was not long before the trade press rounded upon me in full force. A new menace had loomed on their horizon: the Menace of Jessica Mitford. Headlines began to appear in the undertakers' journals: JESSICA MITFORD PLANS ANTI-FUNERAL BOOK, AND MITFORD DAY DRAWS CLOSER!

When *Mortuary Management* began referring to me as Jessica *tout court,* I felt I had arrived at that special pinnacle of fame where the first name only is sufficient identification, as with Zsa Zsa, Jackie, or Adlai. Greedily I gobbled up the denunciations: "the notorious Jessica Mitford"; "shocker"; "stormy petrel."

In an article headlined WHO'S AFRAID OF THE BIG, BAD BOOK? the editor of *Mortuary Management* said there was little to fear because books about "the Profession" never enjoy large sales. He knew this because his dad once wrote a book about funeral service, and although he took an ad in the *Saturday Evening Post,* it sold only three hundred copies.

My husband Bob and I were inclined to agree with his estimate; we did not anticipate a readership much beyond Unitarians, funeral society members, and other advocates of funeral reform, a relatively tiny group. Not so Bob Gottlieb. A few months before publication, he rang up to say the first printing would be 7,500. Some days later, he told us this had been increased to 15,000. Then he telephoned again: the first printing was now set at 20,000. I found this slightly worrying; "Aren't you afraid that we'll end up with a final chapter, 'Remainders To Be Seen'?" I asked him. I need not have worried. On publication day in August 1963, the book went out of stock, the first printing having been sold out.

The response was nothing short of thrilling. To my extreme pleasure, the reviewers not only lavished unstilted praise, they also got the joke. Thus the *New York Times:* "A savagely witty and well-documented exposé . . ." *New York Herald Tribune:* "Bizarre and fantastic . . . a wry account of the death business." *San Francisco Chronicle:* "Explosive. Continually absorbing. Often very funny."

Cosmopolitan: "A brilliant book . . . written so wryly it is difficult to consider it an exposé . . ." *National Guardian:* "One of the strangest and funniest things in literature . . . astonishing, but exceedingly funny." *The Reporter:* "She has the rare ability to make the macabre hilariously funny." *Denver Sunday Post:* "Sane observations and witty . . . sardonic commentary . . ."

The American Way of Death zoomed to No. 1 on the *New York Times* best-seller list, where it stayed for some weeks. CBS broadcast an hour-long documentary, "The Great American Funeral," based on the book. Major newspapers *(Miami Herald; New York Herald Tribune; Denver Post; San Francisco Chronicle; Chicago Tribune; Cleveland Plain Dealer)* published in-depth reports on funeral costs and practices in their respective communities. For a while, funerals were topic A on radio talk shows, with listeners calling in to relate their own dismal experiences at the hands of morticians. Walt Kelly and Bill Mauldin mocked the funeral industry in syndicated cartoons. Elaine May and Mike Nichols produced a televised skit on "That Was the Week That Was" starring Elaine as "your Grief Lady." TV and radio stations around the country featured debates between funeral directors and myself. Clergy of all faiths reinforced the major theme of *The American Way of Death* and denounced ostentatious, costly funerals as pagan. Membership in the nonprofit consumer-run funeral and memorial societies rose from seventeen thousand families to close to a million.

There came a delightful moment when a textbook for college students entitled *The Essential Prose* came clattering into my mailbox—an anthology, according to the editors, of "prose of the first order from the past and present." There, tucked between Plato and Sir Thomas Browne, was the very description of embalming upon which my book had almost foundered. Furthermore, as of this writing, some fifty textbook editors in the past four years alone have chosen this selfsame passage for inclusion in their anthologies. Is there a moral here for the neophyte writer in his dealing with editors?

For me, most rewarding of all was the response of the funeral industry. The trade journals reacted with furious invective, devoting reams on how to combat "the Mitford syndrome," as one put it. *Mortuary Management* was of the opinion that "actually, the danger to the equilibrium of funeral service is not in the book per se. It is in the residual use of Miss Mitford's material. . . . Newspapers, large and small, are reviewing the Mitford volume, passing and repassing its poisons among the citizenry," which I thought was a good point.

Month after month, the funeral mags fulminated against "the Mitford bomb," "the Mitford war dance," "the Mitford missile," "the Mitford blast," and "the Mitford fury." They condemned the movement for cheaper, simpler funerals as a Red plot, and found an ally in Congressman James B. Utt of Santa Ana, California. He read a two-page statement about my subversive background into the *Congressional Record.* As for the purpose of my book, "she is really striking another blow at the Christian religion. Her tirade against morticians is simply the vehicle to carry her anti-Christ attack. . . ." His statement ended with the ringing words, "I would rather place my mortal remains, alive or dead, in the hands of any American mortician than to set foot on the soil of any Communist nation." (In 1970 Mr. Utt exercised that option. His obituary in the *New York Times,* with subhead "Attacked Mitford Book," records that during his ten terms in Congress "his most newsworthy action came when he called Jessica Mitford a 'pro-communist anti-American.' ") The Utt utterance had backfired when the *New York Times* ran an editorial captioned "How Not to Read a Book." The *Times* derided Utt's "McCarthyite attack" and noted that the book had "evoked high praise from Catholic, Protestant and Jewish clergymen, as well as from reviewers and other commentators in all parts of the country," and declared that Utt's "credentials as a book critic can safely be dismissed as nil."

Nor was the subject neglected abroad. German television asked me to go on camera in a documentary they wanted to produce. "But I don't speak German." "No matter, we will send a text for you to study." They sent a camera crew as well, and so it was that I found myself reciting, *"Ein teures Begräbnis* [a costly funeral] *ist ein status symbol, wie ein luxus Auto, ein schwimming pool im Garten, oder ein weekend in Miami Beach für hundert Thaler pro Tag."*

Enjoyable though it is to look back nostalgically at the immediate aftermath of publication of *The American Way of Death,* the basic question remains: Did it result in any fundamental improvements, any alleviation of the lot of the funeral purchaser? For a while, the answer seemed to be a qualified "Yes." In 1977, fourteen years after

The American Way of Death was published, I did further research on the funeral scene for an afterword entitled "Post Mortem" to a new paperback edition. Although the average cost, nationwide, of a funeral exclusive of burial plot had risen from $750 in 1963 to $1,650, in 1977, two major developments offered some hope for those who preferred a less cluttered and expensive send-off. The Federal Trade Commission's Consumer Protection Bureau had promulgated a "trade rule" which promised to go far to protect the unwary funeral buyer in his dealings with undertakers. Cremation had almost doubled in thirteen years; seeing the potential profitability in this trend, an enterprising businessman founded the Neptune Society, a for-profit direct-cremation venture that enjoyed immediate success and soon attracted imitators throughout the country.

However, more recent changes on the funeral front should go far to dispel any feeling of complacency on the part of consumers. Cremation, once the best hope for a low-cost, simple getaway, has become increasingly expensive; furthermore, morticians are fast developing techniques for upgrading this procedure into a full-fig funeral. The Federal Trade Commission's much heralded trade rule has huge loopholes. Most sinister of all is the emergence over the last fifteen years of monopoly ownership of hitherto independent mortuaries and cemeteries.

These developments are the main reason for this updated version of *The American Way of Death*.

The American Way of Death Revisited

1

Not Selling

When funeral directors have taxed me—which they have, and not infrequently—with being beastly about them in my book, I can affirm in good conscience that there is hardly an unkind word about them. In fact, the book is almost entirely given over to expounding *their* point of view. It is chock a block with their Wise Sayings, observations, exhortations, and philosophical reflections culled from funeral trade magazines and interviews with individual funeral directors and official spokesmen.

I did mention that "like every other successful salesman, the funeral salesman must first and foremost believe in himself and his product" (pages 151–52), and that "they long to be worthy of high regard, to be liked and understood, a most human longing. . . . Merchants of a rather grubby order, preying on the grief, remorse, and guilt of survivors, or trained professional men with high standards of ethical conduct? The funeral men really would vastly prefer to fit the latter category" (page 155).

To what extent, if any, has their outlook changed over the decades? I had a rare opportunity to observe a representative cross section of the industry in action when to my astonished delight I was invited by Ron Hast, editor of *Mortuary Management,* to be a featured speaker at a two-day Funeral Service Seminar to take place in October 1995 in Tiburon, California. "That's like Ralph Nader being invited to address General Motors!" a friend said. For me, the anticipation was akin to that felt by a five-year-old promised a trip to Disneyland, or a teenager offered a bit part in a Hollywood movie.

The reality did not disappoint. Tiburon is in Marin County, which, aside from being one of the richest communities in the country, has a cremation rate of about three times that of the national average. And thereby hangs a tale; for while the seminar topics could have fit handily into any trade-meeting agenda—"Maintaining an Effective Workforce," "Responding to Community Trends," "Better Public Relations," etc.—the subtext of many a speech was how to extract maximum profit from cremation.

We gathered in the Tiburon Lodge meeting hall overlooking a huge swimming pool, a congenial WASPish crowd consisting of forty-four funeral directors from around the country, five presidents of casket companies, a few insurance men, the president of Dinair Airbrush Systems, and various spouses.

Welcoming the group, our host—Ron Hast—glumly mentioned that there had been plenty of protest about my presence at the seminar, not the least of which was a state funeral directors' association executive's dire threat to have his members cancel their subscriptions to *Mortuary Management*.

The audience was soon put at ease by the first speaker, perhaps appropriately from the world of big business: John Baker, spry young former manager of a United Airlines subsidiary with a staff of one thousand, responsible for all employee programs. His subject: "How to Maintain an Effective Workforce," which he attacked *con brio*, with much folksy banter and down-home humor. His first question to the audience established the tone: "Who's minding the store when you're away?" Someone answered, "My wife." "Are you sure you can trust her?" Gales of laughter. And: "Be sure to chitchat with your customer." "But *our* customers don't talk!" quipped a casket manufacturer to much hilarity.

The rest of his speech was unexceptional, about a Motivation Study he had conducted to find out what employees value most about their jobs. He assured us that job security, wages, and fringe benefits came far down on the list. First and foremost were Appreciation, Inclusion, Being Part of a Team. "People want to be touched, loved, hugged," said Mr. Baker. "Lots of touchy-feely! You can buy toy dinosaurs, three for 99 cents—give one to a worthy employee! Put his name in the firm newsletter! Give them balloons—people are mad for it! Invite them to a staff meeting. . . ."

Our next speaker, Tom Fisher, was a man of many parts: regular feature writer for *Mortuary Management*, owner-director of a North

Dakota funeral home, and, as we learned from his opening remarks, a longtime, much admired radio and TV personality in his home state. "I'm known as Dakota Tom," he told us.

Speaking in the sonorous tones of his calling, he evinced a poignant nostalgia for past glories: "My vocation in funeral services began at a time when the Golden Age of this profession was coming to an end," he said. "Funeral practitioners who brought sophistication, expansion and acceptance of mortuary services, goods, and equipment to the national marketplace were no more. With their passing, the onset of a professional menopause took place. Isolationism, self-protective insulation from outside forces—these were the attitudes encouraged by industry leadership."

As an Outside Force, I shifted uncomfortably in my chair at the thought of having caused a professional menopause. But Dakota Tom now launched into his major theme: the lessons he had learned from his radio and TV career. "Basically, this gave me a unique opportunity. The rewards were immeasurable in terms of experience because radio/television accorded me the chance to appreciate the full extent of the power of media image-making. Here is the point I make to you. We, as funeral directors and suppliers, have all kinds of problems on our respective plates these days, but I am here to tell you the greatest of these is based in our lack of *identity* and *image*. The public we serve—those consumers we market—aren't buying into our programming. When we witness a high-profile funeral on television, it warms our hearts. Those occasions are not frequent enough in their occurrence to build consumer image."

The solution, he believes, is for funeral directors and suppliers to "scrap the present inefficient marketing methods," pool their resources, and produce fifteen- to thirty-second commercials which "could be delivered by a respected, recognized spokesperson such as a Lloyd Bridges type." The commercials would "affirm the personality of the industry. They should speak of memorialization, the reason for American funeral service. We could finally become the *professionals* we want to be and should be." Ideal network programs for these commercials would be "Today," "Good Morning America," and "Regis and Kathie Lee": "We should target the 18-to-25-year-olds. Remember, they are the ones who will be making arrangements for their parents. This is a passionate cause for me. . . ."

His peroration: "Funeral service may be listing a bit under the strain of too much undue criticism. But I don't think we have anyone to blame for that but ourselves. We don't have to apologize to consumers, to critics or to anyone else. . . .

"When *The American Way of Death* became a best-seller, funeral service went on a diet from which it never recovered. She was trying to tell us we should do something positive about ourselves. We have nothing to apologize for."

Next up, the wondrously named Enoch Glascock offered what he described as "an odyssey." Graduating from mortuary school at the age of twenty-three, his first job was in Greenwood Park, San Diego. "It's the Forest Lawn of San Diego," he told us, with three crematoria on the premises. But its selling methods were hopelessly wrong. People would ask for cremation—and there was stiff competition among the staff as to how quickly they could get rid of a cremation family. Some employees bragged that they could do it in twelve minutes! "That wasn't right," said Mr. Glascock. "I started talking with the cremation families, explaining their many options. When they realized the possibilities, some wanted the deceased present for the service. Some found it of value to purchase a cremation casket.

"As we went forward, management asked me to meet with all the cremation families. We only had two urns, tucked away on a shelf. I built an urn display and got a rental casket. We had a beautiful statue of Christ near the display, and niches by a babbling brook—those sold like hotcakes! We taught the rest of the staff these techniques. Families are served when there are options. But it's tragically wrong to *sell* anything," Mr. Glascock emphasized. "We go for *informed buying* choices."

Mr. Glascock's next job was with Pierce Brothers in Los Angeles. By then he had become an expert in the cremation business, and his new employer sought his advice on developing a cremation market. "Pierce did very few cremations, although they had the first crematory in Los Angeles. They just weren't doing it right." His first step was to conduct a community survey in which respondents were asked three questions: (1) Do you know the name Pierce? Many answered "Yes," as Pierce had high name recognition in the area. (2) What do you know about cremation—can you have a traditional funeral with cremation? Most people answered "No" to that. (3)

What does one do with the ashes? Almost everyone thought that ashes should be scattered.

The last two answers showed where the trouble lay—and pointed to the solution. "I'd spend at least an hour with the cremation family, and I'd come out with an urn, a memorial plaque, flowers."

Over the years, Mr. Glascock continued to perfect his methods. "We came up with '$495 Forever Cremation,' although this $495 didn't last forever," he told us. (Too true. Checking later with Pierce Brothers, I learned that the rock-bottom price in 1995 was $728.) He listed Pierce Brothers under "Cremation" in the Yellow Pages and in the obit pages of the newspapers. He put the emphasis on urns; at that time, the urns were too small, so he arranged for bigger ones.

Further outlining his strategy, he explained, "I welcome the family as I would guests to my own home. I offer the rest room, soda, hospitality. Today, I'd come out with embalming, dressing, visitation. At the end of the arrangements conference, we hold hands, say a prayer, have coffee. I'm a tour guide! We are starting to see more memorialization with cremation. We must *all* be tour guides."

He gives the family the vital statistics form and tells them he will obtain the death certificate. "I say that we are required to show them a price list. So I give them the price list and tell them I'm leaving them to read it; go out of the room for about five minutes, or as long as needed to smoke a cigarette. I ask if they have any questions. We don't accept cash—we take checks or credit cards. We don't do accounts receivable." And when it's all over, "we send a card and a little tree."

He left us with a final anecdote: "A family came from Pacific Palisades. Later, we heard from the daughter, who told me, 'You took care of our mother. We had discussed your firm among others. I want to share a thought: we almost didn't use you, your prices were so *low*. But then we talked with you and your staff multiple times and concluded you are 'Our Sort of People.'"

As introduced in the program notes, Ron Hast "created the Casket Airtray, and presented it to funeral service in May of 1960—a design that continues unchanged." (There is a color photo of "The Air Casketray Combination" and the "Original Casket Airtray" on the back of *Mortuary Management* under the headline FRATERNAL TWINS. They are cardboard shipping boxes, each in a wooden tray fitted for the purpose.) Publisher of *Mortuary Management, Funeral Monitor,* and *Mortuary Science Monitor,* he is also part owner of Abbot & Hast funeral homes. His topic for the seminar: "Easy, Low-Cost Methods of Public Relations."

For starters, how to achieve name recognition? One funeral home gives turkeys at Thanksgiving and Christmas to deserving families—that is, to doctors, hospital executives, and others in a position to steer cases their way. (I remember in the dim past being told by a physician friend of receiving such gifts; his only complaint was that the turkey was delivered in a hearse, which he felt caused his patients some uneasiness.)

Ron Hast suggested that there are "more subtle ways of building real strength in your community. The important factor is to give something which allows everyone to participate.

"For example, apples cost 39 cents a pound with a discount by the case. You could buy ten cases at Lucky's and make up packages of these with enough apples for everybody to get one. You could give a package to the employees of the local police station with a card saying, 'We appreciate your fine service, with thanks from XYZ Chapel.' Then—the officer on the next death call will remember XYZ! It's cheap and easy. Take some to the ambulance service, the nurses' lounge, the city health department—with a card, 'Thanks for your good service.' It's cheap, it goes right to the heart of people in a position to remember your name. This concept *works.*"

Then there is that all-important matter of gaining patronage via the clergy. For this, Mr. Hast hit on the simple and highly effective scheme of having a photo taken of each local church. He showed samples of these, which cost 80 cents apiece. "We give hundreds of these to the minister, who can sell them to the parishioners for $10 apiece, thus raising $1,000 for the church fund," he explained.

There was more to come. The Hast mortuary hired students for an hour or so after school to do odd jobs around the premises. Mr. Hast estimates that each student brings in an average of two cases a year.

Lastly—"*System.* Remember the word System." Too many people, he explained, find it difficult to write letters; they keep putting it off, the moment passes, the letter never gets written. To overcome this obstacle, one can get five hundred cards and envelopes inscribed with the name of the sender for $100. He flourished some sample cards. "Send one to the lady at Kaiser who referred a death, and simply write on it, 'The family appreciated your kindness to them.' "

The brothers Kevin and Mark Waterston titled their talk "Niche Marketing," a double entendre for those attuned to mortuary-speak; a niche is a repository for cremation ashes but also a specific area of commerce, geddit? The Waterston Funeral Home in Minneapolis was started by their father, a "traditional" funeral director, Ron Hast told us in his introduction; but Kevin and Mark are very *non*traditional. "They operate out of one building that will serve more than 2,000 a year, over five percent of all the deaths in Minnesota. They are true marketers," he said. "They have a pre-need backlog of more than 20,000. And in the last several years they've served more than 1,000 new families each year."

Like Tom Fisher, the brothers see "*identity* as the major problem in funeral service." They learned much from the books *Marketing Warfare* and *Bottom-up Marketing* by Jack Trout and Al Ries, which led them to establish a cremation marketing "niche" in Minnesota. "We don't treat cremation as a stepchild, we treat all families the same," said Mark Waterston. "We put the *service* into cremation. Other funeral homes don't do this. It's strictly a volume-type operation." They are also devoted believers in the power of advertising. "We spend $200,000 on advertising. If you want to get into my niche, can you top $75,000 in mailing brochures?"

Aside from the set speeches, there were a couple of early morning treats before the regular meeting got under way.

First of these was a "60 Minutes" documentary dated December 20, 1980, on the subject of the Neptune Society. The video shows Colonel Denning, known as Colonel Cinders (now on his ninth wife, we are told), proclaiming on camera that in eight years he has saved the public $40 million by providing cremations for $400. Much scornful comment from the assemblage, as the rock-bottom minimum offered by Neptune has risen in fifteen years to over $1,000.

Of greater interest was the live demonstration by Dina Ousley, luscious blond president of Dinair Airbrush Systems, of her maquillage as applied to corpses. Dinair offers a range of products to actors on stage or screen, plus a "Fantasy Kit" and "Theme Park & Large Event Systems" with spray makeup in turquoise, black, and white plus glitter. Their price list offers a large variety of stencils, including stars, whales, skeletons, skulls and crossbones. . . .

An appreciative audience clustered round as Ms. Ousley deftly sprayed the face of Max Carroll, owner of a Stockton funeral parlor standing in (or rather lying in) for the cadaver. Later, she told me something of her recent successes in progressing from show biz to mortuary work. "I've had a wonderful response on the Internet," she said. "I've sold to mortuaries from Ireland to Argentina, and was at the National Funeral Directors Association annual meeting in Florida this year. Rose Hills in Whittier, California, bought three systems. They're big business—buried a hundred in one day!"

The "Glamour Kit" consists of a compressor, airbrush hose, cleaner, holder, and makeup in a tote case. "It's the ultimate camouflage, a technique comparable to pointillism in art," she said. An important feature is its use after the embalmer has completed restorative work on an accident case, in which replacements are used to repair the injured face. "The airbrush can create little frown lines, wrinkles, crow's-feet, to give a more natural look."

Once the mortician has acquired the system, which sells for $850, the cost per customer is minimal; the makeup bottles cost $15.75, each containing up to forty applications. "We have a portable system in a little carrying case that can be taken to a church or other site of the funeral."

Ms. Ousley thinks there would be much less demand for direct cremation if "people didn't look so dead—if they looked more alive. People choose cremation with no viewing because the body didn't look good before my method was in use." She told me that a recent survey showed that 75 percent of mortuary customers are unhappy with the appearance of the deceased. "I want to help them grieve properly. I myself want to look good leaving here! I just think it helps."

As for my part, I was the last speaker, billed in the program as having had "a profound impact on the changes experienced in postdeath-care services." Ron Hast told the audience that "she will share her insights about funeral service," so I shared away, much to the displeasure of some of my listeners.

First, I gave them a rundown on the origins of *The American Way of Death*—how I came to write the book, as described in the introduction to the present revised volume. Next, I quoted from some of the reviews that appeared when the book was first published: the favorable ones from a dozen mainstream newspapers and magazines, followed by the unforgettable fulminations of the funeral trade press inveighing against "the notorious Jessica Mitford," "the Mitford blast," "the Mitford missile." But the main point, and the reason I had been invited to speak, was a preview of the forthcoming revised *American Way of Death,* based on recent developments in the death industries such as huge price increases, ingenious methods of extracting the maximum from cremation customers, and monopolization of the industry.

After my talk, the first question was, "How much money did you make from *The American Way of Death*?" "Absolute tons," I answered. "So much I can't even count it—it made my fortune." Audible groans from the audience.

There were a few more questions, some about the Federal Trade Commission, some about the anticipated response to the Service Corporation International (SCI) invasion of Britain. In answer to the latter, I tried to explain that I thought it unlikely that the Brits would ever fall for the American way—the idea of people gathering to gaze at a corpse in a coffin wouldn't catch on. Nor would they embrace the notion of undertakers as grief therapists. The session ended with a short, sharp interchange in which a funeral director refused to tell the assemblage what his exact prices were because, as he explained, he did not wish to divulge this information to his competitors.

Later that day, some of us gathered round the lodge swimming pool for a chat with Tom Fisher. Karen Leonard, my researcher, asked him to elaborate on the point he had made at the meeting about outside forces. "Since you were in the business in 1963, can you talk a bit about the reaction to *The American Way of Death*?" she asked.

In his Dakota Tom mode, Mr. Fisher replied: "I said in my speech that I applaud Jessica Mitford. She did us the greatest favor this industry ever experienced. We were flaccid and a little fat around our waist, and I said we were a little smug up here. I said that cleansed us of that. It put us on a diet. The problem was that the funeral directors overreacted so badly, the diet became a starvation diet, and they never found the strength, you know, for almost twenty-five years, to find their way out—how to do something for themselves—so I always applaud her."

Enclosed in the seminar program was a sheet in which participants were asked to rate the speakers, with a space for comments on each. Avid to hear how I had scored, a few days later I rang up Ron Hast. Enoch Glascock came in first of the seven speakers, he said, but I was No. 2. The comments on my talk ranged from "very complimentary" to "very adverse." He read out a few examples. Under complimentary: "A true brush with history, a wonderful perspective." "Delightful, but she appeared to irritate many in the audience." Adverse: "She's still a cancer—how easily we forget all the damage she did, making a mockery of funeral service." "Most unnecessary to provide a platform for a critic of our profession." There had also been some phone calls, Mr. Hast told me: "One was somebody from Michigan State Funeral Directors Association, a pompous numskull, I couldn't repeat his language!"

In a subsequent *Mortuary Management* editorial entitled "Tuning In or Out," Ron Hast made some of the same points as Tom Fisher had in his poolside chat. He stoutly defended his decision to invite me; as to those who threatened to stop their subscriptions to *Mortuary Management,* he would "encourage them to call us at our expense to cancel their subscriptions—then go and put their heads back in the sand."

"We may or may not agree with the beliefs or expressions of Jessica Mitford," he wrote. ". . . Statistics now demonstrate throughout North America that simplicity or funeral avoidance *is* now the tradition in many regions. The American funeral-buying public has changed, and continues to change. . . . Ms. Mitford asked questions and listened to the answers more than thirty years ago, and produced something the public wanted to hear. Is it not time for us to do the same? . . .

"Can we expect to receive bouquets and laudatory cheers from Jessica Mitford in her new book? I think not. In fact, it is sensible to anticipate volatile criticism of current practices and agendas targeting death-care providers."

Reflecting on what I had gleaned from the Tiburon experience, I have concluded that not much has changed over the years in the way undertakers see their world. They would still "vastly prefer" to be looked on as "trained professional men with high standards of ethical conduct," but the exigencies of their trade still force them into the role of "merchants of a rather grubby order." Enoch Glascock's exposition of how to manipulate a family bent on a simple cremation into buying a full-fledged funeral was for me a high point of the seminar—I agreed with the No. 1 rating accorded him by his colleagues. But how does that fit in with Ron Hast's perception that "simplicity or funeral avoidance *is* now the tradition in many regions"? Or with the general tone of his and Tom Fisher's remarks about the impact of *The American Way of Death*?

Possibly it was the split personality of the calling, arising out of its inherent contradictions, that led to my invitation in the first place.

2

The American Way of Death

> *How long, I would ask, are we to be subjected to the tyranny of custom and undertakers? Truly, it is all vanity and vexation of spirit—a mere mockery of woe, costly to all, far, far beyond its value; and ruinous to many; hateful, and an abomination to all; yet submitted to by all, because none have the moral courage to speak against it and act in defiance of it.*
>
> —LORD ESSEX

O death, where is thy sting? O grave, where is thy victory? Where, indeed. Many a badly stung survivor, faced with the aftermath of some relative's funeral, has ruefully concluded that the victory has been won hands down by a funeral establishment—in a disastrously unequal battle.

Much fun has been poked at some of the irrational "status symbols" set out like golden snares to trap the unwary consumer at every turn. Until recently, little has been said about the most irrational and weirdest of the lot, lying in ambush for all of us at the end of the road—the modern American funeral.

If the Dismal Traders (as an eighteenth-century English writer calls them) have traditionally been cast in a comic role in literature, a universally recognized symbol of humor from Shakespeare to Dickens to Evelyn Waugh, they have successfully turned the tables in recent years to perpetrate a huge, macabre, and expensive practical joke on the American public. It is not consciously conceived of as a joke, of course; on the contrary, it is hedged with admirably contrived rationalizations.

Gradually, almost imperceptibly, over the years the funeral men have constructed their own grotesque cloud-cuckoo-land where the trappings of Gracious Living are transformed, as in a nightmare, into the trappings of Gracious Dying. The same familiar Madison Avenue language, with its peculiar adjectival range designed to anesthetize sales resistance to all sorts of products, has seeped into the funeral industry in a new and bizarre guise. The emphasis is on the same desirable qualities that we have been schooled to look for in our daily search for excellence: comfort, durability, beauty, craftsmanship. The attuned ear will recognize, too, the convincing quasi-scientific language, so reassuring even if unintelligible.

So that this too too solid flesh might not melt, we are offered "solid copper—a quality casket which offers superb value to the client seeking long-lasting protection," or "the Colonial Classic beauty—18 gauge lead coated steel, seamless top, lap-jointed welded body construction." Some are equipped with foam rubber, some with innerspring mattresses. Batesville offers "beds that lift and tilt." Not every casket need have a silver lining, for one may choose among a rich assortment of "color-matched shades" in nonabrasive fabrics. Shrouds no longer exist. Instead, you may patronize a grave-wear couturiere who promises "handmade original fashions—styles from the best in life for the last memory-dresses, men's suits, negligees, accessories." For the final, perfect grooming: "Nature-Glo—the ultimate in cosmetic embalming." And where have we heard that phrase "peace-of-mind protection" before? No matter. In funeral advertising, it is applied to the Wilbert Burial Vault, with its 3/8-inch precast asphalt inner liner plus extra-thick, reinforced concrete—all this "guaranteed by Good Housekeeping." Here again the Cadillac, status symbol par excellence, appears in all its gleaming glory, this time transformed into a sleek funeral hearse. Although lesser vehicles are now used to collect the body and the permits, the Cad is still the conveyance of choice for the Loved One's last excursion to the grave.

You, the potential customer for all this luxury, are unlikely to read the lyrical descriptions quoted above, for they are culled from *Mortuary Management* and other trade magazines of the industry. For you there are the ads in your daily newspaper, generally found on the obituary page, stressing dignity, refinement, high-caliber professional service, and that intangible quality, sincerity. The trade advertisements are, however, instructive, because they furnish an important clue to the frame of mind into which the funeral industry has hypnotized itself.

A new mythology, essential to the twentieth-century American funeral rite, has grown up—or rather has been built up step-by-step—to justify the peculiar customs surrounding the disposal of our dead. And just as the witch doctor must be convinced of his own infallibility in order to maintain a hold over his clientele, so the funeral industry has had to "sell itself" on its articles of faith in the course of passing them along to the public.

The first of these is the tenet that today's funeral procedures are founded in "American tradition." The story comes to mind of a sign on the freshly sown lawn of a brand-new Midwestern college: "There is a tradition on this campus that students never walk on this strip of grass. This tradition goes into effect next Tuesday." The most cursory look at American funerals of past times will establish the parallel. Simplicity to the point of starkness, the plain pine box, the laying out of the dead by friends and family who also bore the coffin to the grave—these were the hallmarks of the traditional American funeral until the end of the nineteenth century.

Secondly, there is the myth that the American public is only being given what it wants—an opportunity to keep up with the Joneses to the end. "In keeping with our high standard of living, there should be an equally high standard of dying," says an industry leader. "The cost of a funeral varies according to individual taste and the niceties of living the family has been accustomed to." Actually, choice doesn't enter the picture for average individuals faced, generally for the first time, with the necessity of buying a product of which they are totally ignorant, at a moment when they are least in a position to quibble. In point of fact, the cost of a funeral almost always varies, not "according to individual taste" but according to what the traffic will bear.

Thirdly, there is an assortment of myths based on half-digested psychiatric theories. The importance of the "memory picture" is stressed—meaning the last glimpse of the deceased in an open casket, done up with the latest in embalming techniques and finished off with a dusting of makeup. Another, impressively authentic-sounding, is the need for "grief therapy," which is big now in mortuary circles. A historian of American funeral directing hints at the grief-therapist idea when speaking of the new role of the undertaker—"the dramaturgic role, in which the undertaker becomes a stage manager to create an appropriate atmosphere and to move the funeral party through a drama in which social relationships are stressed and an emotional catharsis or release is provided through ceremony."

Lastly, a whole new terminology, as ornately shoddy as the rayon satin casket liner, has been invented by the funeral industry to replace the direct and serviceable vocabulary of former times. "Undertaker" has been supplanted by "funeral director" or "mortician." (Even the classified section of the telephone directory gives recognition to this; in its pages you will find "Undertakers—see Funeral Directors.") Coffins are "caskets"; hearses are "coaches" or "professional cars"; flowers are "floral tributes"; corpses generally are "loved ones," but mortuary etiquette dictates that a specific corpse be referred to by name only—as "Mr. Jones"; cremated ashes are "cremains." Euphemisms such as "slumber room," "reposing room," and "calcination—the kindlier heat" abound in the funeral business.

If the undertaker is the stage manager of the fabulous production that is the modern American funeral, the stellar role is reserved for the occupant of the open casket. The decor, the stagehands, the supporting cast are all arranged for the most advantageous display of the deceased, without which the rest of the paraphernalia would lose its point—Hamlet without the Prince of Denmark. It is to this end that a fantastic array of costly merchandise and services is pyramided to dazzle the mourners and facilitate the plunder of the next of kin.

Grief therapy, anyone? But it's going to come high. According to the funeral industry's own figures, the average undertaker's bill—$750 in 1961 for casket and "services"—is now $4,700, to which must be added the cost of a burial vault, flowers, clothing, clergy and musician's honorarium, and cemetery charges. When these costs are added to the undertaker's bill, the total average cost for an adult's funeral today is $7,800.

The question naturally arises, is this what most people want for themselves and their families? For several reasons, this has been a hard one to answer until recently. It is a subject seldom discussed. Those who have never had to arrange for a funeral frequently shy away from its implications, preferring to take comfort in the thought that sufficient unto the day is the evil thereof. Those who have acquired personal and painful knowledge of the subject would often rather forget about it. Pioneering "funeral societies" or "memorial associations" dedicated to the principle of funerals at reasonable cost do exist in a number of communities throughout the country, but until recently their membership was limited to the more sophisticated element in the population—university people, liberal intellectuals—and those who, like doctors and lawyers, come up against problems in arranging funerals for their clients.*

Some indication of the pent-up resentment felt by vast numbers of people against the funeral interests was furnished by the astonishing response to Roul Tunley's 1961 *Saturday Evening Post* article. As though a dike had burst, letters poured in from every part of the country to the funeral societies, to local newspapers. They came from clergymen, professional people, old-age pensioners, trade unionists. Three months after the article appeared, an estimated six thousand had taken pen in hand to comment on some phase of the high cost of dying. Many recounted their own bitter experiences at the hands of funeral directors; hundreds asked for advice on how to establish a consumer organization in communities where none exists; others sought information about prepayment plans. Thirty years later, the situation seems worse. In 1993 I wrote a letter encouraging funeral simplicity which appeared in a "Dear Abby" column. More than thirty thousand people wrote asking for information about funeral-planning societies. The funeral industry, finding itself in the glare of the public spotlight, continues to engage in serious debate about its own future course—as well it might.

Some entrepreneurs are already testing the waters with stripped-down, low-cost operations. One, calling itself "Church and Chapel Funeral Service," contracts with conventional funeral homes to lower costs by doing the unthinkable—moving the service out of the mortuary to a church, a cemetery chapel, even a nursing home.

In 1994 Russ Harman launched Affordable Funeral Service in a Washington, D.C., suburb. Taking the low-cost approach to the extreme, he operates with no facilities outside his own home. He uses private residences, churches, or, if viewing the deceased is desired, a rented mortuary. The basic strategy, according to Ron Hast's *Funeral Monitor,* is to keep overhead low. A white, unmarked van is used

---

*See chapter 20, "New Hope for the Dead," and page 275 for a list of nonprofit societies that will provide advice and information to nonmembers as well as to members.

instead of a hearse. There are no limos. Business is booming, with three vans patrolling the nation's capital and lone vans in five other cities. Harman's next project is to take the operation nationwide. Will Affordable Funeral Service be able to do it? It seems likely, since late word is that it has been swooped into the net of SCI, whose worldwide operations are the subject of chapter 16.

Is the funeral inflation bubble ripe for bursting? Back in the sixties, the American public suddenly rebelled against the trend in the auto industry towards ever more showy cars, with their ostentatious and nonfunctional fins, and a demand was created for compact cars patterned after European models. The all-powerful U.S. auto industry, accustomed to telling customers what sort of car they wanted, was suddenly forced to listen for a change. Overnight, the little cars became for millions a new kind of status symbol. Could it be that the same cycle is working itself out in the attitude towards the final return of dust to dust, that the American public is becoming sickened by ever more ornate and costly funerals, and that a status symbol of the future may indeed be the simplest kind of "funeral without fins"?

3

The Funeral Transaction

A funeral is not an occasion for a display of cheapness. It is, in fact, an opportunity for the display of a status symbol which, by bolstering family pride, does much to assuage grief. A funeral is also an occasion when feelings of guilt and remorse are satisfied to a large extent by the purchase of a fine funeral. It seems highly probable that the most satisfactory funeral service for the average family is one in which the cost has necessitated some degree of sacrifice. This permits the survivors to atone for any real or fancied neglect of the deceased prior to his death. . . .

—*National Funeral Service Journal*

The sellers of funeral service have, one gathers, a preconceived, stereotyped view of their customers. To them, the bereaved person who enters the funeral establishment is a bundle of guilt feelings, a snob, and a status seeker. Funeral directors feel that by steering the customer to the higher-priced caskets, they are administering the first dose of grief therapy. In the words of the *National Funeral Service Journal:* "The focus of the buyer's interest must be the casket, vault, clothing, funeral cars, etc.—the only tangible evidence of how much has been invested in the funeral—the only real status symbol associated with a funeral service."

Whether or not one agrees with this rather unflattering appraisal of the average person who has suffered a death in the family, it is nevertheless true that the funeral transaction is generally influenced by a combination of circumstances which bear upon the buyer as in no other type of business dealing: the disorientation caused by bereavement, the lack of standards by which to judge the value of the commodity offered by the seller, the need to make an on-the-spot decision, general ignorance of the law as it affects disposal of the dead, the ready availability of insurance money to finance the transaction. These factors predetermine to a large extent the outcome of the transaction.

The funeral seller, like any other merchant, is preoccupied with price, profit, selling techniques. Mr. Leon S. Utter, a former dean of the San Francisco College of Mortuary Science, has written, "Your selling plan should go into operation as soon as the telephone rings and you are requested to serve a bereaved family. . . . Never preconceive as to what any family will purchase. You cannot possibly measure the intensity of their emotions, undisclosed insurance, or funds that may have been set aside for funeral expenses."

The selling plan should be subtle rather than high-pressure, for the obvious "hard sell" is considered inappropriate and self-defeating by industry leaders. Two examples of what not to say to a customer are given in the *Successful Mortuary Operation Service Manual:* "I can tell by the fine suit you are wearing, that you appreciate the finer things, and will want a fine casket for your Mother," and "Think of the beautiful memory picture you will have of your dear Father in this beautiful casket."

At the same time, nothing must be left to chance. The trade considers that the most important element of funeral salesmanship is the proper arrangement of caskets in the selection room (where the customer is taken to make his purchase). The sales talk, while preferably dignified and restrained, must be designed to take maximum advantage of this arrangement.

The uninitiated, entering a casket-selection room for the first time, may think he is looking at a random grouping of variously priced merchandise. Actually, endless thought and care are lavished on the development of new and better selection-room arrangements, for it has been found that the placing of the caskets materially affects the amount of the sale. There are available to the trade a number of texts devoted to the subject, supplemented by frequent symposiums, seminars, study courses, visual aids, scale-model selection rooms complete with miniature caskets that can be moved around experimentally. All stress the desired goal: "selling consistently in a bracket that is above average."

The relationship between casket arrangement and sales psychology is discussed quite fully by Mr. W. M. Krieger, former managing director of the influential National Selected Morticians association, in his book *Successful Funeral Management*. He analyzes the blunder of placing the caskets in order of price, from cheapest to the most expensive, which he calls the "stairstep method" of arrangement. As he points out, this plan "makes direct dollar comparisons very easy." Or, if the caskets are so arranged that the most expensive are the first ones the buyer sees, he may be shocked into buying a very cheap one. A mistake to be avoided is an "unbalanced line" with too many caskets in the low price range: "The unbalanced line with its heavy concentration of units under $300 made it very easy for the client to buy in this area with complete satisfaction."*

In developing his method of display, Mr. Krieger divides the stock of caskets for convenience into four "quartiles," two above and two below the median price, which in his example is $400. The objective is to sell in the third, or just above median, quartile. To this end the purchaser is first led to a unit in this third quartile—about $125 to $150 *above* the median sale, in the range of $525 to $550. Should the buyer balk at this price, he should next be led to a unit providing "strong contrast, both in price and quality," this time something well below the median, say in the $375 to $395 range. The psychological reasons for this are explained. They are twofold. While the difference in quality is demonstrable, the price is not so low as to make the buyer feel belittled. At the same time, if the buyer turns his nose up and indicates that he didn't want to go *that* low, now is the time to show him the "rebound unit"—one priced from $25 to $50 above the median, in the $425 to $450 bracket.

Mr. Krieger calls all this the "Keystone Approach," and supplies a diagram showing units 1, 2, and 3 scattered with apparent artless abandon about the floor. The customer, who has been bounced from third to second quartile and back again on the rebound to the third, might think the "Human Tennis Ball Approach" a more appropriate term.

Should the prospect show no reaction either way on seeing the

---

*While most of the sales techniques described in this chapter have not changed, the prices quoted should be increased tenfold to reflect current costs. The average mortuary bill in 1961, $400 to $750, is now, according to the National Funeral Directors Association's latest survey, $4,700 ($7,800 with cemetery charges included).

first unit—or should he ask to see something better—the rebound gambit is, of course, "out." "In" is the Avenue of Approach. It seems that a Canadian Mountie once told Mr. Krieger that people who get lost in the wild always turn in a great circle to their right. Probably, surmises Mr. Krieger, because 85 percent of us are right-handed. In any event, the Avenue of Approach is a main, wide aisle leading to the right in the selection room. Here are the better-quality third- and fourth-quartile caskets.

For that underprivileged, or stubborn, member of society who insists on purchasing below the median (but who should nevertheless be served "graciously and with just as much courtesy and attention as you would give to the buyer without a limit on what he can spend"), there is a narrow aisle leading to the *left,* which Mr. Krieger calls "Resistance Lane." There is unfortunately no discussion of two possible hazards: what if an extremely affluent prospect should prove to be among the 15 percent of left-handed persons, and should therefore turn automatically into Resistance Lane? How to extricate him? Conversely, what if one of the poor or stubborn, possibly having at some time in his past been lost in Canada, should instinctively turn to the broad, right-handed Avenue of Approach?

The Comprehensive Sales Program Successful Mortuary Operation is designed along the same lines as Mr. Krieger's plan, only it is even more complicated. Everything is, however, most carefully spelled out, beginning with the injunction to greet the clients with a warm and friendly handshake and a suggested opening statement, which should be "spoken slowly and with real sincerity: 'I want to assure you that I'm going to do everything I can to be helpful to you!' "

Having made this good beginning, the funeral director is to proceed with the arrangement conference, at each stage of which he should "weave in the service story"—in other words, impress upon the family that they will be entitled to all sorts of extras, such as ushers, cars, pallbearers, a lady attendant for hairdressing and cosmetics, and the like—all of which will be included in the price of the casket, which it is now their duty to select. These preliminaries are very important, for "the Arrangement Conference can *make* or *break* the sale."

The diagram of the selection room in this manual resembles one of those mazes set up for experiments designed to muddle rats. It is here that we are introduced to the Triangle Plan, under which the buyer is led around in a triangle, or rather in a series of triangles. He is started off at position A, a casket costing $587, which he is told is "in the $500 range"—although, as the manual points out, it is actually $13 short of $600. He is informed that the average family buys in the $500 range—a statement designed to reassure him, explain the authors, because "most of the people believe themselves to be above average." Suppose the client does not react either way to the $587 casket. He is now led to position B on the diagram—a better casket priced at $647. However, this price is not to be mentioned. Rather, the words "sixty dollars additional" are to be used. Should the prospect still remain silent, this is the cue to continue upward to the most expensive unit.

Conversely, should the client demur at the price of $587, he is to be taken to position C—and told that "he can save a hundred dollars by choosing this one." Again, the figure of $487 is not to be mentioned. If he now says nothing, he is led to position D. Here he is told that "at sixty dollars additional, we could use this finer type, and all of the services will be just exactly the same." This is the crux of the Triangle Plan; the recalcitrant buyer has now gone around a triangle to end up unwittingly within forty dollars of the starting point. It will be noted that the prices all end in the number seven, "purposely styled to allow you to quote as 'sixty dollars additional' or 'save a hundred dollars.' "

Some grieving families will be spared this tour altogether, for a sales technique of the nineties is to sell caskets by catalogue only. One might not think of a casket as "photogenic," but morticians exclaim with enthusiasm that families are choosing more expensive caskets when they don't have to look at the real thing. The buyer is not likely to have caught the significance of this guided tour, whether it be through the catalogue or the display room. As a customer, he finds himself in an unusual situation, trapped in a set of circumstances peculiar to the funeral transaction. His frame of mind will vary, obviously, according to the circumstances which brought him to the funeral establishment. He may be dazed and bewildered, his young wife having just been killed in an accident; he may be rather relieved because a crotchety old relative has finally died after a long and painful illness. The great majority of funeral buyers, as they are led through their paces at the mortuary—whether shaken and grief-stricken or merely looking forward with pleasurable anticipation to the reading of the will—are assailed by many a nagging question: What's the *right* thing to do? I am arranging a funeral, but surely this is no time to indulge my own preferences in taste and style; I feel I know what she would have preferred, but what will her family and friends expect? How can I avoid criticism for inadvertently doing the wrong thing? And, above all, it should be a nice, decent funeral—but what is a nice, decent funeral?

Which leads us to the second special aspect of the funeral transaction: the buyer's almost total ignorance of what to expect when he enters the undertaker's parlor. What to look for, what to avoid, how much to spend. The funeral industry estimates that the average individual has to arrange for a funeral only once in fifteen years. The cost of the funeral is the third-largest expenditure, after a house and a car, in the life of an ordinary American family. Yet even in the case of the old relative whose death may have been fully expected and even welcomed, it is most unlikely that the buyer will have discussed the funeral with anybody in advance. It just would not seem right to go around saying, "By the way, my uncle is very ill and he's not expected to live; do you happen to know a good, reliable undertaker?"

Because of the nature of funerals, the buyer is in a quite different position from the one who is, for example, in the market for a car. Visualize the approach. The man of prudence and common sense who is about to buy a car consults a Consumers' Research bulletin or seeks the advice of friends; he knows in advance the dangers of rushing into a deal blindly.

In the funeral home, the man of prudence is completely at sea, without a recognizable landmark or bearing to guide him. It would be an unusual person who would examine the various offerings and then inquire around about the relative advantages of the Keystone casket by York and the Valley Forge by Batesville. In the matter of cost, a like difference is manifest. The funeral buyer is generally not in the mood to compare prices here, examine and appraise quality there. He is anxious to get the whole thing over with—not only is he anxious for this, but the exigencies of the situation demand it.

The third unusual factor which confronts the buyer is the need to make an on-the-spot decision. Impulse buying, which should, he knows, be avoided in everyday life, is here a built-in necessity. The convenient equivocations of commerce—"I'll look around a little and let you know," "Maybe I'll call you in a couple of weeks if I decide to take it"—simply do not apply in this situation. Unlike most purchases, this one cannot be returned in fifteen days and your money refunded in full if not completely satisfied.

In 1994 the FTC amended the Funeral Rule to prohibit undertakers from charging a special "casket-handling fee" to customers who purchased caskets from the storefront discount outlets that were beginning to make their appearance. In the few years since, there has been an explosion of these outlets, and one may now even shop for a casket on the Internet. But just as most funeral buyers feel barred by circumstances from shopping around for a casket, they are likewise barred by convention from complaining afterwards if they think they were overcharged or otherwise shabbily treated. The reputation of the TV repairman, the lawyer, the plumber is public property, and their shortcomings may be the subject of dinner-party conversation. The reputation of the undertaker is relatively safe in this respect. A friend, knowing I was writing on the subject, reluctantly told me of her experience in arranging the funeral of a brother-in-law. She went to a long-established, "reputable" undertaker. Seeking to save the widow expense, she chose the cheapest redwood casket in the establishment and was quoted a low price. Later, the salesman called her back to say the brother-in-law was too tall to fit into this casket, she would have to take one that cost a hundred dollars more. When my friend objected, the salesman said, "Oh, all right, we'll use the redwood one, but we'll have to cut off his feet." My friend was so shocked and disturbed by the nightmare quality of this conversation that she never mentioned it to anybody for two years.

Popular ignorance about the law as it relates to the disposal of the dead is a factor that sometimes affects the funeral transaction. People are often astonished to learn that in no state is embalming required by law except in certain special circumstances, such as when the body is to be shipped by common carrier.

The funeral men foster these misconceptions, sometimes by coolly misstating the law to the funeral buyer and sometimes by inferentially investing with the authority of law certain trade practices which they find it convenient or profitable to follow. This free and easy attitude to the law is even to be found in those institutions of higher learning, the colleges of mortuary science, where the fledgling undertaker receives his training. For example, it is the law in most states that when a decedent bequeaths his body for use in medical research, his survivors are bound to carry out his directions. Nonetheless, an embalming textbook, *Modern Mortuary Science,* disposes of the whole distasteful subject in a few misleading words: "Q: Will the provisions in the will of a decedent that his body be given to a medical college for dissection be upheld over his widow? A: No. . . . No one owns or controls his own body to the extent that he may dispose of the same in a manner which would bring humiliation and grief to the immediate members of his family."

I had been told so often that funeral men tend to invent the law as they go along (for there is a fat financial reward at stake) that I decided to investigate this situation firsthand. Armed with a copy of the California Code, I telephoned a leading undertaker in my community with a concocted story: my aged aunt, living in my home, was seriously ill—not expected to live more than a few days. Her daughter was coming here directly; but I felt I ought to have some suggestions, some arrangements to propose in the event that . . . Sympathetic monosyllables from my interlocutor. The family would want something very simple, I went on, just cremation. Of course, we can arrange all that, I was assured. And since we want only cremation and there will be no service, we should prefer not to buy a coffin. The undertaker's voice at the other end was now alert, although smooth. He told me, calmly and authoritatively, that it would be "illegal" for him to enter into such an arrangement. "You mean, it would be against the law?" I asked. Yes, indeed. "In that case, perhaps we could take a body straight to the crematorium in our station wagon?" A shocked silence, followed by an explosive outburst: "Madam, the average lady has neither the facilities nor the inclination to be hauling dead bodies around!" (Which was actually a good point, I thought.)

I tried two more funeral establishments and was told substantially the same thing: cremation of an uncoffined body is prohibited under California law. This was said, in all three cases, with such a ring of conviction that I began to doubt the evidence before my eyes in the state code. I reread the sections on cremation, on health requirements; finally I read the whole thing from cover to cover. Finding nothing, I checked with an officer of the Board of Health, who told me there is no law in California requiring that a coffin be used when a body is cremated. He added that indigents are cremated by some county welfare agencies without benefit of coffin.

It was just this sort of tactic described above that moved the FTC to rule in 1984 that morticians may no longer lie to the public. Anecdotal reports, however, indicate that honesty is still an elusive quality in the trade. One family that wanted to carry the ashes to the cemetery for burial was told, "You used to be able to do that. But it's against the law now."

Cemetery salesmen are also prone to confuse fact with fiction to their own advantage in discussing the law. Cemeteries derive a substantial income from the sale of "vaults." The vault, a cement enclosure for the casket, is not only a moneymaker; it facilitates upkeep of the cemetery by preventing the eventual subsidence of the grave as the casket disintegrates. In response to my inquiry, a cemetery salesman (identified on his card as a "Memorial Counselor") called at my house to sell me what he was pleased to call a "pre-need memorial estate," in other words, a grave for future occupancy. After he quoted the prices of the various graves, the salesman explained that a minimum of $520 must be added for a vault, which, he said, is "required by law."

"Why is it required by law?"

"To prevent the ground from caving in."

"But suppose I should be buried in one of those Eternal caskets made of solid bronze?"

"Those things are not as solid as they look. You'd be surprised how soon they fall apart."

"Are you *sure* it is required by law?"

"I've been in this business fifteen years; I should know."

"Then would you be willing to sign this?" (I had been writing on a sheet of paper, "California state law requires a vault for ground burial.")

The Memorial Counselor gathered up his color photographs of memorial estates and walked out of the house.

The fifth unusual factor present in the funeral transaction is the availability to the buyer of relatively large sums of cash. The family accustomed to buying every major item on time—car, television set, furniture—and spending to the limit of the weekly paycheck, suddenly finds itself in possession of insurance funds and death-benefit payments, often from a number of sources. It is usually unnecessary for the undertaker to resort to crude means to ascertain the extent of insurance coverage; a few simple and perfectly natural questions put to the family while he is completing the vital statistics forms will serve to elicit all he needs to know. For example, "Occupation of the deceased?" "Shall we bill the insurance company directly?"

The undertaker knows, better than a schoolboy knows the standings of the major-league baseball teams, the death-benefit payments of every trade union in the community, the Social Security and workmen's compensation scale of death benefits: Social Security payment, $255; if the deceased was a veteran, $300 more and free burial in a national cemetery; an additional funeral allowance of up to $5,000 under some state workers' compensation laws if the death was occupationally connected; and so on and so on.

The undertaker has all the information he needs to proceed with the sale. The widow, for the first time in possession of a large amount of ready cash, is likely to welcome his suggestions. He is, after all, the expert, the one who knows how these things should be arranged, who will steer her through the unfamiliar routines and ceremonies ahead, who will see that all goes as it should.

At the lowest end of the scale is the old-age pensioner, most of whose savings have long since been spent. He is among the poorest of the poor. Nevertheless, most state and county welfare agencies permit him to have up to $2,500 in cash; in some states he may own a modest home as well, without jeopardizing his pension. The funeral director knows that under the law of virtually every state, the funeral bill is entitled to preference in payment as the first charge against the estate. There is every likelihood that the poor old chap will be sent out in high style unless his widow is a very, very cool customer indeed.

The situation that generally obtains in the funeral transaction was summed up by former Surrogate Court Judge Fowler of New York in passing upon the reasonableness of a bill which had come before him: "One of the practical difficulties in such proceedings is that contracts for funerals are ordinarily made by persons differently situated. On the one side is generally a person greatly agitated or overwhelmed by vain regrets or deep sorrow, and on the other side persons whose business it is to minister to the dead for profit. One side is, therefore, often unbusiness-like, vague and forgetful, while the other is ordinarily alert, knowing and careful."

There are people, however, who know their own minds perfectly well and who approach the purchase of a funeral much as they would any other transaction. They are, by the nature of things, very much in the minority. Most frequently they are not in the immediate family of the deceased but are friends or representatives of the family. Their experiences are interesting because to some extent they throw into relief the irrational quality of the funeral transaction.

In 1961 Mr. Rufus Rhoades, a retired manufacturer of San Rafael, California, was charged with arranging for the cremation of a ninety-two-year-old friend who died in a rest home. He telephoned the crematorium and was quoted the price of $75 for cremation, plus $15 for shipping the ashes to Santa Monica, where his friend's family had cemetery space. He suggested hiring an ambulance to pick up the body, but this idea was quickly vetoed by the crematorium. He was told that he would have to deal through an undertaker, that the body could not be touched by anyone but a licensed funeral director, that a "container" would have to be provided. This he was unaware of; and no wonder, for these were "regulations" of the crematorium, not requirements of California law.

Mr. Rhoades looked in the San Rafael telephone directory and found five funeral establishments listed. He picked one at random, called, and was told that under no circumstances could price be discussed over the telephone, as it was "too private a matter"; that he should come down to the funeral home. There he found that the cheapest price, including "a low-priced casket and the complete services," was $480. Mr. Rhoades protested that he did not want the complete services, that there was to be no embalming, that he did not want to see the coffin. He merely wanted the body removed from the rest home and taken to the crematorium, some five miles away. Balking at the $480, Mr. Rhoades returned home and telephoned the other four funeral establishments. The lowest quotation he could obtain was $250.

Not unnaturally, Mr. Rhoades felt that he had paid a fee of $50 a mile to have his friend's body moved from the rest home to the crematorium. The undertaker no doubt felt, for his part, that he had furnished a service at well below his "break-even" point, or, in his own terminology, "below the cost at which we are fully compensated."*

The point of view of the funeral director must here be explored. In 1962 I talked with Mr. Robert MacNeur, owner of a Grant Miller Mortuary, the largest funeral establishment in the Oakland area, with a volume of one thousand funerals a year. Their cheapest offering at the time was the standard service with redwood casket, at $485. "My firm has never knowingly subjected a person to financial hardship," Mr. MacNeur declared. "We will render a complete funeral service for nothing if the circumstances warrant it. The service is just the same at no charge as it is for a $1,000 funeral." Mr. MacNeur produced a copy of the "Grant Miller Co-operative Plan," in which this philosophy was spelled out.

> If a family finds the First Standard Complete Funeral Arrangement including the finer type redwood casket at $495 to be beyond their present means or wishes, Grant Miller Mortuaries stand ready to reduce costs with the following co-operative plan chart, rather than use one or a series of cheap or inferior caskets.

There followed a descending price scale, culminating in "$0 for persons in Distress Circumstances."

A recent inquiry as to the availability of the plan produced a puzzled response: "We have no such plan, never heard of it." The redwood box, which many today would find attractive, is available now only as a "rental unit," at $795 for one to two days' occupancy. Today's low-cost receptacle is a pine box, listed on the Grant Miller casket price list at $2,425, which brings the minimum cost of a Grant Miller funeral to $3,420.

Service Corporation International (see chapter 16, "A Global Vil-

---

*Current crematory charges run from $200 to $350. In the Santa Rosa area today, Mr. Rhoades would have to pay $1,000 or more to move his friend's body from the rest home to the crematory.

lage of the Dead") has a "no-walk" policy and will do "whatever is necessary" to keep the family from going to a competitor, according to one disaffected employee. But trying to find out what kind of discount is offered and who might qualify is as difficult today as it was with Grant Miller thirty years ago. The rare customer who has the wit and gumption need only stand up and head for the door until the price has dropped to an acceptable level.

The guiding rule in funeral pricing appears to be "from each according to his means," regardless of the actual wishes of the family. A funeral director in San Francisco says, "If a person drives a Cadillac, why should he have a Pontiac funeral?" The Cadillac symbol figures prominently in the mortician's thinking. This kind of reasoning is peculiar to the funeral industry. A person can drive up to an expensive restaurant in a Cadillac and can order, rather than the $40 dinner, a $2 cup of tea and he will be served. It is unlikely that the proprietor will point to his elegant furnishings and staff and demand that the Cadillac owner order something more commensurate with his ability to pay so as to help defray the overhead of the restaurant.

There is, however, one major difference between the restaurant transaction and the funeral transaction. It is clear that while the Cadillac owner may return to the restaurant tomorrow with a party of six and order $40 dinners all around, this will not be true of his dealings with the undertaker. In the funeral business it's strictly one to a customer. Very likely many a funeral director has echoed with heartfelt sincerity the patriotic sentiments of Nathan Hale: "I only regret that I have but one life to lose for my country." But if the undertaker fails to move in and strike while the iron is hot, the opportunity is literally lost and gone forever. (The only exception to this is noted by the Clark Grave Vault people, who in their advertisements advance the startling thought: "DISINTERMENTS—RARE BUT REWARDING. It needn't be a problem. It can lead to repeat business. . . .")

The funeral industry faces a unique economic situation in that its market is fixed, or inelastic, which leads to practices such as those deplored by Emily Post, that famed arbiter of taste and custom, in the first edition of *Etiquette,* published in 1923:

Whether the temptation of "good business" (on the part of the funeral director) gradually undermines his character . . . knowing as he does that bereaved families ask no questions . . . or whether his profession is merely devoid of taste, he will, if not checked, bring the most ornate and expensive casket in his establishment; he will perform every rite that his professional ingenuity for expenditure can devise; he will employ every attendant he has; he will order vehicles numerous enough for the cortege of a President; he will even, if thrown in contact with a bewildered chief-mourner, secure a pledge for the erection of an elaborate mausoleum.

Evidently, Mrs. Post got a reaction from the undertakers, for in the 1942 edition of *Etiquette* she prefaced her remarks about funerals with this statement: "Because of the criticism of a certain not admirable type of funeral director in the earlier editions of this book, it must at once be said that this was not meant to apply to any of the directors of high reputation, who are consciously considerate not only of the feelings of the family but also of their pocketbooks." However, she then goes on not only to repeat the offending paragraph but to strengthen it: "The wrong type of director will refuse to give an itemized list of costs, but will, instead, do his best to hypnotize the family into believing that the more expensive the casket, the more elaborate the preparations, the greater the love and honor shown the deceased." In a later edition, revised in 1955, the offending passage is, without explanation, deleted in its entirety.

4

The Artifacts

Men have been most phantasticall in the singular contrivances of their corporal dissolution. . . .

—SIR THOMAS BROWNE,
Urne-Buriall

"The No. 280 reflects character and station in life. It is superb in styling and provides a formal reflection of successful living." This is quoted from the catalogue of Practical Burial Footware of Columbus, Ohio, and refers to the Fit-a-Fut Oxford, which comes in patent, calf, tan, or oxblood with lace or goring back. The same firm carries the Ko-Zee, with its "soft, cushioned soles and warm, luxurious slipper comfort, but true shoe smartness." Just what practical use is made of this footwear is spelled out. Burial footwear demonstrates "consideration and thoughtfulness for the departed." The closed portion of the casket is opened for the family, who on looking see that "the ensemble is complete although not showing. You will gain their complete confidence and good will." The women's lingerie department of Practical Burial Footwear supplies a deluxe package, in black patent box with gold-embossed inscription, of "pantee, vestee," and nylon hose, "strikingly smart—ultimate in distinction." Also for the ladies are custom burial gowns, bootees, stole, and bra "for post mortem form restoration," offered by Lipari Gowns of Johnstown, Pennsylvania.

Florence Gowns of Cleveland, Ohio, exhibited their line of "streetwear type garments and negligees," together with something new, a line of "hostess gowns and brunch coats," at a convention of the National Funeral Directors Association. (However, the devotional set exhibit at the same meeting, put on by Kelco Supplies of

Minneapolis, while it included "The Last Supper," failed to come through with a "Last Brunch.")

Casket styles range from classic (that is, the "urn theme") to Colonial to French provincial to futuristic—the "Transition" casket, styled for the future—surely, something here to please everybody. The patriotic theme comes through very strong, finding its most eloquent expression in the Batesville Casket Company's "Valley Forge," designed to reflect the rugged, strong, soldierlike qualities associated with that historic theme. . . . "Its charm lies in the warm beauty of the natural grain and finish of finest maple hardwoods. A casket designed indeed for a soldier—one that symbolizes the solid, dependable, courageous American ideals so bravely tested at Valley Forge." For all its soldierlike qualities, it looks most comfortable, with its nice beige linen pillow and sheets. On the wall behind it hangs a portrait of George Washington, who is looking, as usual, rather displeased.

For the less rugged, the bon vivant who dreams of rubbing shoulders with the international smart set, the gay dog who would risk all on the turn of a card, there is the "Monaco," a Duraseal metal unit "with Sea Mist Polished Finish, interior richly lined in 600 Aqua Supreme velvet, magnificently quilted and shirred, with matching jumbo bolster and coverlet." Set against a romantic background depicting a brilliant Riviera sky, its allure heightened by suggestions of tropical ferns and a golden harp, this model can be had for not much more than a first-class airfare to Monte Carlo.

And for the homebody who is neither rugged nor daring, but is interested in solid comfort, medium-priced metal caskets are now equipped with the "Beautyrama Adjustable Soft-Foam Bed. Quality mattress fabric is used and height and adjustment is accomplished by patented means which eliminate cranking. Modified during a year of product development, the bed is soft and buoyant, but will hold firm without slipping."

Well, there is a great deal more to it. The observer, confronted for the first time by the treasures and artifacts of this unfamiliar world, may well feel something akin to the astonishment of Bernal Díaz del Castillo at his first glimpse of the hitherto undiscovered court of Montezuma: "We were amazed," he declared, "and some of the soldiers even asked whether the things we saw were not a dream."

And not to be outdone in trendiness, Doric offers "a feminine alternative in burial vaults . . . products with soft rose and white exterior finishes in a range of prices to suit every family's needs." Top of the line is the Rose Patrician, with "all matching carapace with a formed rose emblem and nameplate."

Then there is Brocatelle, one of the Batesville Casket Company's decorator fabrics, "hand-loomed in the traditional European manner, custom designed, typical of the rich heavy-figured fabrics used by royalty during the seventeenth, eighteenth and nineteenth centuries. These fabrics are color oriented with sculptured panels of complementary hues, an interpretation of the finest art and sculpture, usually found only in the world's leading decorator houses."

The burial vault is a relative newcomer in funeral wares. As late as 1915, it was used in only 5 to 10 percent of all funerals—a far cry from today's proud slogan of a leading vault manufacturer, "A Wilbert Burial Vault Every Minute" (based, a footnote tells us, on an eight-hour workday). Since the word "vault" may connote to the uninitiated a burial chamber, a word of explanation is in order. The vault we are describing here is designed as an outer receptacle to protect the casket and its contents from the elements during their eternal sojourn in the grave. Vaults are made of a variety of materials; they may be of concrete, pre-asphalt-lined; of aluminum; of a copper, asphalt, and concrete mixture; of fiberglass. In any case, a good vault is a "symbolic expression of affection." They are getting more beautiful by the year, may be had in a variety of colors including polished stripes, and are frequently decorated with all sorts of lovely things—foreverness symbols like trees of life or setting suns—leading one to speculate as to whether the time may not be ripe for the introduction of a sur- or super- or supra-vault, and so on and on, like those little wooden eggs-within-eggs we used to find in our Christmas stockings.

I happened to have had a bracing confrontation with a vault salesman. Vidalia, Georgia—a very small town south of Savannah—is the home of the Ohoopee Public Library which was having a symposium on death—very big in recent years at colleges, library associations, and the like.

The death meetings were scheduled on successive Tuesdays, to be addressed by ministers on religious aspects, philosophers, etc. . . . and I was the leadoff speaker on the death industries. Brought in, I suppose, as a bit of comic relief.

But then the American Legion attacked. They blasted the Ohoopee Public Library for giving a platform to a well-known subversive. And they sent copies of all the old House Un-American Activities Committee reports to the newspapers. So the newspapers, even in far-off Savannah, sprang into life and carried the releases.

The librarians fought back. "Everybody can have his or her say at the Ohoopee Public Library," they said. They also had the clever idea of sending special invitations with free tickets to all the funeral directors and associated industries for miles around . . . underlining the free-speech message and urging them to come.

As a result of this totally unexpected publicity, which blanketed the area, the lecture had to be moved from a small meeting hall to the high school auditorium, which was absolutely packed. The chairman led off, repeating the free-speech stand of the library and asking, "Are there any members of the funeral profession here?" Upon which, twelve black suits stood up, all in a row, and then sat down.

I gave my talk, which seemed to be well received because most people in Vidalia as elsewhere have at one time or another suffered from the machinations of the funeral industry. When the question period came, I asked first whether there were any questions from the funeral contingent. A black suit rose up and he said, "I am a vault man. I sell vaults. I listened to Mrs. Mitford's speech and she never said that when Jesus Christ our Lord was crucified, a rich man gave him his vault." And then he sat down. I replied that since I spend a lot of time in motels where the only reading matter supplied was a Bible, I was indeed familiar with the story of Joseph of Arimathea and his gift to Jesus of his vault. But if you read further, it seems he didn't stay there all that long. I mean he was up and out in three days.

At this point the black suits rose up, all twelve of them, and walked out. I was expecting people to follow because we were, after all, in the Bible Belt. Deep Bible Belt in Vidalia, Georgia. But rather to my pleasure, not a soul stirred. They were all keen to discuss their mother's funeral.

Cemeteries now compete with the funeral directors for the lucrative vault business. Most require the use of vaults in all burials for the ostensible reason that the vault prevents the caving in of the grave due to the eventual disintegration of the casket. The selling point made to the customer is, of course, the eternal preservation of the dead. It seems that the Midwest is a particularly fruitful territory for the sale of metal vaults. "Must be the psychological reason brought about by thoughts of extreme heat and cold, stormy weather, snow and frozen ground," muses *Mortuary Management*.

An appropriate showcase setting for all these treasures assumes a special importance. Gone forever are the simple storefront undertaking establishments of earlier days. They have been replaced by elaborate structures in the style of English country houses, French provincial châteaux, Spanish missions, split-level suburban executive mansions, or Byzantine mosques—frequently, in a freewheeling mixture of all these. A Gothic chapel may be carpeted with the latest in wall-to-wall, two-inch-thick, extra-pile Acrilan, and Persian rugs laid on top of this; its bronze-girt door may open onto an authentically furnished Victorian drawing room in one corner of which is a chrome-and-tile coffee bar. The slumber rooms in the same building may stress the light and airy Swedish modern motif.

The funeral home "chapel" has begun to assume more and more importance as the focal point of the establishment. In fact, many now call themselves "chapels." The nomenclature has gradually changed. From "undertaker" to "funeral parlor" to "funeral home" to "chapel" has been the linguistic progression; "chapel" has the additional advantage of circumventing the word "funeral." Chapel of the Chimes, Chapel of Memories, Little Chapel of the Flowers—these are replacing Snodgrass Funeral Home. The chapel proper is a simulated place of worship. Because it has to be all things to all people, it is subject to a quick change by wheeling into place a "devotional chapel set" appropriate to the religion being catered to at the moment—a Star of David, a cross, a statue of the Virgin, and so on. Advertisements and promotional brochures generally emphasize the chapel and its features: "Enter the chapel. Note how the sun pours its diffused glory through Gothic windows, and how the blue and amber, ruby and amethyst tones of glass play smilingly on walls and ceiling . . ." (Chapel of the Chimes brochure).

The slumber rooms are elusively reminiscent of some other feature of American life. What familiar establishments also boast such eclecticism of design, from medieval to futuristic, combined with the most minute attention to comfort? In what category of building are you sure to find voluptuous carpeting underfoot, floor-length draw drapes, skillfully arranged concealed lighting to please the eye, temperature expertly adjusted by push button for maximum well-being—the soothing atmosphere of restful luxury pervading all? The answer was suggested by a funeral director with whom I was discussing costs. He was explaining the items that go to make up a total. "So then you've got a slumber room tied up for three days or more," he said. "Right there's a consideration: How much would it cost you to stay in a good motel for three days?"

Motels for the dead! That's it, of course—a swimming pool and TV the only missing features.

The selection room is the portion of the mortuary where the caskets are displayed and offered for sale. It is here that all of the previous efforts of the funeral director—his advertising, his living the good life in the community, the impression he has made on the bereaved family during the arrangement conference—will be crowned with success or doomed to failure. It is here that the actual price of the funeral will be settled.

The decor and lighting of the selection room and particularly the arrangement of merchandise are matters of greatest importance, for these, as we have seen, materially condition and affect the conduct of the transaction itself. As an interior decorator writes, "Being the financial foundation of mortuary income, caution should be exercised in every detail and appointment, employing the finest selling qualities of color lighting effects, proper placement of caskets and special background features; the psychological effect producing a feeling of security and confidence that results in the sale of higher grade caskets, and the return of families for additional service when needed."

Further on decor, one writer advises that warm colors are said to be *advancing* colors; and cold colors are *receding* colors. She recommends cool backgrounds to set off the warm walnut, mahogany, copper shades of the caskets. Another prefers touches of red about the place, possibly decorative wallpaper panels, and a bone-white ceiling to give a good distribution of light. The matter of good lighting is most important because in dim light it is hard to distinguish between low-grade rayon and transparent velvet casket linings. Throughout, "color, life and light" will provide the right atmosphere for people "conditioned to modern environment." A *minimum* of forty square feet of floor space is needed to display a burial casket, although if possible sixty square feet should be allowed for each unit.

We have glimpsed the chapel, the slumber rooms, the casket-selection room, all designed for public inspection and edification. We have examined some of the choice and curious artifacts and their uses. There is one door we have not yet opened, through which the public may not enter and behind which certain procedures take place—procedures indispensable to the proper utilization of the funeral director's merchandise and premises. What goes on in that forbidden territory, and why, can only be understood in context if we "weave in the service story."

5

The Story of Service

There was a time when the undertaker's tasks were clear-cut and rather obvious, and when he billed his patrons accordingly. Typical late-nineteenth-century charges, in addition to the price of merchandise, are shown on bills of the period as: "Services at the house (placing corpse in the coffin), $1.25," "Preserving remains on ice, $10," "Getting permit, $1.50." It was customary for the undertaker to add a few dollars to his bill for being "in attendance," which seems only fair and right. The cost of embalming was around $10 in 1880. An undertaker, writing in 1900, recommends these minimums for service charges: washing and dressing, $5; embalming, $10; hearse, $8 to $10. As Robert W. Habenstein and William M. Lamers, the historians of the trade, have pointed out, "The undertaker had yet to conceive of the value of personal service offered professionally for a fee, legitimately claimed." Well, he has now so conceived with a vengeance.

When weaving in the story of service as it is rendered today, spokesmen for the funeral industry tend to become so carried away by their own enthusiasm, so positively lyrical and copious in their declarations, that the outsider may have a little trouble understanding it all. There are indeed contradictions. Preferred Funeral Directors International has prepared a talk designed to inform people about service: "The American public receive the services of employees and proprietor alike, nine and one half days of labor for every funeral handled, they receive the use of automobiles and hearses, a building including a chapel and other rooms which require building maintenance, insurance, taxes and licenses, and depreciation, as well as heat in the winter, cooling in the summer, light and water." The writer goes on to say that while the process of embalming takes only about three hours, "it would be necessary for one man to work two forty-hour weeks to complete a funeral service. This is coupled with an additional forty hours of service required by members of other local allied professions, including the work of the cemeteries, newspapers, and, of course, the most important of all, the service of your clergyman. These some 120 hours of labor are the basic value on which the cost of funerals rests."

Our informant has lumped a lot of things together here. To start with "the most important of all, the service of your clergyman": the average religious funeral service lasts no more than twenty-five minutes. Furthermore, it is not, of course, paid for by the funeral director. The "work of the cemeteries" presumably means the opening and closing of a grave. This now mechanized operation, which takes fifteen to twenty minutes, is likewise not billed as part of the funeral director's costs. The work of "newspapers"? This is a puzzler. Presumably, reference is made here to the publication of an obituary notice on the vital statistics page. It is, incidentally, surprising to learn that newspaper work is considered an "allied profession."

Just how insurance, taxes, licenses, and depreciation are figured in as part of the 120 man-hours of service is hard to tell. The writer does mention that his operation features "65 items of service." In general, the funeral salesman is inclined to chuck in everything he does under the heading of "service." For example, in a typical list of "services" he will include items like "securing statistical data" (in other words, completing the death certificate and finding out how much insurance was left by the deceased), the "arrangements conference" (in which the sale of the funeral to the survivors is made), and the "keeping of records," by which he means his own bookkeeping work. Evidently, there is some confusion here between items that properly belong in a cost-accounting system and items of actual service rendered in any given funeral. In all likelihood, the idle time of employees is figured in and prorated as part of the "man-hours." The up-to-date funeral home operates on a twenty-four-hour basis, and the prepared speech contains this heartening news:

> The funeral service profession of the United States is proud of the fact that there is not a person within the continental limits

of the United States who is more than two hours away from a licensed funeral director and embalmer. That's one that even the fire-fighting apparatus of our country cannot match.

While the hit-or-miss rhetoric of the foregoing is fairly typical of the prose style of the funeral trade as a whole, and while the statement that 120 man-hours are devoted to a single funeral may be open to question, there really is a fantastic amount of service accorded the dead body and its survivors.

Having decreed what sort of funeral is right, proper, and nice, and having gradually appropriated to himself all the functions connected with it, the funeral director has become responsible for a multitude of tasks—beyond the obvious one of "placing corpse in the coffin" recorded in our nineteenth-century funeral bill. His self-imposed duties fall into two main categories: attention to the corpse itself, and the stage-managing of the funeral.

The drama begins to unfold with the arrival of the corpse at the mortuary.

Alas, poor Yorick! How surprised he would be to see how his counterpart of today is whisked off to a funeral parlor and is in short order sprayed, sliced, pierced, pickled, trussed, trimmed, creamed, waxed, painted, rouged, and neatly dressed—transformed from a common corpse into a Beautiful Memory Picture. This process is known in the trade as embalming and restorative art, and is so universally employed in the United States and Canada that for years the funeral director did it routinely, without consulting corpse or kin. He regards as eccentric those few who are hardy enough to suggest that it might be dispensed with. Yet no law requires embalming, no religious doctrine commends it, nor is it dictated by considerations of health, sanitation, or even of personal daintiness. In no part of the world but in North America is it widely used. The purpose of embalming is to make the corpse presentable for viewing in a suitably costly container; and here too the funeral director routinely, without first consulting the family, prepares the body for public display.

Is all this legal? The processes to which a dead body may be subjected are, after all, to some extent circumscribed by law. In most states, for instance, the signature of next of kin must be obtained before an autopsy may be performed, before the deceased may be cremated, before the body may be turned over to a medical school for research purposes; or such provision must be made in the decedent's will. In the case of embalming, permission is required (under Federal Trade Commission rules) only if a charge is to be made for the procedure. Embalming is not, as funeral providers habitually claim, a legal requirement even when the body of the deceased is to be on display in an open casket. A textbook, *The Principles and Practices of Embalming,* comments on this: "There is some question regarding the legality of much that is done within the preparation room." The author points out that it would be most unusual for a responsible member of a bereaved family to instruct the mortician, in so many words, to "embalm" the body of a deceased relative. The very term "embalming" is so seldom used that the mortician must rely upon custom in the matter. The author concludes that unless the family specifies otherwise, the act of entrusting the body to the care of a funeral establishment carries with it an implied permission to go ahead and embalm.

Embalming is indeed a most extraordinary procedure, and one must wonder at the docility of Americans who each year pay hundreds of millions of dollars for its perpetuation, blissfully ignorant of what it is all about, what is done, and how it is done. Not one in ten thousand has any idea of what actually takes place. Books on the subject are extremely hard to come by. You will not find them in your neighborhood bookshop or library.

In an era when huge television audiences watch surgical operations in the comfort of their living rooms, when, thanks to the animated cartoon, the geography of the digestive system has become familiar territory even to the nursery-school set, in a land where the satisfaction of curiosity about almost all matters is a national pastime, surely the secrecy surrounding embalming cannot be attributed to the inherent gruesomeness of the subject. Custom in this regard has within this century suffered a complete reversal. In the early days of American embalming, when it was performed in the home of the deceased, it was almost mandatory for some relative to stay by the embalmer's side and witness the procedure. Today, family members who might wish to be in attendance would certainly be dissuaded by the funeral director. All others, except apprentices, are usually barred by law from the preparation room.

A close look at what actually does take place may explain in large measure the undertaker's intractable reticence concerning a procedure that has become his major raison d'être. Is it possible he fears that public information about embalming might lead patrons to wonder if they really want this service? If the funeral men are loath to discuss the subject outside the trade, the reader may, understandably, be equally loath to go on reading at this point. For those who have the stomach for it, let us part the formaldehyde curtain. Others should skip to the bottom of page 49.

The body is first laid out in the undertaker's morgue—or, rather, Mr. Jones is reposing in the preparation room to be readied to bid the world farewell.

The preparation room in any of the better funeral establishments has the tiled and sterile look of a surgery, and indeed the embalmer/restorative artist who does his chores there is beginning to adopt the term "dermasurgeon" (appropriately corrupted by some mortician-writers as "demi-surgeon") to describe his calling. His equipment—consisting of scalpels, scissors, augers, forceps, clamps, needles, pumps, tubes, bowls, and basins—is crudely imitative of the surgeon's, as is his technique, acquired in a nine- or twelve-month post–high school course at an embalming school. He is supplied by an advanced chemical industry with a bewildering array of fluids, sprays, pastes, oils, powders, creams, to fix or soften tissue, shrink or distend it as needed, dry it here, restore the moisture there. There are cosmetics, waxes, and paints to fill and cover features, even plaster of Paris to replace entire limbs. There are ingenious aids to prop and stabilize the cadaver: a VariPose Head Rest, the Edwards Arm and Hand Positioner, the Repose Block (to support the shoulders during the embalming), and the Throop Foot Positioner, which resembles an old-fashioned stocks.

Mr. John H. Eckels, president of the Eckels College of Mortuary Science, thus describes the first part of the embalming procedure: "In the hands of a skilled practitioner, this work may be done in a comparative short time and without mutilating the body other than by slight incision so slight that it scarcely would cause serious inconvenience if made upon a living person. It is necessary to remove the blood, and doing this not only helps in the disinfecting, but removes the principal cause of disfigurements due to discoloration."

Another textbook discusses the all-important time element: "The earlier this is done, the better, for every hour that elapses between death and embalming will add to the problems and complications encountered. . . ." Just how soon should one get going on the embalming? The author tells us, "On the basis of such scanty information made available to this profession through its rudimentary and haphazard system of technical research, we must conclude that the best results are to be obtained if the subject is embalmed before life is completely extinct—that is, before cellular death has occurred. In the average case, this would mean within an hour after somatic death." For those who feel that there is something a little rudimentary, not to say haphazard, about this advice, a comforting thought is offered by another writer. "Speaking of fears entertained in the early days of premature burial," he points out, "one of the effects of embalming by chemical injection, however, has been to dispel fears of live burial." How true; once the blood is removed, chances of live burial are indeed remote.

To return to Mr. Jones, the blood is drained out through the veins and replaced by embalming fluid pumped in through the arteries. As noted in *The Principles and Practices of Embalming*, "Every operator has a favorite injection and drainage point—a fact which becomes a handicap only if he fails or refuses to forsake his favorites when conditions demand it." Typical favorites are the carotid artery, femoral artery, jugular vein, and subclavian vein. There are various choices of embalming fluid. If Flextone is used, it will produce a "mild, flexible rigidity. The skin retains a velvety softness, the tissues are rubbery and pliable. Ideal for women and children." It may be blended with B. and G. Products Company's Lyf-Lyk tint, which is guaranteed to reproduce "nature's own skin texture . . . the velvety appearance of living tissue." Suntone comes in three separate tints: Suntan; Special Cosmetic Tint; moderately pink.

About three to six gallons of a dyed and perfumed solution of formaldehyde, glycerin, borax, phenol, alcohol, and water is soon circulating through Mr. Jones, whose mouth has been sewn together with a "needle directed upward between the upper lip and gum and brought out through the left nostril," with the corners raised slightly "for a more pleasant expression." If he should be buck-toothed, his teeth are cleaned with Bon Ami and coated with colorless nail polish.

His eyes, meanwhile, are closed with flesh-tinted eye caps and eye cement.

The next step is to have at Mr. Jones with a thing called a trocar. This is a long, hollow needle attached to a tube. It is jabbed into the abdomen and poked around the entrails and chest cavity, the contents of which are pumped out and replaced with "cavity fluid." This done, and the hole in the abdomen having been sewn up, Mr. Jones's face is heavily creamed (to protect the skin from burns which may be caused by leakage of the chemicals), and he is covered with a sheet and left unmolested for a while. But not for long—there is more, much more, in store for him. He has been embalmed, but not yet restored, and the best time to start the restorative work is eight to ten hours after embalming, when the tissues have become firm and dry.

The object of all this attention to the corpse, it must be remembered, is to make it presentable for viewing in an attitude of healthy repose. "Our customs require the presentation of our dead in the semblance of normality . . . unmarred by the ravages of illness, disease or mutilation," says Mr. J. Sheridan Mayer in his *Restorative Art*. This is rather a large order since few people die in the full bloom of health, unravaged by illness and unmarked by some disfigurement. The funeral industry is equal to the challenge: "In some cases the gruesome appearance of a mutilated or disease-ridden subject may be quite discouraging. The task of restoration may seem impossible and shake the confidence of the embalmer. This is the time for intestinal fortitude and determination. Once the formative work is begun and affected tissues are cleaned or removed, all doubts of success vanish. It is surprising and gratifying to discover the results which may be obtained."

The embalmer, having allowed an appropriate interval to elapse, returns to the attack, but now brings into play the skill and equipment of sculptor and cosmetician. Is a hand missing? Casting one in plaster of Paris is a simple matter. "For replacement purposes, only a cast of the back of the hand is necessary; this is within the ability of the average operator and is quite adequate." If a lip or two, a nose, or an ear should be missing, the embalmer has at hand a variety of restorative waxes with which to model replacements. Pores and skin texture are simulated by stippling with a little brush, and over this cosmetics are laid on. Head off? Decapitation cases are rather routinely handled. Ragged edges are trimmed, and head joined to torso with a series of splints, wires, and sutures. It is a good idea to have a little something at the neck—a scarf or high collar—when time for viewing comes. Swollen mouth? Cut out tissue as needed from inside the lips. If too much is removed, the surface contour can easily be restored by padding with cotton. Swollen neck and cheeks are reduced by removing tissue through vertical incisions made down each side of the neck. "When the deceased is casketed, the pillow will hide the suture incisions. . . . [A]s an extra precaution against leakage, the suture may be painted with liquid sealer."

The opposite condition is more likely to present itself—that of emaciation. His hypodermic syringe now loaded with massage cream, the embalmer seeks out and fills the hollowed and sunken areas by injection. In this procedure, the backs of the hands and fingers and the under-chin area should not be neglected.

Positioning the lips is a problem that recurrently challenges the ingenuity of the embalmer. Closed too tightly, they tend to give a stern, even disapproving expression. Ideally, embalmers feel, the lips should give the impression of being ever so slightly parted, the upper lip protruding slightly for a more youthful appearance. This takes some engineering, however, as the lips tend to drift apart. Lip drift can sometimes be remedied by pushing one or two straight pins through the inner margin of the lower lip and then inserting them between the two front upper teeth. If Mr. Jones happens to have no teeth, the pins can just as easily be anchored in his Armstrong Face Former and Denture Replacer. Another method to maintain lip closure is to dislocate the lower jaw, which is then held in its new position by wire run through holes which have been drilled through the upper and lower jaws at the midline. As the French are fond of saying, *il faut souffrir pour être belle*.

If Mr. Jones has died of jaundice, the embalming fluid will very likely turn green. Does this deter the embalmer? Not if he has intestinal fortitude. Masking pastes and cosmetics are heavily laid on, burial garments and casket interiors are color-correlated with particular care, and Jones is displayed beneath rose-colored lights. Friends will say, "How *well* he looks." Death by carbon monoxide, on the other hand, can be rather a good thing from the embalmer's viewpoint: "One advantage is the fact that this type of discoloration is an exaggerated form of a natural pink coloration." This is nice because the healthy glow is already present and needs but little attention.

The patching and filling completed, Mr. Jones is now shaved, washed, and dressed. A cream-based cosmetic, available in pink, flesh, suntan, brunette, and blond, is applied to his hands and face, his hair is shampooed and combed (and, in the case of Mrs. Jones, set), his hands manicured. For the horny-handed son of toil, special care must be taken; cream should be applied to remove ingrained grime, and the nails cleaned. "If he were not in the habit of having them manicured in life, trimming and shaping is advised for better appearance—never questioned by kin."

Jones is now ready for casketing (this is the present participle of the verb "to casket"). In this operation his right shoulder should be depressed slightly "to turn the body a bit to the right and soften the appearance of lying flat on the back." Positioning the hands is a matter of importance, and special rubber positioning blocks may be used. The hands should be cupped slightly for a more lifelike, relaxed appearance. Proper placement of the body requires a delicate sense of balance. It should lie as high as possible in the casket, yet not so high that the lid, when lowered, will hit the nose. On the other hand, we are cautioned, placing the body too low "creates the impression that the body is in a box."

Jones is next wheeled into the appointed slumber room, where a few last touches may be added—his favorite pipe placed in his hand, or, if he was a great reader, a book propped into position. (In the case of little Master Jones, a teddy bear may be clutched.) Here he will hold open house for a few days, visiting hours 10 a.m. to 5 p.m.

All now being in readiness, the funeral director calls a staff conference to make sure that each assistant knows his precise duties. Mr. Wilber Krieger writes: "This makes your staff feel that they are a part of the team, with a definite assignment that must be properly carried out if the whole plan is to succeed. You never heard of a football coach who failed to talk to his entire team before they go on the field. They have been drilled on the plays they are to execute for hours and days, and yet the successful coach knows the importance of making even the bench-warming third-string substitute feel that he is important if the game is to be won." The winning of *this* game is predicated upon a glass-smooth handling of the logistics. The funeral director has notified the pallbearers, whose names were furnished by the family, has arranged for the presence of a clergyman, organist, and soloist, has provided transportation for everybody, has organized and listed the flowers sent by friends. In *Psychology of Funeral Service,* Mr. Edward A. Martin points out: "He may not always do as much as the family thinks he is doing, but it is his helpful guidance that they appreciate in knowing they are proceeding as they should. . . . The important thing is how well his services can be used to make the family believe they are giving unlimited expression to their own sentiment."

The religious service may be held in a church or in the chapel of the funeral home; the funeral director vastly prefers the latter arrangement, for not only is it more convenient for him, but it affords him the opportunity to show off his beautiful facilities to the gathered mourners. After the clergyman has had his say, the mourners queue up to file past the casket for a last look at the deceased. The family is not asked whether they want an open-casket ceremony; in the absence of instruction to the contrary, this is taken for granted. Consequently, well over 68 percent of all American funerals in the mid-1990s featured an open casket—a custom unknown in other parts of the world. Foreigners are astonished by it. An Englishwoman living in San Francisco described her reaction in a letter to the writer:

> I myself have attended only one funeral here—that of an elderly fellow worker of mine. After the service I could not understand why everyone was walking towards the coffin (sorry, I mean casket), but thought I had better follow the crowd. It shook me rigid to get there and find the casket open and poor old Oscar lying there in his brown tweed suit, wearing a suntan makeup and just the wrong shade of lipstick. If I had not been extremely fond of the old boy, I have a horrible feeling that I might have giggled. Then and there I decided that I could never face another American funeral—even dead.

The casket (which has been resting throughout the service on a Classic Beauty Ultra Metal Casket Bier) is now transferred by a hydraulically operated device called Porto-Lift to a balloon-tired,

Glide Easy casket carriage which will wheel it to yet another conveyance, the Cadillac Funeral Coach. This may be lavender, cream, light green. Black, once de rigueur, is coming back into fashion. Interiors, of course, are color-correlated, "for the man who cannot stop short of perfection."

At graveside, the casket is lowered into the earth. This office, once the prerogative of friends of the deceased, is now performed by a patented mechanical lowering device. A "Lifetime Green" artificial grass mat is at the ready to conceal the sere earth, and overhead, to conceal the sky, is a portable Steril Chapel Tent ("resists the intense heat and humidity of summer and the terrific storms of winter . . . available in Silver Grey, Rose or Evergreen"). Now is the time for the ritual scattering of the earth over the coffin, as the solemn words "earth to earth, ashes to ashes, dust to dust" are pronounced by the officiating cleric. This can today be accomplished "with a mere flick of the wrist with the Gordon Leak-Proof Earth Dispenser. No grasping of a handful of dirt, no soiled fingers. Simple, dignified, beautiful, reverent! The modern way!" The Gordon Earth Dispenser is of nickel-plated brass construction. It is not only "attractive to the eye and long wearing"; it is also "one of the 'tools' for building better public relations" if presented as "an appropriate non-commercial gift" to the clergy. It is shaped something like a saltshaker.

Untouched by human hand, the coffin and the earth are now united.

It is in the function of directing the participants through this maze of gadgetry that the funeral director has assigned to himself his relatively new role of "grief therapist." He has relieved the family of every detail, he has revamped the corpse to look like a living doll, he has arranged for it to nap for a few days in a slumber room, he has put on a well-oiled performance in which the concept of *death* has played no part whatsoever—unless it was inconsiderately mentioned by the clergyman who conducted the religious service. He has done everything in his power to make the funeral a real pleasure for everybody concerned. He and his team have given their all to score an upset victory over death.

Dale Carnegie has written that in the lexicon of the successful man there is no such word as "failure." So have the undertakers managed to delete the word "death" and all its associations from their vocabulary. They have from time to time published lists of In and Out words and phrases to be memorized and used in connection with the final return of dust to dust; then, still dissatisfied with the result, they have elaborated and revised the list. Thus, a 1916 glossary substitutes "prepare body" for "handle corpse." Today, though, "body" is Out and "remains" or "Mr. Jones" is In.

"The use of improper terminology by anyone affiliated with a mortuary should be strictly forbidden," declares Edward A. Martin. He suggests a rather thorough overhauling of the language; his deathless words include: "service, not funeral; Mr., Mrs., Miss blank, not corpse or body; preparation room, not morgue; casket, not coffin; funeral director or mortician, not undertaker; reposing room, not showroom; baby or infant, not stillborn; deceased, not dead; autopsy or post-mortem, not 'post'; coach, not hearse; shipping case, not shipping box; flower car, not flower truck; cremains or cremated remains, not ashes; clothing, dress, suit, etc., not shroud; drawing room, not parlor."

This rather basic list was refined in 1956 by Victor Landig in his *Basic Principles of Funeral Service*. He enjoins the reader to avoid using the word "death" as much as possible, even when such avoidance may seem impossible; for example, a death certificate should be referred to as a "vital statistics form." One should speak not of the "job" but rather of the "call." We do not "haul" a dead person, we "transfer" or "remove" him—and we do this in a "service car," not a "body car." We "open and close" his grave rather than dig and fill it, and in it we "inter" rather than bury him. This is done not in a graveyard or cemetery, but rather in a "memorial park." The deceased is beautified, not with makeup, but with "cosmetics." Anyway, he didn't die, he "expired." An important error to guard against, cautions Mr. Landig, is referring to "cost of the casket." The phrase "amount of investment in the service" is a wiser usage here.

Miss Anne Hamilton Franz, writing in *Funeral Direction and Management*, adds an interesting footnote on the use of the word "ashes" to describe (in a word) ashes. She fears this usage will encourage scattering (for what is more natural than to scatter ashes?), and prefers to speak of "cremated remains" or "human remains." She does not like the word "retort" to describe the container in which cremation takes place, but prefers "cremation chamber" or "cremation vault," because this "sounds better and softens any harshness to sensitive feelings."

As for the Loved One, poor fellow, he wanders like a sad ghost through the funeral men's pronouncements. No provision seems to have been made for the burial of a Heartily Disliked One, although the necessity for such must arise in the course of human events.*

---

*The funeral people, ever alert to fill a need, have come up with a casket that can be written on. The York "Expressions" casket, introduced at the 1996 convention of the National Funeral Directors Association, features "a smooth surface with a special coating on which those who gather may write one last farewell to the departed." The caskets come with a set of permanent markers and a Memorial Guide that rashly invites "those who gather" to "make known their hidden thoughts." As happens when chums are invited to autograph a schoolmate's surgical cast, there will predictably be the occasional nonconformist who is unable to resist the temptation to use the permanent marker to express his hidden thoughts, however derogatory.

6

The Rationale

A funeral service is a social function at which the deceased is the guest of honor and the center of attraction.... A poorly prepared body in a beautiful casket is just as incongruous as a young lady appearing at a party in a costly gown and with her hair in curlers.

—CLARENCE G. STRUB AND L. G. FREDERICK,
The Principles and Practices of Embalming

The words "costly gown" are the operative ones in the above paragraph, culled from a standard embalming-school textbook. The same thought is often expressed by funeral men: "Certainly, the incentive to select quality merchandise would be materially lessened if the body of the deceased were not decontaminated and made presentable," says *De-Ce-Co,* the publication of a funeral supply company. And Mr. T. E. Schier, president of the Settegast-Kopf Funeral Home in Houston, Texas, says, "The majority of the American people purchase caskets, not for the limited solace from their beauty prior to funeral service, or for the impression that they may create before their friends and associates. Instead, they full-heartedly believe that the casket and the vault give protection to that which has been accomplished by the embalmer."

One might suppose—and many people do—that the whole point of embalming is the long-term preservation of the deceased. Actually, although phrases like "peace-of-mind protection" and "eternal preservation" crop up frequently in casket and vault advertising, the embalmers themselves know better. For just how long is an embalmed body preserved? The simple truth is that a body *can* be preserved for a very long time indeed—probably for many years, depending upon the strength of the fluids used, and the temperature and humidity of the surrounding atmosphere. Cadavers prepared for use in anatomical research may outlast the hardiest medical student. The trouble is, they don't look very pretty; in fact they tend to resemble old shoe leather.

The more dilute the embalming fluid, the softer and more natural-appearing the guest of honor. Therefore, the usual procedure is to embalm with about enough preservative to ensure that the body will last through the funeral—generally, a matter of a few days. "To the ancient embalmer permanent preservation was of prime importance and the maintenance of a natural color and texture a matter of minor concern; to us the creation and maintenance of a lifelike naturalness is the major objective, and post-burial preservation is incidental. . . . The Egyptian embalmer's subjects have remained preserved for thousands of years—while the modern embalmer sometimes has to pray for favorable climatic conditions to help him maintain satisfactory preservation for a couple of days." The same textbook, *The Principles and Practices of Embalming,* cautioning the neophyte embalmer on the danger of trying to get by with inadequate embalming, says, "But if we were to approach the average embalmer and tell him that the body he had just embalmed would have to be kept on display for a month or two during the summer, what would his reaction be? To fall in a dead faint from fright, no doubt."

No matter what the more gullible customers may be led to believe about eternal preservation in the privacy of the arrangements-room conference, undertakers do not try to mislead the serious investigator about this. They will generally admit quite readily that their handiwork is not even intended to be permanent.

If long-term preservation is not the embalmer's objective, what then is?

Clearly, some rather solid-sounding justifications for the procedure had to be advanced, above and beyond the fact that embalming is good business for the undertaker because it helps him to sell more expensive caskets.

The two grounds chosen by the undertaking trade for defense of embalming embrace two objectives near and dear to the hearts of Americans: hygiene, and mental health. The theory that embalming is an essential hygienic measure has long been advanced by the funeral industry. A much newer concept, that embalming and restoring the deceased are necessary for the mental well-being of the survivors, is now being promoted by industry leaders; the observer who looks closely will discover a myth in the making here. "Grief therapy," the official name bestowed by the undertakers on this aspect of their work, has long been a second line of defense for the embalmers.

The primary purpose of embalming, all funeral men will tell you, is a sanitary one, the disinfecting of the body so that it is no longer a health menace. More than one writer, soaring to wonderful heights of fantasy, has gone so far as to attribute the falling death rate in this century to the practice of embalming (which, if true, would seem a little shortsighted on the part of the practitioners): "It is a significant fact that when embalming was in its infancy, the death rate was 21 to every 1,000 persons per year, and today it has been reduced to 10 to every 1,000 per year." The writer magnanimously bestows "a great deal of credit" for this on the medical profession, adding that funeral directors are responsible for "about 50 percent of this wonderful work of sanitation which has so materially lowered the death rate." When embalmers get together to talk among themselves, they are more realistic about the wonderful work of sanitation. In a panel discussion reported by the *National Funeral Service Journal,* Dr. I. M. Feinberg, an instructor at the Worsham College of Mortuary Science, said, "Sanitation is probably the farthest thing from the mind of the modern embalmer. We must realize that the motives for embalming at the present time are economic and sentimental, with a slight religious overtone."

Whether or not the undertakers themselves actually believe that embalming fulfills an important health function (and there is evidence that most of them really do believe it), they have been extraordinarily successful in convincing the public that it does. Outside of medical circles, people who are otherwise reasonably knowledgeable and sophisticated take for granted not only that embalming is done for reasons of sanitation but that it is required by law.

In an effort to sift fact from fiction and to get an objective opinion on the matter, I sought out Dr. Jesse Carr, chief of pathology at San Francisco General Hospital and professor of pathology at the University of California Medical School. I wanted to know specifically how, and to what extent, and in what circumstances, an unembalmed cadaver poses a health threat to the living.

Dr. Carr's office is on the third floor of the San Francisco General Hospital, its atmosphere of rationality and scientific method in refreshing contrast to that of the funeral homes. To my question "Are undertakers, in their capacity of embalmers, guardians of the public health?" Dr. Carr's answer was short and to the point: "They are not guardians of anything except their pocketbooks. Public health virtues of embalming? You can write it off as inapplicable to our present-day conditions." Discussing possible injury to health caused by the presence of a dead body, Dr. Carr explained that in cases of communicable disease, a dead body presents considerably less hazard than a live one. "There are several advantages to being dead," he said cheerfully. "You don't excrete, inhale, exhale, or perspire." The body of a person who has died of a noncommunicable illness, such as heart disease or cancer, presents no hazard whatsoever, he explained. In the case of death from typhoid, cholera, plague, and other enteric infections, epidemics have been caused in the past by the spread of infection by rodents and seepage from graves into the city water supply. The old-time cemeteries and churchyards were particularly dangerous breeding grounds for these scourges. The solution, however, lies in city planning, engineering, and sanitation, rather than in embalming, for the organisms which cause disease live in the organs, the blood, and the bowel, and cannot all be killed by the embalming process. Thus was toppled—for me, at least—the last stronghold of the embalmers; for until then I had confidently believed that their work had value, at least in the rare cases where death is caused by such diseases.

Dr. Carr has carried on his own campaign for a decent, common-sense approach to cadavers. The morgue in his hospital was formerly a dark retreat in the basement, "supposedly for aesthetic and health reasons; people think bodies smell and are unhealthy to have around." Objecting strongly to this, Dr. Carr had the autopsy rooms moved up to the third floor along with the offices. "The bodies aren't smelly, they're not dirty—bloody, of course, but that's a normal part of medical life," he said crisply. "We have so little apprehension of disease being spread by dead bodies that we have them up here right among us. It is medically more efficient, and a great convenience in student teaching. Ten to twenty students attend each autopsy. No danger here!"

A body will keep, under normal conditions, for twenty-four hours unless it has been opened. Floaters, explained Dr. Carr in his commonsense way, are another matter; a person who has been in the Bay for a week or more ("shrimps at the orifices, and so forth") will decompose more rapidly. They used to burn gunpowder in the morgue when floaters were brought in, to mask the smell, but now they put them in the Deepfreeze, and after about four hours the odor stops (because the outside of the body is frozen) and the autopsy can be performed. "A good undertaker would do his cosmetology and then freeze," said Dr. Carr thoughtfully. "Freezing is modern and sensible."

Anxious that we not drift back to the subject of the floaters, I asked about the efficacy of embalming as a means of preservation. Even if it is very well done, he said, few cadavers embalmed for the funeral (as distinct from those embalmed for research purposes) are actually preserved.

"An exhumed embalmed body is a repugnant, moldy, foul-looking object," said Dr. Carr emphatically. "It's not the image of one who has been loved. You might use the quotation 'John Brown's body lies a-moldering in the grave'; that really sums it up. The body itself may be intact, as far as contours and so on; but the silk lining of the casket is all stained with body fluids, the wood is rotting, and the body is covered with mold." The caskets, he said, even the solid mahogany ones that cost thousands of dollars, just disintegrate. He spoke of a case where a man was exhumed two and a half months after burial: "The casket fell apart and the body was covered with mold, long whiskers of penicillin—he looked ghastly. I'd rather be nice and rotten than covered with those whiskers of mold, although the penicillin is a pretty good preservative. Better, in fact, than embalming fluid."

Will an embalmed corpse fare better in a sealed metal casket? Far from it. "If you seal up a casket so it is more or less airtight, you seal in the anaerobic bacteria—the kind that thrive in an airless atmosphere, you see. These are the putrefactive bacteria, and the results of their growth are pretty horrible." He proceeded to describe them rather vividly, and added, "You're a lot better off to be buried in an aerobic atmosphere; otherwise the putrefactive bacteria take over. In fact, you're really better off with a shroud, and no casket at all."

Like many another pathologist, Dr. Carr has had his run-ins with funeral directors who urge their clients to refuse to consent to postmortem medical examinations. The funeral men hate autopsies; for one thing, it does make embalming more difficult, and also they find it harder to sell the family an expensive casket if the decedent has been autopsied. There are, said Dr. Carr, three or four good concerns in San Francisco that understand and approve the reasons for postmortem examination; these will help get the needed autopsy permission from the family, and employ skilled technicians. "It's generally the badly trained or avaricious undertaker who is resistant to the autopsy procedure. They all tip the hospital morgue men who help them, but the resistant ones are obstructive, unskilled, and can be nasty to the point of viciousness. They lie to the family, citing all sorts of horrible things that can happen to the deceased, and while they're usually very soft-spoken with the family, they are inordinately profane with hospital superintendents and pathologists. In one case where an ear had been accidentally severed in the course of an autopsy, the mortician threatened to *show* it to the family."

In a 1959 symposium in *Mortuary Management* on the attitudes of funeral directors towards autopsies, some of this hostility to doctors erupts into print. One undertaker writes, "The trouble with doctors is that they think they are little tin Gods, and anything they want, we should bow to, without question. My feeling is that the business of the funeral director is to serve the family in the best way he knows how, and if the funeral director knows that an autopsy is going to work a hardship, and result in a body that would be difficult to show, or that couldn't be shown at all, then I think the funeral director has not only the right, but the duty, to advise the family against permitting an autopsy." Another, defending the pathologists ("After all, the medical profession as a whole is reasonably intelligent"), describes himself as a "renegade embalmer where the matter of autopsies is concerned." He points to medical discoveries which have resulted from postmortem examination; but he evidently feels he is in a minority, for he says, "Most funeral directors are still 'horse and buggy undertakers' in their thinking and it shows up glaringly in their moronic attitude towards autopsies."

To get the reaction of the funeral men to the views expressed by Dr. Carr now became my objective. I was not so much interested, at this point, in talking to the run-of-the-mill undertaker, as in talking to the leaders of the industry, those whose speeches and articles I had read in the trade press—in short, those who might be termed the theoreticians of American funeral service. They, I felt, would have at their fingertips any facts that might bolster the case for embalming, and would be in a position to speak authoritatively for the industry as a whole.

In this, I was somewhat disappointed. The discussions seemed inconclusive, and the funeral spokesmen themselves often appeared to be unclear about the points they were making.

My first interview was with Dr. Charles H. Nichols, a Ph.D. in education from Northwestern University, who became the educational director of the National Foundation of Funeral Service. Among his published works are "The Psychology of Selling Vaults" and "Selling Vaults," which appeared in the *Vault Merchandiser* in 1954 and 1956 respectively. His duties at the foundation include lecturing to undertakers at the School of Management on such subjects as "Counseling in Bereavement."

Dr. Nichols readily volunteered the information that embalming has made an enormous contribution to public health and sanitation, that if done properly it can disinfect the dead body so thoroughly that it is no longer a source of contamination. "But *is* a dead body a source of infection?" I asked. Dr. Nichols replied that he didn't know. "What about foreign countries where they do not as a rule embalm; is much illness caused by failure to do so?" Dr. Nichols said he didn't know.

Mr. Wilber Krieger was an important figure in funeral circles, for he was not only managing director of an influential trade association, National Selected Morticians, but also director of the National Foundation of Funeral Service. To my question "Why is embalming universally practiced in the United States?" he answered that there is a public health factor: germs do not die with the host, and embalming disinfects. I told him of my conversation with Dr. Jesse Carr, and of my own surprise at learning that even in typhoid cases, embalming is ineffective as a safety measure against contagion; upon which he burst out with, "That's a typical pathologist's answer! That's the sort of thing you hear from so many of them." Pressed for specific cases of illness caused by failure to embalm, Mr. Krieger recalled the death from smallpox of a prominent citizen in a small Southern community where embalming was not practiced. Hundreds went to the funeral to pay their respects, and as a result a large number of them came down with smallpox. Unfortunately, Mr. Krieger had forgotten the name of the prominent citizen, the town, and the date of this occurrence. I asked him if he would check on these details and furnish me with the facts; however, he has not yet done so.

I had no better luck in a subsequent conversation with Mr. Howard C. Raether, executive secretary of the National Funeral Directors Association (to which the great majority of funeral directors belong), and Mr. Bruce Hotchkiss, vice president of that organization and himself a practicing undertaker. In this case, our conversation was recorded on tape. I asked what health hazard is presented by a dead body which has not been opened up, for purposes of either autopsy or embalming.

MR. RAETHER: Well, as an embalmer, Bruce, aren't there certain discharges that come from the body without it having been opened up?
MR. HOTCHKISS: Yes, most assuredly from—orally—depending upon the mode or condition preceding death.

Then I asked, "Can you give any place, then, where the public health has been endangered—give us the place and the time?"

They could not. We talked around the point for several minutes, but these two leaders of an industry built on the embalming process were unable to produce a single fact to support their major justification for the procedure. I told them what Dr. Carr had said about embalming and public health. "Do you have any comment on that?" I asked. Mr. Raether answered, "No; but we can take a look-see and try to give you some instances."

When the results of the look-see arrived, eight weeks later, in the form of an impressive-looking document titled "Public Health and Embalming," I was surprised to find that it was the work not of a medical expert but of Mr. Raether (who is a lawyer) himself. The approach was curiously oblique:

I confronted some teachers in colleges of mortuary science with the opinion of your San Francisco pathologist that embalming in no way lessens the spread of communicable disease. Their first reaction was "who is he, what is his proof?" And, rightly so. Then they add that it is not contended embalming destroys all microbes.

What *is* contended? We are not told. An authority is cited that seems vaguely irrelevant. It is recommended that I read *Public Health in Boston, 1630–1822;* I am assured that the dean of the American Academy of Funeral Service "has documented proof," but no further evidence is offered. This reminds me of the old trial lawyers' maxim: "When the law is against you, argue the facts; when the facts are against you, argue the law; when the law and the facts are against you, give the opposing counsel hell."

A health officer, in the single reference to a source outside the funeral industry, is quoted as advancing a startlingly novel argument for embalming. It is efficacious, he declares, not only from a public health standpoint but "from the standpoint of man's ages-long concern with life after death," a proposition that is hard to argue against.

The only specific information offered Mr. Raether by spokesmen for the National Funeral Directors Association (NFDA)—to support the contention that embalming has value as a sanitary measure—concerned "the procedures followed at the famous Mayo Clinic, where they have a standing rule that no autopsy shall be conducted on a body unless that body is embalmed—unless they need tissue immediately. This is a standing rule for the protection of doctors and pathologists who might be working with the body."

Unversed though I am in the procedures of doctors and pathologists, this sounded very strange to me. I wrote to the clinic in question to ask if it was true. Their answer: "Unfortunately, it appears that Mr. Raether has been misinformed concerning the attitude of the Mayo Clinic toward the embalming of bodies. We have no rule which requires that bodies be embalmed before an autopsy is performed. It is true that frequently bodies are embalmed prior to the performance of an autopsy, but this is done more for the convenience of the funeral directors than because of any insistence on our part."

Kenneth V. Iserson is a professor of surgery and director of the bioethics program at the Medical School of the University of Arizona. After twenty years in practice treating dying patients and counseling professionals and families about sudden death, he realized, when preparing an ethics paper on teaching with donated remains, that there were huge gaps in his knowledge about what happened to dead bodies. He was prompted to investigate, and the results of his exploration were published as *Death to Dust: What Happens to Dead Bodies?* (Galen Press, 1994).

Dr. Iserson's massive, comprehensive volume is easily the best work on the subject that has appeared in recent years, and it is written with a fluency that makes it accessible to the lay reader as well as the professional.

He was initially stymied by what he felt was a cover-up by a funeral industry that systematically conceals its methods. He says now, in words which have a familiar ring to me, "At the time I was writing, I had to work with several Deep Throats."

Like Dr. Carr, Dr. Iserson has no patience with the argument that embalming is necessary because of the health hazard posed by unembalmed bodies. He quotes with approval Dr. Carr's discussion with me, adding that the Arizona Auditor General's Office, in a review of funeral industry practices, concluded that "the public health risks associated with the disposal of human remains are minimal"; also, a Canadian health minister, "Embalming serves no useful purpose in preventing the transmission of communicable disease."

The clincher for Dr. Iserson is the acknowledged failure of embalmers universally to apply measures for their own protection. If embalmers are not concerned about protecting themselves, he reasons, what message does that send to the public about the claim that embalming is necessary as a public health measure? The true purpose of embalming, he suggests, is to facilitate an open-casket funeral—with the emphasis on *casket*. Embalming, he suggests, is a procedure that boils down to sales and profits.

The only "authoritative" voice the industry has been able to produce in rebuttal belongs to one John Kroshus, identified only as having a connection with the University of Minnesota's program of mortuary science. Mr. Kroshus is quoted in *Funeral Monitor* (April 1996) as denouncing "the book" (again a phrase familiar to me) by posing the question: "If embalming is taken out of the funeral, then viewing the body will also be lost. If viewing is lost, then the body itself will not be central to the funeral. If the body is taken out of the funeral, then what does the funeral director have to sell?"

I could not have put it better.

In a curious, perhaps inevitable, reversal, the decades spent persuading the public that embalming is a sound public health measure have come back to haunt the funeral folk. Angrily protesting new Occupational Safety and Health Administration (OSHA) regulations that end the practice of dumping bodily wastes and embalming fluids down drains or in Dumpsters, one mortician, according to Mortuary Management, ridiculed the "illogic of it all." It seems, he claims, "that waste from dead people is now deemed to be more dangerous than that which comes from the living." He goes on to protest that not one case of infection has been reported as resulting from the longstanding practice of dumping bodily wastes and embalming fluids down sewers.

If the public health benefits of embalming are elusive, ten times more so is the role of "grief therapy," which is fast becoming a favorite with the funeral men. Trying to pin down the meaning of this phrase is like trying to pick up quicksilver with a fork, for it apparently has no meaning outside funeral trade circles. Although it sounds like a term picked up from the vocabulary of psychiatry, psychiatrists of whom I inquired were unable to enlighten me because they had never heard of it.

"Grief therapy" is most commonly used by funeral men to describe the mental and emotional solace which, they claim, is achieved for the bereaved family as a result of being able to "view" the embalmed and restored deceased.

The total absence of authoritative sources on the subject does not stop the undertakers and their spokesmen from donning the mantle of the psychiatrist when it suits their purposes. As an embalming textbook says, "In his care of each subject the embalmer has a heavy responsibility, for his skill and interest will largely determine the degree of permanent mental trauma to be suffered by all those closely associated with the deceased."

Lately, the meaning of "grief therapy" has been expanded to cover not only the Beautiful Memory Picture but any number of aspects of the funeral. Within the trade, it has become a catchall phrase, its meaning conveniently elastic enough to provide justification for all of its dealings and procedures. Phrases like "therapy of mourning" and "grief syndrome" trip readily from industry tongues. The most "therapeutic" funeral, it seems, is the one that conforms to their pattern, that is to say, the one arranged under circumstances guaranteeing a maximum profit.

I had a long discussion with Mr. Raether about "grief therapy," in which I sought to know what medical or psychiatric backing he could produce to substantiate the funeral industry theory that viewing the restored and embalmed body has psychotherapeutic value. He spoke of grief and ceremony; he mentioned some clergymen of his acquaintance who thought viewing the body was a valuable experience; but no qualified psychiatric reference was forthcoming.

Eventually he referred me to an article by Stanford University professor Edmund H. Volkart which had appeared in *Explorations in Social Psychiatry* and which allegedly supported the proposition that "viewing" was therapeutically valuable to the bereaved. Since Professor Volkart's article was the only authoritative published work cited by Mr. Raether, it seemed advisable to check with him. Professor Volkart, who was at the time director of Stanford's program in medicine and the behavioral sciences, wrote to me as follows:

> I know of no evidence to support the view that "public" viewing of an embalmed body is somehow "therapeutic" to the bereaved. Certainly there are no statistics known to me comparing the outcomes of such a process in the United States with the outcomes of England where public viewing is seldom done. Indeed, since the public viewing of the corpse is part and parcel of a whole complex of events surrounding funerals, it would be difficult, if not impossible, to ascertain either its therapeutic or contra-therapeutic effect.
>
> The phrase "grief therapy" is not in common usage in psychiatry, so far as I know. That the loss of any loved object frequently leads to depressions and malfunctioning of the organism is, of course, well known; what is not well known or understood are the conditions under which some kind of intervention should be made, or even the nature of the intervention.

My general feeling is that the phenomena of grief and mourning have appeared in human life long before there were "experts" of any kind (psychiatric, clerical, etc.) and somehow most, if not all, of the bereaved managed to survive. The interesting problem to me is why it should be that so many modern Americans seem more incapable of managing loss and/or grief than other peoples, and why we have such reliance upon specialists. My own hunch is that morbid problems of grief arise only when the relevant laypersons (family members, friends, children, etc.) somehow fail to perform their normal therapeutic roles for the bereaved—or may it be that the bereaved often break down because they simply do not know how to behave under the circumstances? Very few of us, I think, would be capable of managing sustained, ambiguous situations.

Demonstrably flimsy and absurd as the justifications for universal embalming and "viewing" may have been, these patently fraudulent claims of undertakers for their product remained immune from government intervention until 1984, when the Federal Trade Commission's funeral rules were adopted. These provided, among other things, that:

It is a deceptive act or practice for a funeral provider to:
- Represent that state or local law requires that a deceased person be embalmed when such is not the case;
- Fail to disclose that embalming is not required by law except in certain special cases.

The rule went on to provide that prior approval for embalming must be obtained from a family member.

The howls of dismay that greeted these seemingly innocuous rulings were pitiful to behold. They echoed, indeed, the eruption, five years earlier, that followed the introduction of a similar requirement at a meeting of California's State Board of Funeral Directors and Embalmers. I had special reason to take note of it at the time, because the proposer was my husband, Bob Treuhaft, who had been appointed to the board by then governor Jerry Brown.

The proposed regulation required that a responsible party confirm that he or she understood that:

Arterial embalming requires cutting into an artery and drain-
ing the blood, which is replaced by chemical preservatives for
the temporary preservation of the body while awaiting interment. I understand that embalming is not required by law.

Bud Noakes, an editor of *Mortuary Management,* responded
emotionally in a leading editorial:

I thought I had reached a time of life at which I do not shock
easily, but I realize now I had not fully plumbed the depths to
which Mr. Treuhaft is capable of descending. I was shocked
that an individual, who is sworn to act in the best interest of
California, could be so wholly insensitive to the emotional
state of bereaved families.

Anyone who wants to know how embalming is accomplished can easily find out simply by asking funeral directors.
But the answer will be given in a tactful and diplomatic manner, and in consideration of the emotional state of the person
making the inquiry. For anyone to assume that the same explanation could be given to everyone under any and all circumstances is to confess abysmal ignorance of the tender
sensitivities of people in a state of bereavement.

There follows a call to action. There will be a hearing at the state
capitol (date and address given) to vote on the proposal. "It is incumbent upon all funeral directors to take immediate action to protect
the best interests of the bereaved public we are dedicated to serving."

So the brethren rallied, and the lobbyists lobbied, and the proposal was defeated. Dead, yes, but destined to be reincarnated five
years later in the Federal Trade Commission's Funeral Rule.

The funeral folk soon had another opportunity to show their tender concern for the feelings of those in bereavement. When, in the
early eighties, the outbreak of AIDS became a matter of public anxi-
ety, there was panic on the part of funeral directors and embalmers
for their own safety. Most mortuaries refused to accept cases where it
was believed that the deceased had been exposed to the HIV virus;
those that did accept AIDS victims refused to wash, dress, or embalm
the victim.

The New York State Funeral Directors Association (NYSFDA),

on June 17, 1983, advised members to institute a moratorium on the embalming of AIDS victims. Reaction was quick.

Peter Slocum, a spokesman for the State Department of Health, said that funeral directors had previously been advised to handle the bodies of victims of AIDS as they handle victims of hepatitis B—that is, to wear latex gloves, a procedure that had already been prescribed to prevent spread of any contagious disease and required for health care workers under all circumstances when working with dead bodies. "We have not seen anything that suggests that there needs to be any precautions beyond that."

Governor Mario Cuomo introduced a bill in the state legislature which would make funeral directors liable to loss of license if they refused to embalm AIDS victims, saying, "We must not permit AIDS sufferers and their families to be subjected to irrational and unscientific behavior born out of fear, not fact." One week later, the NYSFDA lifted its moratorium on embalming, and the bill died in committee.

This, however, is by no means the end of the story. It is now cash-in time. The mortuaries that did take AIDS cases began charging healthy "AIDS handling fees," usually $200 to $500. Others used subcontractors to do the embalming, covertly adding the cost by inflating the basic service fee. When the problem began to reach crisis proportions in New York City, the Gay Men's Health Crisis (GMHC), with the help of volunteers, surveyed the city's five-hundred-odd licensed funeral homes to identify their AIDS policies. With that information in hand, it put together a guide recommending only forty-two of the five hundred mortuaries to the thousands of friends and relatives of people with AIDS.

The New York City Human Rights Commission got involved in the matter and, as reported in the *Boston Phoenix* (March 12, 1993), published GMHC's list, which fanned public outrage. Loss of business and some successful damage actions helped produce a turn-around, and many mortuaries asked to be added to the referral list.

Elsewhere, however, the AIDS surcharge persisted in one form or another, despite its illegality under the Americans with Disabilities Act (ADA), which requires funeral homes to "provide their services on a non-discriminatory basis to persons who have had AIDS." Since the government was doing nothing to ensure compliance, California assemblywoman Jackie Speier, prodded by the funeral and memorial societies, in 1992 introduced two antisurcharge measures in the state legislature. The leaders of the campaign—Ann Tompkins, president of the California-Hawaii Federation of Funeral and Memorial Societies, and Karen Leonard (dubbed by the *Boston Globe* the "scourge of the funeral industry")—feeling that something was needed to waken the legislators from their lethargy, had Ann appear dressed in a "state-of-the-art" protective suit, the outfit that coroners wear when opening and dissecting bodies for autopsies . . . a far more invasive procedure than embalming. Ann then did her striptease, removing the entire "protective" outfit down to the latex gloves, while Karen explained that the gloves were the sum total of protection needed, or prescribed by OSHA (Occupational Safety and Health Administration), for handling supposedly diseased cadavers. Wholesale cost: two dollars per hundred pair.

Everyone enjoyed the performance except the funeral directors, who were there en masse. The bills passed and were signed into law, the first such legislation in the nation.

7

The Allied Industries

The undertaker, who pockets slightly more than half of the funeral dollar, has generally drawn the spotlight upon himself when the high cost of dying has come under scrutiny. But he is not the whole show. Behind the scenes, waiting for their cue, are the cemeteries, florists, monument makers, vault manufacturers. The casket-manufacturing companies, to whom the undertakers are perennially and heavily in debt, are often lurking in the wings like ambitious understudies waiting to move in and assume control of the funeral establishments should financial disaster strike.

The cast in this drama is not always one big happy family. There are the usual backstage displays of irritation, pique, jealousy, a certain vying and jockeying for position. There are lawsuits and scathing denunciations which arise because of the stiff competition. These can be submerged in the interests of a common endeavor, for the show must go on, and the common goal must be served: that of extracting the maximum admission fee from the paying audience.

The casket companies reported that the alarming condition of the industry's accounts receivable was "far more aggravated in the casket field than in any other manufacturing endeavor." Back in 1961, the funeral establishments owed the casket makers more than $39 million, 20 percent of the year's production, an amount equal to about 317,000 caskets, of which, groaned the creditors, some 40 percent had "already been interred!" Presumably making repossession a most inconvenient remedy for the creditor.

The answer to this problem is, of course, to sell in ever-higher brackets. As Herbert L. Stein, vice president of the National Casket Company and president of the Casket Manufacturers Association, said, "Since the public's purse limits funeral expenditures and nature limits the number of funerals . . . skillful merchandising of quality goods is about the only avenue for upping profits anywhere along the line."

Selling the public on the "quality" of his merchandise can tax the ingenuity of the undertaker. The costliest caskets are those built of the thickest metal. The cheaper lines of metal caskets, constructed of thin sheet metal over a wooden frame, achieve the same look of massive elegance, and can hardly be distinguished (except by grateful pallbearers) from the heavyweights that weigh hundreds of pounds more and sell for thousands of dollars more. A writer in *Mortuary Management* described the average run of lightweight metal caskets as "nothing more or less than stovepipes. Stovepipe gauges are always misleading the public. . . . 'Metal is metal,' says John Public."

The method hit upon by the casket makers to solve this knotty problem is essentially the method used by furniture manufacturers (whose direct descendants they are): that is, to make the cheaper lines so hideous that only customers who can afford the barest minimum will buy them. Mr. John Beck, then president of the Balanced Line Casket Company and of Elgin Associates,* carefully explained the position:

> In most cases where funeral directors are not showing enough profit, they are showing too many low price metal caskets that look too good, are embellished up entirely too much for their price position. . . . We call the items "profit robbers." For right in the area where people do have the money to buy better funerals and will do so when given the proper selection and opportunity, the better sale is lost. The second area where opportunity is lost is in the sealer† area. If the lowest price sealer looks as good as the best one, of course most people will buy the lowest price one. . . . This is the region

---

*Elgin is no more, nor is Merit; they along with many other manufacturers, have been swallowed up by the industry's Big Three: Batesville, Aurora, and York. The number of casket manufacturers has plummeted from 520 in 1976 to fewer than 100 primary producers today.

†A sealer is a casket with a gasket.

where greater profits can be made as this is the one where people who have the money to buy will do so if they are given the proper incentive.

And Mr. Leroy R. Derr, president of the Boyertown Casket Company:

> We can make cheaper caskets, certainly. You can make them and so can I. However, each one helps underwrite the failure of our funeral directors. Too many "cheapies" will ruin the funeral directors completely.

So well did the anti-cheapie program succeed that sales of metal caskets soared. The significance of this industry-engineered change in funeral fashions lies in the circumstance that the wholesale cost of a metal "sealer" casket is today $350, while a cloth-covered softwood wholesales at about $160. Grained-hardwood caskets, which wholesale on an average for about as much as metal ones, have held their own over the years, accounting for about 15 percent of unit sales. The metals, however, which can be mass-produced more cheaply than the hardwoods, are the ones that are pushed most vigorously by the manufacturers.

Here again, what is good for one segment of the burial business has its odd and painful repercussions in another. So enthusiastically are metal caskets pushed that fairly often they are sold even in cases where the deceased is to be cremated. This is most irksome to the crematories, whose equipment—designed for the expeditious combustion of wood—is not geared to the combustion of metal receptacles.

One crematory operator told me how they solve the problem: the lightweight metal caskets are put into the retort, where they eventually buckle and partially melt. "The remains are actually baked," he explained. The heavier and costlier grades cannot be disposed of in this way because they are likely to ruin the crematory equipment. The body is removed from this type of casket and cremated as is— which leaves the problem of disposing of the casket. "State law prohibits the reuse of them," the crematory operator said. "You can't very well take it out to the city dump, because what if the family should happen to pass by and see it there? So we have to break them up and scrap them."

The significance to the consumer of wholesale casket costs lies in the use of "formula pricing," which means in its simplest application that the price of the funeral is arrived at by marking up the wholesale casket cost anywhere from 400 to as much as 900 percent or higher. The markup is usually steepest in the lower price ranges.

Funeral directors have always been jealous guardians of the secrets of wholesale costs. The first official act of the California Undertakers and Funeral Directors Association at its founding convention in 1882 was the adoption of a resolution "that this Association earnestly request all manufacturers and wholesale dealers in undertakers' goods . . . to refrain from sending out catalogues and price lists to any parties who are not undertakers or funeral directors in good standing." Seventy years later, this concern was still uppermost; *Mortuary Management* in 1952 reported, "The National Funeral Directors Association has for a number of years had a policy which states that all catalogues, catalogue sheets, and other advertisements which give wholesale prices for funeral merchandise, when mailed, should be sent in sealed envelopes as first class mail." The same policy applies to funeral directors who mail price lists offering shipping services, embalming services, etc.

Over the years, the occasional hardy storefront casket retailer attempted to compete with the mortuaries in the sale of caskets. These efforts largely failed because the mortuaries resorted to various anticompetitive measures, among them the imposition of a "casket handling fee" when the casket was purchased from a third party. When in 1994 the FTC adopted a rule prohibiting the practice, retail casket sellers, offering substantial discounts, began to flourish. The media—fascinated by the trend—provided publicity, and consumers began to shop around.

Industry response was predictable. Gordon Fairclough in the *Wall Street Journal* interviewed a funeral director in the neighborhood of one new casket emporium. The mortician reports that he met the competition by the simple expedient of lowering his casket prices while at the same time raising his service fees.

The conflict between cemetery and funeral director is of a different nature, for they are in direct competition for the dead man's dollar. The funeral director is here in the choice position, since he ordinarily gets to the prospect first. By the time he gets through with him, there won't be much money left over for a grave. The cemetery people come in a poor second, often finding that by the time their particular commodity is offered to the prospect, the funeral director has skimmed the cream from the top. He has not only induced the bereaved family to spend its all on the casket, but he may steer them away from direct contact with the cemetery and take it upon himself to order a cheap grave by telephone. This can all be very annoying and not at all good for grave sales.

The *American Cemetery* reports a discussion on "immediate-need" selling in which suggestions were made about how the cemeteries can get around this problem. The first thing is to insist that the family make a personal visit to the cemetery and not permit the purchase of the grave to be handled through the funeral director. Mr. David E. Linge, executive vice president of Cedar Memorial Park, Cedar Rapids, Iowa, is quoted as saying: "We don't feel a funeral director's position is such that he can call a cemetery and say, 'Open a thirty-five-dollar single [at least $350 today],' any more than we would call him and say, 'Provide the family with your hundred-dollar casket [$1,000 or more today].' For that reason we will not take, under any circumstances, a sale over the telephone in an at-need situation."

The funeral director should, however, be asked to supply as much information as possible about the family—"their names, relationship to the deceased, financial background, social and economic status in the community." Once he has done so, the article continues, he can safely be dismissed while the arrangements proceed. At this time the funeral director is tactfully drawn away from the family group, since Mr. Linge feels that "as a matter of professional courtesy, he should not be present at the conference."

The family visit also gives the cemetery personnel an opportunity "to describe its other services, such as bronze memorials, flowers, mausoleum crypts and cremation facilities." If the family does not buy a memorial then and there, chances are they will do so in the very near future; for Cedar Memorial Park has a "carefully planned program to provide counsel and assistance for lot owners after the at-need sale has been made." The program works like this: first a letter is sent to the family announcing that the Cedar Park memorial counselor and director of the Family Counseling Service will call upon them shortly "to secure the information necessary for the Historical

Record and present you with a photographic record of the services at Cedar Memorial." Three days later, the counselor arrives at the home and "suggests the purchase of a bronze memorial." But that is not all; in the middle of the month following the service, the counselor is after the family again, this time to invite them to a "counseling program" at the cemetery chapel. This in turn is followed up by yet another personal visit; "Dr. Dill always visits them if a memorial has not been selected."

Another cemetery writer describes the conflict of interest between undertaker and cemetery: "You are all familiar with the situation wherein the mortician gives a telephone order for your bare minimum, telling you to put it on his bill and not contact the family? He is trying to be a good fellow in the eyes of the family he is serving, but more than that, he is scared to death that if we see them, we'll oversell them, and he will suffer in his sale or will have to wait for his money."*

The cemeteries are not taking it lying down. They have developed their own potent counterweapon—"pre-need" sales, for which salesmen roam the neighborhoods of metropolis and suburb like thieving schoolboys in an orchard, snatching the fruit before it has fallen from the tree. They have outflanked their adversary here by getting to the prospect not hours ahead—but probably *years* ahead—of the undertaker. Worse yet, they have begun to establish their own mortuaries for the "one-stop" funeral.

Robert Waltrip of SCI, Ray Loewen of the Loewen Group, and Charles Stewart of Stewart Enterprises, the head honchos of the Big Three of the corporate funeral world, have been pitted in a worldwide race to buy up cemeteries with integrated undertaking establishments. Known in the trade as combos, these have proven to be prodigious money mills.

That such combinations may be illegal in states such as Pennsylvania, Wisconsin, Michigan, and New York, which acknowledge the traditional view that cemeteries are not meant to be for-profit

---

*Mortuary Management stated editorially that it is the funeral director's traditional prerogative to "get first whack at the family." *Concept: The Journal of Creative Ideas for Cemeteries* was quick to take issue with this statement, calling it a "shocking blunder" and adding, "Regardless of the truth in the statement, isn't it improper to talk that way?"

enterprises, has thus far not been seen by the corporate buccaneers as a deterrent.

Louisiana-based Stewart recently negotiated an agreement with the Catholic archdiocese of Los Angeles, the nation's largest (home to nearly 4 million Catholics), to build and operate mortuaries in its six biggest cemeteries. In return for this invaluable endorsement, the Church, to the anguished distress of the independent Catholic funeral directors in the diocese, will receive a percentage of the proceeds from each funeral Stewart performs at the cemeteries.

"Sinful," Father Henry Wasielewski (whose crusade against funeral profiteers is addressed in chapter 14, "The Nosy Clergy") calls the deal. "Most Stewart mortuaries charge thousands more than many independents for the same funeral." It seems unlikely that Stewart, in its new role as purveyor of Catholic funerals in southern California, will share Father Henry's view that a funeral is a sacred ritual that belongs in church. "It should be as simple as the white pall that covers a Catholic casket, signifying man's equality and humility in death."

Then there's the touchy problem of who gets to sell the vault. Vaultmanship is very big these days; at least 60 percent of all Americans wind up in one of these stout rectangular metal or concrete containers, which may cost anywhere from several hundred to a few thousand dollars. Vault selling is ordinarily the prerogative of the funeral director, to whom the vault manufacturers address their message: "Think of your last ten clients. Think how many of that ten had the means and would actually have welcomed an opportunity to choose a finer vault. Makes sense, doesn't it, to give them that opportunity? You'll be surprised how many will choose this finer Clark Vault and be grateful to you for recommending it."

Vault men, when they get together among themselves, can be a convivial and jolly lot, prone to their own kind of family jokes; the Wilbert Burial Vault Company, for instance, gives an annual picnic featuring barbecued chicken, ribs, and "vaultburgers." This bonhomie does not extend to their relations with the cemetery people, whom they are constantly hauling into court. At one time, lawsuits were raging in various parts of the country, brought by vault manufacturers against the cemeteries, to enjoin the latter from going into the business of selling vaults. The theory is that the cemeteries, operating as nonprofit organizations, have no business selling things. The monument makers, too, have entered the fray with the same complaint, for the cemeteries have lately taken to banning the old-fashioned tombstones and selling their own bronze markers. They are slowly driving the monument makers out of business. In some cases, the monument makers have secured injunctions prohibiting the cemeteries from selling monuments, markers, or memorials of any kind. This is a cruel blow to the cemeteries, for they count heavily on the sale of bronze markers.

The cemeteries fight back by making things as rough as possible for both vault and monument companies. They may charge an arbitrary toll for use of their roads in connection with vault installations. They may require that all vaults be installed by cemetery personnel. They won't permit monument makers to install the foundations for their Smiling Christs, Rocks of Ages, and other Items of Dignity, Strength, and Lasting Beauty; instead, they insist that these be installed by the cemetery, which sets a stiff fee for the service.

The backstage squabbling among the various branches of the funeral business has long been a matter of concern to some of the more farsighted industry leaders, who are understandably fearful that the customer will eventually catch on.

These leaders believe that, rather than engage in such unseemly quarrels over the customer's dollar, they should instead concertedly strive to upgrade the standard of dying. A cemetery spokesman, decrying the friction between cemetery and undertaker, writes:

> How simple it is to sell a product or an idea if we but believe in it. If we have the opportunity to foster the sentiment behind the funeral service, we must not fail to do so. Strengthen the idea behind the funeral customs, committals and the like. The family will receive additional mental satisfaction and comfort when the service is complete and in keeping with the deceased's station in life; and from a strictly mercenary angle, it will pay big dividends in establishing the thought of perpetuity and memorialization in the mind of the family.

He acknowledges the funeral director's pioneering role in conditioning the market:

Without question, the tremendous advancement in funeral customs in America must be credited to the funeral director and not to the demands of the public, not even ourselves. He has carried on assiduously an educational campaign which has resulted indirectly in a public desire for funeral sentiment and memorialization.

The lesson to be learned, then, is to promote harmony backstage for a smooth and profitable public performance. Another cemetery writer, reproving his fellow cemetery operators for their jealousy of "the success and dollar income of the funeral directors," suggests one good way in which the cemetery men can effect a rapprochement with these rivals: "Have a yearly meeting with them. Feed them a good dinner, distribute a small token. Last year, we gave them all a set of cuff links made of granite from our mausoleum. Last but not least set up a memorial council. It won't cure all ills, but I can assure you it will help. I believe it can control legislation. . . ."

The memorial council idea actually originated in another quarter, with the flower industry, which had long been urging that industries that profit from funerals unite in common cause. As the president of the Society of American Florists said, "Funeral directors, as well as florists, are in danger of being swept away along with sentiment and tradition by those who do not realize the true value of the traditional American funeral practice. . . . Cooperation between florists and funeral director is essential as it is only one step from 'no flowers' to 'no funeral.' "

The florists, whose language is often pretty flowery, convened the first meeting of the allied funeral industries under the alliterative designation "Symposium on Sentiment." The announced purpose of the symposium was "to combat the forces which are attacking sentiment, memorialization and the rights of the individual in freedom of expression"—in blunter words, to combat the religious leaders and the memorial societies who advocate simpler, less expensive funerals. As the editor of the *American Funeral Director,* weightiest of the industry's trade journals, put it, "The present movement is broad and sweeping. It threatens not only funeral directors, but the entire American concept of memorialization. This means that the supply men, cemeteries, florists, memorial dealers and everyone else dedicated to the care and memorialization of the dead have genuine cause for alarm."

The sentimental gentlemen who rallied to the Symposium on Sentiment (they were in fact the only ones summoned) were an elite group, the top executives of the funeral industry's major trade associations. The names of the associations describe their respective areas of concern: National Funeral Directors Association, National Selected Morticians, American Cemetery Association, National Association of Cemeteries, Florists Telegraph Delivery Association, Monument Builders of America, and Casket Manufacturers Association.

The symposium heard a "Statement on Memorialization" prepared by the florists, who had quite a lot to say about the Dignity of Man, the United States as champion of freedom and leader of the democratic nations of the world, the importance of the individual, the profound traditions of the centuries, and so on: "The final rites, memorial tributes, the hallowed pageant of the funeral service all speak for the dignity of man. . . . Memorialization is love. It records a love so strong, so happy, so enduring that it can never die. It is the recognition of the immortality of the human spirit, the rightful reverence earned by the good life. It is the final testimony to the dignity of man." Just what else went on at the Symposium on Sentiment is a little hard to say, for those participants in the hallowed pageant of the funeral service who attended the meeting have not told us what was said. I asked Mr. Howard Raether, who represented the funeral directors, what sort of agreements were reached. "No agreements." And are copies of the proceedings available? "No." Which is a pity, because from what one can learn of the florists and their ways, the symposium must have been a most colorful meeting.

Funeral flowers accounted for 65 to 70 percent of the cut-flower industry's revenue in 1960, and many funeral homes either had an ownership interest or a commission "arrangement" with the local florist. By 1970 the market share had dropped to 40 percent, and it has, according to trade sources, gone down steadily since then. By 1995 sales had further declined to 14 percent of what was now a $14 billion industry (up from $414 million in 1960). While the floral industry has no statistics on how many flower shops are owned by undertakers, one can assume that the "arrangement" (or a markup) continues to be a sideline source of income for the mortuary.

A current survey of newspaper death notices (and yes, Virginia, there is a trade publication called *Obits and Pieces*) confirms the rout of the "please omit" rubric. One-half to two-thirds of the notices contain requests such as "Donations to (charity) preferred." As before, among the major dailies only the *New York Times* and the *Washington Post* will accept the proscribed words. The *San Francisco Chronicle* will accept "in lieu of" in lieu of "please omit."

What then was achieved by the florists' huge advertising campaign and massive deployment of forces in the War of the Roses? Having won the battle and lost the war, whom can they blame for the distressing decline in sales of funeral flowers?

"Donations to . . . preferred," a formulation devised by the florists themselves to curtail the use of "please omit," must certainly have played a part. "Preferred to what?" is inescapably suggestive.

There are other culprits, of course—no doubt the major ones are the parallel decline of the "standard" open-casket funeral and the sixfold increase in cremations since 1960. These are developments which the florists, with all their resources, have been unable to influence.

8

God's Little
Million-Dollar Acre

In the interment industry there have been a great many revolutionary changes taking place in the last twenty years. More progress has been made during this period than had been made in the previous two thousand years. . . . Today we face an era of unprecedented development in our industry through the use of progressive methods, materials and educational techniques.

—Concept: The Journal of Creative Ideas for Cemeteries

There's gold in them thar verdant lawns and splashing fountains, in them mausoleums of rugged strength and beauty, in them distinctive personalized bronze memorials, in them museums and gift shops. *Concept: The Journal of Creative Ideas for Cemeteries*—the very title vibrates with the thunder of progress—circulated in 1963 to America's five thousand then operating cemeteries, to whom it imparted many an idea on how the gold can best be mined and minted.

The cemetery as a moneymaking proposition is new in this century. The earliest type of burial ground in America was the churchyard. This gave way in the nineteenth century to graveyards at the town limits, largely municipally owned and operated. Whether owned by church or municipality, the burial ground was considered a community facility; charges for graves were nominal, and the burial ground was generally not expected to show a profit.

Prevailing sentiment that there was something special and sacred about cemetery land, that it deserved special consideration and should not be subjected to such temporal regulation as taxation, was reflected in court decisions and state laws. A cemetery company is an association formed for "a pious and public use," the United States Supreme Court said in 1882, and more recently the New Jersey Supreme Court ruled that a cemetery, even if privately owned, is a public burial ground "whose operation for purposes of profit is offensive to public policy." Other rulings have affirmed that land acquired for cemetery purposes becomes entirely exempt from real estate taxes the moment it is acquired, even before a dead body is buried in it.

This traditional view of cemetery land proved a blessing to the land speculators who began to enter the field, and whose handiwork can now be seen on the outskirts of thousands of American communities.

The major premises which, evolved over the years, lie behind modern cemetery operation are all, on the face of it, sound and intelligent enough. Cemetery land is tax-free, which is as it should be, since in theory the land is not to be put to gainful use. Cheap land which for one reason or another does not easily lend itself to such needs of the living as housing and agriculture is commonly used for cemeteries. The purchase of a grave for future occupancy is, surely, a rational and sensible act, showing foresight and prudence on the part of the buyer who wishes to spare his family the trouble and expense of doing so when the need arises. Innovations which result in more economical upkeep of cemeteries, such as dispensing with upright tombstones to facilitate mechanical mowing, seem practical and commendable; so does the establishment of an endowment fund for the future upkeep of the cemetery.

Economies achieved by new and efficient operating methods, tax exemptions such as only schools and churches enjoy, dedication to "pious and public use"—these would all seem to point in the direction of continuously reducing the cost of burial. The opposite has been the case. The cost of burial has soared, at a rate outstripping even the rise in undertakers' charges. The winning combination that has transformed the modern cemetery into a wildly profitable commercial venture is precisely its tax-free status, the adaptability of cheap land to its purposes, the almost unlimited possibilities of subdividing the land, the availability for reinvestment of huge "perpetual care" resources, and the introduction of "pre-need" installment selling. Given these propitious conditions, there is really no end to the creative ideas that can be put to work by the cemetery promoter.

A very creative idea for cemeteries is to establish them as nonprofit corporations. In California and in many other states, virtually all commercial cemeteries enjoy this privilege. At first glance it would seem an act of purest altruism that somebody should go to all the trouble, at absolutely no profit to himself, to start a cemetery wherein his fellow man may be laid to eternal rest. A second glance discloses that the nonprofit aspect removes the necessity to pay income tax on grave sales. And a really close look discloses that the profits that are now routinely extracted by the promoters of "nonprofit" cemeteries are spectacular beyond the dreams of the most avaricious real estate subdivider.

There is nothing actually illegal about the operation. It works like this: Foreverness Lawn Memory Gardens, Inc., is organized as a nonprofit cemetery corporation, closely controlled by the promoters. Foreverness owns not a scrap of land. The acreage it will use for burial plots is owned by the promoters, either in their own names or, more commonly, in the name of a closely held land company. They enter into a contract with themselves—that is, the land company has a contract with Foreverness which provides that Foreverness will operate the cemetery and sell the graves, the promoters to receive for each grave sold 50 percent of the selling price, and for each mausoleum crypt, 60 percent. Since Foreverness out of its half of the income must bear all of the cemetery's operating, sales, and maintenance costs, there is little danger that it will lose its chaste nonprofit character. The promoters, for their part, rake in hundreds of thousands of dollars per acre for their low-cost land.*

Modern transportation has made it possible for the cemetery, like the supermarket, to be at some distance from commercial centers and high-priced residential sections; therefore land for the vast new "park" cemeteries can often be acquired for a modest cash outlay—sometimes for as little as $300 an acre, more commonly for $500 to $1,500 an acre. (Sometimes, of course, particularly when a mausoleum sales program is planned, the promoters will go higher. A California cemetery announced the purchase of "100 acres of ocean

*See end-of-chapter note.

view property" for a reported $5,000 an acre, for the development of "patio-style" mausoleum crypts.)

Having acquired his tax-free, bargain land, the cemeterian (as he likes to be called) starts to get his property ready for occupancy. It is here that creativity begins to come into play.

A real estate promoter who subdivides land for live occupancy may be quite pleased if he can break an acre of land into 50-by-100-foot lots suitable for resale to people who can afford to buy and build. He counts himself lucky if he can squeeze six such lots out of an acre. But consider the cemetery promoter, who routinely breaks his acreage into easy-to-own little packages measuring 8 feet by 3 feet, fifteen hundred or better to the acre, each parcel guaranteed tax-exempt. Fifteen hundred burial spaces per acre is an estimate that errs on the conservative side and would today be considered old-fashioned. For one thing, it allows space for the accommodation of the now outmoded headstone, and it allows 15 percent for drives, walks, and little spaces between graves so that the fastidious or reverent may avoid stepping on the graves to get from one to another. The modern "lawn-type" cemetery, the most creative idea of all, utilizes all this wasted space by simply eliminating footpaths between graves (the paths of glory now lead but to the gift shop and museum) and by banning tombstones altogether, thus making possible unbroken rows of snugly packed 7-by-3-foot graves. The tombstone is replaced by standard bronze markers set flush with the ground—a creative idea which (a) enables the cemetery owners to appropriate from the sale of the plaques profits that formerly went to the monument makers for tombstones, and (b) by opening up the area to huge power mowers,* eliminates all need for hand-trimming of grave plots and saves 75 percent of the maintenance cost.

To these innovations cemeteries now add a further refinement: the sale of nice, cozy "companion spaces" for occupancy by husband and wife. The advantage to the promoters is that the companions will repose one above the other in a single grave space, dug "double depth," to use the trade expression. One Los Angeles "lawn-type" cemetery gives this estimate of its land use:

---

*Rose Hills (Los Angeles) Memorial Park boasts "the world's largest lawn mower."

Adult graves	1,815 per acre
Additional graves; made available by reserving one-half of each acre for double-depth interments	907
Babyland (three in the space occupied by one adult)	120
Total number of graves	2,842 per acre

Another, also in Los Angeles, projects 3,177 "plantings" per acre on land used for ground burial.

It must not be thought that this sort of overcrowding is always the most profitable use of cemetery land. As in the conventional real estate transaction, it is more profitable to offer variety, something to suit every purse and give rein to every social aspiration, and cemetery land—like real estate for the living—is priced according to desirability. There are "view lots" and "garden locations" for those who aspire to be housed among the comfortably well-to-do; nice, roomy "memorial estates" for the really rich; crowded, plainer quarters for those accustomed to tract housing. Neighborhoods develop here too along lines of status and prestige, as well as along religious lines; lodges and clubs are represented by sections set aside for Masons, Lions, veterans' organizations, and the like.

Prevailing prejudices in the land of the living were at one time mirrored in the land of the dead, and racial segregation as practiced on cemetery land paralleled that which prevailed aboveground. As court decisions forced changes aboveground, cemetery segregation fell back accordingly.

The next trend in cemetery development was upward expansion—the community mausoleum. Here indeed was a breakthrough in the space barrier. There may be limits to how deep one can conveniently dig to bury the dead, but when one is building for aboveground entombment, the sky is literally the limit, and ten thousand mausoleum spaces to an acre is a most realistic yield. Referred to disparagingly by cemeterians as "tenement mausoleums," these are very In and are an enormously lucrative proposition. Structurally and functionally, they lend themselves ideally to the simplest form of block construction, for they consist merely of tier upon tier of cubicles made of reinforced concrete faced with a veneer of marble or granite. Crypt is stacked upon crypt—six or seven high—two deep, on either side of a visitors' corridor. The most advantageous size for crypts, we are told, is 32 inches wide, 25 inches high, and 90 inches long.

One large mausoleum construction firm suggests putting a whole acre into crypts, offering the most alluring figures on property potential to be realized from the crypt-filled acre: potential gross sales, $4,308,000; net potential, $2,808,000.

All of the clever planning to extract the maximum use from each acre of land would avail little if the cemetery promoter then had to sit back and wait upon the haphazard whim of the Grim Reaper. With the death rate at its present level, he might have to wait a very long time indeed to begin to realize profit on his investment. This barrier has been brilliantly surmounted by the massive "pre-need" sales campaign, employing squads of telemarketers seeking an invitation to invade the privacy of your home. One of the most successful devices in the history of merchandising, pre-need selling is the key to the runaway growth of the modern cemetery business.

As pre-need sales continue to zoom, it cannot be long before every living American will own a grave, or at least have contracted to pay for one on the installment plan. Perhaps it is this prospect of a saturated market that spurs competing promoters in the race to get there first, to range ever farther in extending their chains of cemeteries to take in even the remotest hamlet. Only this can account for the prodigious rate at which cemetery development and mausoleum construction have been piling up. No community is too small to attract the attention of the promoters: *Concept* cites the case of a town with a population of less than 750 where a successful 288-crypt mausoleum has been established. A mausoleum building firm reported construction of a 336-crypt "indoor-outdoor" mausoleum in Reserve, Louisiana, which at that time had a population of 1,126.

From the point of view of the cemetery promoter, the special attraction of pre-need selling is its self-financing feature. With little or no cash, he acquires an option on some rural acreage and has it zoned for cemetery use. He has a landscape architect supply him with sketches picturing verdant terraces, splashing fountains, tall cypresses and blooming shrubs, and broad avenues converging on an imposing central "feature" (a word used throughout the trade for "statue"), usually in a religious motif. These can be ordered by catalogue number; popular models are *The Good Shepherd,* Model 221-Z; *Christus; The Sermon on the Mount; The Last Supper.* He gets plans and drawings of his mausoleum-to-be from one of the national organizations that specialize in this form of construction. He then contracts with a sales organization that makes a specialty of pre-need selling to handle his sales, and he is in business.

The money comes rolling in, and up to this point not a spadeful of dirt has been turned at the Beautiful Memory Garden; not a cement slab has been poured at the site of the Sweet Repose Mausoleum. It is standard practice in this business not to start construction until at least one-third of all the projected burial and crypt space has been sold. Since this amount is far more than will ever be spent on development and construction, the buyers of these little burial spaces will have furnished the promoter, in advance, with all the capital he will need, and a handsome advance profit as well.

It is not as hard as one might think to extract outrageoussounding prices from the public, because pre-need payments are customarily made in painless installments over a long period of time. The cemetery owner can, after all, afford to offer generous terms. Unlike any other commodity offered for sale on the installment plan, this one remains always in the seller's possession, and its use may not be called for until many years after it has been paid for in full. "Sunset View's 'Before Need' ownership plan offers the opportunity for purchasing family lots in monthly installments so small that they are hardly noticeable," says a circular mailed to me by a local cemetery.

Pre-need selling is a costly proposition, and it is the customer, of course, who ultimately foots the bill. The sales organization usually works on a 50 percent commission; the individual salesman gets 20 to 40 percent of the selling price. "In most cemeteries which have pre-arrangement sales programs, four to ten times more is spent for direct selling than is spent for the total cost of planning, development, and landscaping," complains a cemetery architect.

The major conglomerates, such as SCI, Loewen, and Stewart, are able to circumvent these high costs by advertising for salespeople, "No experience required." The hungry hopefuls, once enticed, learn that they will be obliged to meet a sales quota set by the company— one easily met by the novices when they sign up their kith and kin, but impossible to continue once that has been done. It's a cruel but effective way to market a community at low cost, with no regular employees, no employee benefits.

The "space and bronze deal," as it is called by the sales specialists, is exciting, heady work. The exuberant buoyancy, the spirit of confidence, the zeal and joie de vivre reflected in the soaring prose of the *American Cemetery* are in marked contrast to the embattled gloom, the righteous martyrdom, that stalks the pages of the undertaker's trade magazines.

Before the advent of the commercial cemetery, the principal cemetery executive was the superintendent or head groundskeeper. Today, the unassuming fellow who kept up the cemetery grounds has been supplanted in place of first importance by a more dashing breed—a Memorial Counselor, who in this capacity must quickly acquire a few new postures. An executive of the California Interment Association sees the Memorial Counselor as walking a sort of tightrope: "Exploitation of cemetery sales achievements must assume the proper place in the delicate balance of ethical cemetery practices and the natural American drive to achieve the strongest possible business posture."

Luckily, it takes only about a week for a person to acquire the right amount of sincerity and truth at a school for Memorial Counselors. The trainee is "schooled in the best methods of gaining access into a home. He must be in a problem-solving frame of mind, and must be one who has come to render a service and not one who has come to sell something. During the week he is reviewed constantly on trial closes and answering objections." At the end of the week the student is presented with his certificate as "Professional Memorial Consultant."

In a typical sales argument, the idea of inflation is the first concern to plant in the prospect's mind:

Mr. Jones, if something should happen to me in the years to come, my wife, bless her heart, would feel inclined to go out and emotionally overspend. She would use money I left for her comfort and protection and buy cemetery property at its then INFLATED price to show her love for me. That's why I have tied her hands and protected her against her own affection and the rolling surge of INFLATION. This protection is possible only by acting now. I'm sure we husbands all agree on this point, don't we?

And another:

Mr. and Mrs. Jones, our birth certificate is a purchase contract for our cemetery property. We must have a place to be buried. Furthermore the laws of all 50 states confirmed the sale. We must be buried in a duly approved cemetery.* The only choice left to us is which of the two prices we desire to pay. If we wait we pay the inflated price—all cash—yes we buy in an emergency. If we act now we stop inflation—under this program we even roll the price back. As good businessmen, we know which makes more sense, don't we?

Why do the customers buy? The aura of genteel respectability conferred by ownership of cemetery property (often the only piece of real estate the prospect will ever own), the wisdom and economy of advance planning for a contingency that must inevitably arise, are powerful arguments. It sounds good, but the "economy" is a myth and the "wisdom" a snare. The customer in the pre-need era pays far more for burial than he would have in pre-pre-need days. Years ago, while there was no pre-need selling, there was a certain amount of pre-need buying (a most important distinction), generally by those solid citizens—staid families of substantial means—who were accustomed, in this as in other matters, to planning in advance. Acquisition of a "family plot" was not a costly transaction; if a family paid $100 for a four-grave plot, it was paying a lot. Single graves ran from $1 to $20. Even today, people who live in communities that have not yet been invaded by the commercial pre-needers can buy from municipal, denominational, or other noncommercial cemeteries burial space either in advance or when death occurs at a fraction of what they would have to pay a commercial solicitor.

*Not true. In many states, home burial is still permissible in rural areas; and in all states, cremated remains may be buried on private property. In every state except California, cremated remains may be scattered at will or with the landowner's permission.

Frequently people do not know of the existence in their community of a publicly owned cemetery; and few take the trouble to go there to make advance arrangements. Those who do so are prosaically just buying a grave, whereas the stay-at-homes, who wait for the Memorial Counselor to call, get so much *more* for their money: "Ideally a couple in their early years of married life will benefit by making arrangements at that time, affording them protection and economic benefits when they need it most and often creating a psychological bond that may enrich their marital relationship," says the Interment Association of America.

The advent of the mausoleum boom added a new dimension to the pre-need sales rhetoric. "Talk Mausoleum!" urged *Concept;* and evaluating the results of a recent direct-mail campaign, it reported, "It was agreed that prestige and horror of ground burial motivated the bulk of replies."

Mausoleum advertising reaches back into history for its theme—Abraham's cave, the Pyramids, the tomb of King Mausolus, the Taj Mahal (usually referred to as "the $15,000,000 Taj Mahal"), the "$3,000,000 Lincoln Memorial," Grant's Tomb. *Concept* quotes Tressie Johnson of Texas ("she is a volume producer in mausoleum sales; sincerity plays a great part in her success") on how to make the most of the historical theme. She suggests mentioning the Taj Mahal, Napoleon, Lincoln, Grant, and Lenin: "But what means even more to the family, tell them Jesus was supposed to have been placed in a rock tomb belonging to Joseph of Arimathea."

In real life, the brand-new mausoleums mushrooming in communities across the country do not look very much like the Taj Mahal. They look a good deal more like giant egg crates, and the little receptacles have a certain sameness about them—which is not surprising, since they are identical. However, since purchasing power varies from customer to customer, and since those able to pay more should be given every opportunity to do so, distinction and desirability have been conferred on some of the receptacles by the magic of the sales talk.

Like uncounted millions of other Americans, I was visited by a cemetery "Memorial Counselor." He spread out for my delectation page after page of shiny color representations of rolling lawns, limpid pools, statues of the Good Shepherd, of sundry Apostles; "And here are some of our special Babyland features," he announced proudly, producing a folder of statues of toddlers and lambs. On each picture was printed in small letters "Artist's Conception."

"Can I go out and see it?" I asked.

"Well, there won't be anything much to see for a while yet; most of it is still in the planning stage. Here's how the mausoleum is going to look." He pulled out a folder showing "Preconstruction Corridor" in pink and gray marble, and "Sunshine Garden—An Innovation in Out-of-doors Memorial Construction" in cream and blue. It was gratifying to note that the brochure advertised "Mausoleum staff to serve you every day of the year from sunrise to sunset," and particularly comforting (in view of the purpose of the property I was being offered) to learn that one's crypt would be "Judgement Proof." From the counselor and his brochures I began to get an inkling of how the pricing is established; how liabilities can be transformed into assets, and economies—convenient for the cemetery promoters—made attractive. The crypts facing the corridor are called "mausoleum crypts." The ones facing outside, and forming in fact the outside wall of the structure, once less salable and therefore lower in price, are now called "garden crypts"—a stroke of creative genius—and often command even higher prices than the stuffy old indoor ones. "It's all part of the trend towards outdoor living," explained the counselor. The pavement of the corridors does not go to waste, either. A crypt below floor level has none of the associations of the bargain basement if it is labeled "Westminster Crypt"— on the contrary, it conjures up flattering thoughts of reposing eternally cheek by jowl with the great and famous. Likewise, the cost of a dividing wall between two crypts can be eliminated if they are advertised as a "True Companion Crypt—permits husband and wife to be entombed in a single chamber without any dividing wall to separate them. Here, husband and wife may truly be 'Together Forever.' "

"Then, the corridor crypts would all be one price, the garden crypts another, and so on?" I asked. Oh no, said the counselor, there's quite a difference. The corridor crypts vary considerably; the cheapest are the ones near the top. "And the most expensive?" "Heart level," he replied, tapping that organ with his right hand and giving one of his sincere looks.

Later, when I went to see the cemetery, I could see why the counselor was not too anxious to have prospects go out there. It was merely an expanse of dusty, dried-out California hillside, with a fine view of the factories and warehouses of the industrial section below. The Lifetime Green artificial grass mats stacked near the office offered a lurid contrast to the vistas of brown land on either side; the mausoleum was a stunted dwarf compared with the massive structure of the "Artist's Conception." The "features" were apparently also in the future, except for a rather forlorn-looking huge tin Bible at the entrance. A small slope, about the size of a town dweller's back garden, was already converted into graves; I counted seventeen of them, and six occupied crypts in the mausoleum. The Memorial Counselor had accurately told me that of fifteen hundred burial places sold, only twenty-three were actually in use.

The profit potential of a cemetery does not by any means end with the sale of burial space. Adjuncts of cemetery operation, such as the digging, planting, trimming, and general maintenance of graves, which fifty years ago (before the advent of the commercial cemetery) were looked upon simply as chores to be handled by the groundskeeper or the sexton, are today systematically turned to good account. And there are today many extra profit items for the cemetery owner which played no part in cemetery operation or finance in the days before Forest Lawn became the arbiter of fashion in the burial world—the sale of vaults, bronze grave markers, flowers, postcards, and statuary, and the collection, control, and management of huge "perpetual care" funds.

A generation ago, gravedigging and markers were provided by cemeteries at a nominal cost. *Park and Cemetery* (a fuddy-duddy forerunner of *Concept*) reported in 1921 that cemeteries in Seattle were charging $7 for opening and closing a grave. Now a mechanized operation, opening and closing a grave can be completed in about fifteen minutes. Today, cemeteries are charging $600 to $900 for this service, even more on Sundays and holidays. Opening a mausoleum vault, which means simply removing the 25-by-32-inch faceplate, will cost a comparable amount. Zestiest of all for the cemetery are the charges made for opening niches to contain urns in the columbarium. The faceplate of a small niche measures 14 by 14 inches; the charge for opening it in the Neptune Society's San Francisco columbarium is $300. What needs to be done to open it? I asked an undertaker. "It's all in the wrist," he replied. The cost of a niche runs upward from $3,500, but this, I was assured, includes all charges for care "in perpetuity."

Other profit items which the commercial cemetery tries to pre-empt for itself are the sale of vaults, grave liners, and markers.

The cement marker, once a threat to bronze sales, is no longer a problem. The commercial cemeteries, authorized by law to make their own rules, simply prohibit their use. The cemetery's specifications for the size, shape, and installation of the bronze, granite, or granite-and-bronze markers which they now require are likely to be so stringent as to make it inconvenient to buy this commodity elsewhere, or to have it installed by an outside supplier. The ordinary bronze marker, inscribed with the name of the deceased and his dates of birth and demise, sells for about $350 for a single grave. The standard cemetery markup is 100 to 200 percent.

In areas already saturated with grave and mausoleum sales, a second pressing of the vintage, so to speak, can be harvested by selling bronze markers "in advance of need" to people who have already purchased interment space. Although I find it hard to picture the customer placing the order for his own memorial ahead of time ("How shall I order the inscription? 'To My Dearly Beloved Self,' perhaps, or just simply 'Dear Me'?"), such sales are being made in substantial volume.

The bronze deal, whether pre-, post- or at-need, can be greatly facilitated by the use of sales letters, which are followed up by telephone calls and personal visits from the Bronze-Memorial Counselors. The Matthews Memorial Bronze Company has prepared dozens of suggested sales letters with which the cemetery can pepper lot holders at appropriate intervals:

Dear Friend,

The other day, we and our Maintenance crews were out working the section of the cemetery where your family estate is located. Naturally, we couldn't help but notice that the graves were unmemorialized.

One of the workmen commented that an unmarked grave is a sad thing.

Some of the letters are geared to seasonal use: "Dear Friend, If Winter comes, can Spring be far behind?" . . . "Dear Friend, In a few weeks the forsythia and daffodils will raise their golden horns to the sky and trumpet in the warm winds of spring." . . . "Dear Friend, Soon the year will repeat its old story." . . . "Dear Friend, Soon Easter will be upon us once again." . . . "Dear Friend, The second Sunday in May is Mother's Day." . . . "Dear Friend, Does Memorial Day make you think about a drive in the country?" . . . "Dear Friend, Decoration Day is just a few short weeks away." . . . "Dear Friend, Once again Christmas is almost here." After four or five paragraphs of trumpeting forsythia or happy Mom's Day visits, the point is made: "But if you want bronze memorialization by the holiday, you've got to act swiftly. You see, it takes many weeks to individually handcraft and deliver the memorial of your selection."

Another tactic being used by cemeteries is to contact lot owners, asking them to come in so the cemetery can update its new computer. Once there, the future resident is reminded of the ever-looming threat of inflation and persuaded to purchase vault and memorials "now." Opening and closing can be paid for in advance, too, and one Virginia gentleman was induced to plunk down $900—to cover the weekend or holiday rates, just in case.

Just what happens to the money that is collected on the "pre-need bronze deal" is not quite clear. The pre-need space buyer receives for his money a salable ownership interest in an existing bit of real estate, whereas the pre-need "bronze" buyer receives only a certificate telling him that when he dies a piece of metal will be manufactured and set in his grave. The seller meantime—and it may be a very long time—has the use not only of the money paid for the memorial-to-be, but an additional sum which the purchaser has been obliged to pay for its perpetual care! Regulatory laws that might give the buyer some measure of protection have not yet, in many states, been enacted.

Another idea used by most cemeteries is the "perpetual care fund." The uninitiated might expect that, having paid a pretty penny for a crypt or a grave, the costs of upkeep might be borne by the cemetery. Not at all. There is added to the cost of cemetery and mausoleum space a surcharge of 10 to 20 percent for future care; some mausoleums charge as much as 25 percent of the price of the crypt.

Graves need tending, it is true, but the care that needs to be lavished on a cement crypt is somewhat hard to envisage.

The monies so collected are kept by the cemetery owner, supposedly as an endowment fund to guarantee such care forever in the future, a promise palpably incapable of fulfillment. Nevertheless, the magic of pre-need selling has swelled these funds in many cases to huge proportions. The money held in such funds in the United States totaled over $1 billion in 1961 and has swelled to over $20 billion in the ensuing thirty-five years.

The cemetery operators to whom these funds have been entrusted have not always been as scrupulously honest in their stewardship as one might hope. The itinerant promoter who moves his sales crew into a community to saturate it with pre-need sales is hardly the type one would expect to sit around and wait for his sold-out cemetery to fill up, much less wait forever to lavish perpetual care upon it. And when he moves on to the next community, he has not always been able to resist the temptation to take the perpetual care fund with him—for safekeeping, of course, or at least to dip into it for a loan at low interest to purchase new cemetery property. After all, the money is there to be invested.

A fund of over $20 billion, available for investment at the discretion of cemetery owners, can serve as a powerful political weapon. Only after the misappropriation of funds became a public scandal did a few state legislatures begin to impose legal controls on the investment of cemetery trust funds. The potent cemetery lobby (it is the envy of the funeral directors, who carry less weight in the state legislatures) has contrived to secure laws that are not unduly burdensome, and in some states the regulation of perpetual care funds is placed under the benign authority of a board composed entirely of cemetery owners.

Municipal cemeteries are operated as a public service and are often partially subsidized by public funds. Since they do not as a rule advertise, or send salesmen out on commission, they are able to offer cemetery space and services at moderate cost.

What happens when, for the first time, commercial cemeteries move into a community where there is already a municipal cemetery? A sales team blankets the community, sells pre-need lots at from three to ten times the price charged by the municipal cemetery, which has no advertising or pre-need promotion budget. The reaction of the city fathers is likely to be, "Now that sufficient burial space is available from a private source, why spend money to operate a municipal cemetery?" or, "Let's raise our rates and make it self-supporting—if they can do it, why can't we?" In the latter case, the municipal cemetery gets itself an advertising appropriation, perhaps hires a crew of pre-need salesmen, and up go the charges correspondingly.

Cemetery men have also found in pre-need selling a means of cutting themselves into the veterans' market, a source of business from which they would be excluded by the federal laws which give veterans and their wives the privilege of burial in national cemeteries without charge. Pre-need selling enables the cemetery man to outflank the undertaker. He gets into the home first—years ahead of the undertaker, in fact—seduces the family with his glossy catalogues, and points out that the veteran's $300 burial allowance can be applied to the cost of the grave. That one must die in a VA hospital or nursing home to qualify may never get mentioned.

Pre-need cemetery promoters, in considering whether a particular community is ripe for exploitation, are least of all concerned about whether there is a deficiency of cemetery space. All they want and need to know is how often the town has been previously canvased by pre-need salesmen, and how many householders already own cemetery lots. Consequently, duplication of cemetery facilities goes on apace. Once, in hearings on a cemetery application in Los Angeles, there was testimony from numerous sources that there already existed sufficient cemetery facilities to handle all burials in the Los Angeles area for the next hundred years.

Having saturated a community with pre-need graves, crypts, vaults, and memorials, and having established a perpetual care fund the control of which is firmly under his thumb, how next can the cemetery promoter cash in on his privileged position? It should surprise no one who has come this far that men of vision in the industry have already looked ahead and come up with the ultimate solution: a prepaid package that will include not only burial space and marker but "casket," hearse, undertaking services, and flower shop as well.

We have seen that funeral home charges are today eight to ten times what they were thirty years ago. And while cemetery prices have increased correspondingly, the leap in profitability has been nothing short of spectacular. SCI, for example, reported a profit margin of 34 percent for its cemetery operations in 1995, a performance which would do credit to any corporation in the Fortune 500, compared with a still robust 22 percent for its funeral establishments. And the cemeteries in North America that yield the highest returns are those, like Forest Lawn, that have self-contained mortuaries and flower shops. It is these that the corporate consolidators scramble for most avidly, leading to bidding contests that some securities analysts consider rash.

After Words

Tempest in New York:
Hearing Slams Cemetery Marketing Practices*

By any standard, it has not been a great public relations year for cemeterians. In California, recent headlines have widely spread the story of grim violations at numerous prominent cemeteries, including disinterment, multiple burials, non-maintenance, and fraud/embezzlement. Now comes New York, where the controversy has taken a new direction and focused not so much on cemetery maintenance, but on ownership policy and marketing practices.

Under New York law, cemeteries are not-for-profit enterprises, regulated in part to help ensure that sufficient money is set aside for perpetual care. The current debate therefore centers on the following questions: Is it proper, then, to allow funeral homes, established to make money, to acquire an interest in cemeteries? And could pressures for profit this year endanger the sanctity of care in the years to come? The State Cemetery Board held a hearing in Albany last week to address these and other issues as part of broader legislation on cemetery reform taking shape in both houses of the New York legislature.

---

*This article first appeared in the *Funeral Monitor,* March 25, 1996. Reprinted with permission.

As usual, the hearing placed on public view a distorted image for funeral service. The recent expansion of The Loewen Group and SCI into the New York cemetery market is the underlying factor which has brought the issue to a head. It is no secret that both companies have bought many funeral homes in the region in recent years—and they are increasingly buying cemeteries as well.

The New York State Funeral Directors Association, for one, has mixed feelings about this development. Wayne Baxter testified that his membership is concerned that joint ownership might expose the public to excesses by unscrupulous funeral directors. He said regulations may be needed to ensure that money from the nonprofit cemeteries is not funneled into the profit-making funeral homes—a scenario that is more conceivable with joint ownership. The National Catholic Cemetery Conference, through spokeswoman Ellen Woodbury, also charges "conglomerate ownership" with an "outrageous litany of untruths and misinformation" designed to steer mourners away from religious cemeteries. "We have a 2,000 year old tradition of caring for the dead as a matter of faith, not as a matter of profit," she said. Finally, Rabbi Elchonon Zohn, speaking for the Jewish Community Relations Council, also considered joint ownership problematic, maintaining that there is an incentive to adopt marketing practices that could generate immediate profits (such as selling two-for-one grave sites), but weaken a cemetery's ability to maintain care when its space is sold out.

Whether true or not, recent alleged selling tactics by a Loewen Group sales person have provided ammunition for the reform camp—and made no friends in the major Roman Catholic diocese on Long Island. A Loewen representative, offering a "free crypt" at a nearby Loewen-owned cemetery, made the mistake of approaching Ellen Woodbury, director of cemeteries for the Rockville Centre Catholic Diocese and President of the National Catholic Cemetery Association. It was not a pretty picture—and Ms. Woodbury claims to have captured it all on tape.

"Congratulations," the voice on the phone told Ellen

Woodbury, "You've won a free grave." It was a telemarketer on behalf of The Loewen Group seeking an appointment. As widely reported in the *New York Post,* one of the first things the sales person did upon arrival was hand the promised "free grave" certificate to Woodbury and her husband. She soon made it clear, however, that the giveaway grave was less than desirable. It was in a section of the cemetery where, she said, the graves are sinking. "Wouldn't you rather be in the above-ground crypts under development?" the saleswoman asked. She said the "free grave" certificate could be turned in for a discount in a "better" part of the cemetery—and the cemetery would guarantee the Woodburys a 15% discount at a local Loewen-owned funeral home as long as financing was made in advance. As described, a perfectly legal sales pitch was transformed into a blatant cemetery/funeral home tie-in, not to mention a classic bait-and-switch marketing maneuver.

The Loewen saleswoman did not have the good sense to at least stop right there, and apparently went right on to slander the condition of and long-term outlook for Catholic cemeteries in the area. In a letter obtained by this *Monitor* from Ms. Woodbury to the Diocese of Rockville Centre, she notes: "The part of the presentation which concerned me most was when my husband and I mentioned we were Catholic and felt inclined to choose a Catholic cemetery rather than a non-sectarian one. The counselor insisted that Catholic cemeteries are not maintained as well as Washington Memorial Park, have very limited space, and are definitely not funded, being totally dependent on the diocese in which they are located to support the care and maintenance of the grounds and building in the future. She continued that, as a result of the Church's current financial condition, there would definitely be no funds available in the future for the maintenance of their cemeteries. When approached, she insisted that even Pope John Paul refused to permit a special cemetery collection to help dioceses offset this expense. These are outlandish statements and lies."

The state attorney general is reviewing the tape for possible violations of consumer protection laws and other regulations—and The Loewen Group would also appreciate having a copy. Larry Miller, of The Loewen Group's Cemetery Division, clearly stated that criticism of any religion is not part of the company's sales program—and vowed to investigate and fire any employee found to be engaging in religion bashing. He also said that Loewen telemarketers are trained to follow a carefully written script and "everything is above board." According to Miller, the "free grave" offer is genuine and not part of any bait-and-switch scam, and he noted that "thousands" of people have taken advantage of the offer in 38 states in which the company has holdings.

Marketing, as always, is probably one of the touchiest areas in funeral service—given the volatility of the topic and, often, the vulnerability of the client—and this latest dustup only reconfirms the point. Done correctly, there is nothing illegal about telemarketing: A service or product is available at a fair price and you, Mr. and Mrs. Consumer, should know about it.

Certainly, with 9,000 employees, The Loewen Group or any other large mega-business is going to have its share of overzealous sales people who aggressively cross the line into unfair and/or fraudulent marketing ploys. Is the basic problem a compensation system based on commissions? Does that particular motivating factor impel too many sales people over the line? No easy answers here. In conversation with Loewen cemetery division officials, it became clear that commissioned sales people are the traditional—and proven—way to go, and that straight salary or salary/commission combinations have not yielded the optimum sales results. To this *Monitor,* the key element is to hire the best and insist on sales training—heavy-duty training which explicitly outlines strict limits, largely scripted presentations, and provides no excuse for lack of knowledge about the dos and don'ts.

The Loewen Group and any other deathcare enterprise must maintain a strong company policy against high-pressure selling tactics—and promptly fire those who venture off the reservation. It has been said before: Other businesses can afford their occasional bad apples a lot better than funeral service can.

9

Shroudland Revisited

Nothing in Los Angeles gives me a finer thrill than Forest Lawn. . . . The followers of a triumphant Master should sleep in grounds more lovely than those where they have lived—a park so beautiful that it seems a bit above the level of this world, a first step up toward Heaven.

—BRUCE BARTON,
quoted in *Art Guide to Forest Lawn*

Forest Lawn Memorial-Park of Southern California is the greatest nonprofit cemetery of them all; and without a doubt its creator—Hubert Eaton, the Dreamer, the Builder, inventor of the Memorial Impulse—is the anointed regent of cemetery operators. He has probably had more influence on trends in the modern cemetery industry than any other human being. Mrs. Adela Rogers St. Johns, his official biographer, sees Forest Lawn as "the lengthened shadow of one man's genius." Even as she was writing those words, that long shadow was creeping over much of the cemetery land in the territorial United States; today it spans oceans, extending to Hawaii and even to Australia.

The Dreamer and his brainchild are already known to tens of thousands of readers through *The Loved One,* by Evelyn Waugh—to whom *Mortuary Management* refers as "Evelyn (Bites-The-Hand-That-Feeds-Him) Waugh." If there are skeptics who think that Mr. Waugh may have been guilty of exaggeration, a visit to Forest Lawn should set their minds at rest.

I was among the one and a half million who passed through the entrance gates one year; the guidebook says they are the largest in the world, twice as wide and five feet higher than the ones at Buckingham Palace; and (presumably to warn anyone rash enough to try hefting one) adds that each weighs five thousand pounds.

It is all there, just as Mr. Waugh has described it, although in the intervening years since *The Loved One* was written, there have been many additions, so the overall impression is that today it far transcends his description.

There are the churches, ranging from wee to great, the Wee Kirk o' the Heather incongruously furnished with wall-to-wall carpeting, the Great Mausoleum Columbarium, primarily patriotic in theme, with its Memorial Court of Honor, Hall of History, Freedom Mausoleum, and Court of Patriots. "Does one have to be a citizen or sign a loyalty oath to get into the Hall of Patriots?" I asked a guide. "No, ma'am!" was the answer. "Anyone can be buried there, as long as he's got the money to pay for it." (This is not strictly true; Forest Lawn refused convicted rapist Caryl Chessman's last remains "on moral grounds.")

There are statues, tons of them, some designed to tug at the heartstrings: *Little Duck Mother, Little Pals, Look, Mommy!*, others with a different appeal—partially draped Venuses, seminude Enchantresses, the reproduction of Michelangelo's *David*, to which Forest Lawn has affixed a fig leaf, giving it a surprisingly indecent appearance.

A 1996 visit to Forest Lawn Memorial-Park in the Los Angeles suburb of Glendale confirmed the extraordinary stability and vigor of the business.

There has been no change in style. The Dreamer has been put to rest in the Court of Honor, but the vulgarity of his Dream is being maintained with a sure and faithful hand—shooting-gallery statuary, gift shop, Wee Kirk o' the Heather. Changes are in terms of scale only. There are now five Forest Lawns in Southern California where once there stood one—Hollywood Hills, Cypress, Covina Hills, and Forest Lawn–Long Beach, "formerly Forest Lawn–Sunnyside," complete the roster.

Forest Lawn's "life size replica" of Michelangelo's *David* was toppled from its pedestal and demolished, fig leaf and all, in the Sylmar earthquake of 1971. Another replica, sans fig leaf, installed a decade later fared no better. David was removed when ladies' groups took exception to his full frontal nudity.

While Forest Lawn operates funeral parlors and flower shops in each of its locations, the sale of burial plots is still the core of its business. Medium-priced graves are now priced at $5,580 in the Vale of Faith to $10,900 in the Terrace of Brilliant Star; 15 percent is now added for perpetual care. Should you want something better, $27,000 will get you into the Terrace of Sunlit Skies, and for $31,000 you may join even more select company in the Garden of Honor (which features piped-in pop hymns, a feature that might make it, for some, their idea of perpetual purgatory). You may if you wish install an approved statue, but to do so you must buy four or more grave spaces.

The population of Forest Lawn, over 200,000 in 1961, has been augmented by new arrivals at the rate of 6,500 a year. On all sides one may see the entire cycle of burial unfolding before one's eyes. There is a museum in Chicago containing an exhibit of hatching chicks; the unhatched eggs are in one compartment, those barely chipped in another, next the emerging baby chicks, and finally the fully hatched fledglings. The Forest Lawn scene is vaguely reminiscent of that exhibit. Here is a grass-green tarpaulin unobtrusively thrown over the blocked-out mound of earth removed to ready a grave site for a newcomer. Near it is a brilliant quilt of mixed orchids, gardenias, roses, and lilies of the valley, signifying a very recent funeral. Farther on, gardeners are shoveling away the faded remains of a similar floral display, possibly three or more days old. Between these are scores of flat bronze memorial plaques bearing the names of the old residents. In the distance, the group of people entering one of the churches could be either a wedding party or a funeral party; it's hard to tell the difference at Forest Lawn.

Other sights to visit are the hourly showings of the *Crucifixion* ("largest oil painting in the world") and a stained-glass reproduction of *The Last Supper*. Mrs. St. Johns says of the Dreamer, "In Missouri-ese, he had always been a sucker for stained glass."

Behind the Hall of Crucifixion are the museum and gift shop. The purpose of the museum and the method used to assemble its contents are explained by Eaton in *Comemoral*. If a museum is established, people will become accustomed to visiting the cemetery for instruction, recreation, and pleasure. A museum can be started on a very small—in fact, minimal—scale, perhaps to begin with in just one room with just one statue. Once started, it will soon grow: "I speak from experience. People begin to donate things with their names attached, and bring their friends to see them on display." The result of this novel approach to museology is an odd assortment of knick-knacks—old coins, copies of the shekels paid to Judas for his betrayal of Jesus, a bronze tablet inscribed with the Gettysburg Address, some suits of armor, Balinese carvings, Japanese scrolls, bits of jade, some letters by Longfellow, Dickens, etc., and lots more.

The museum received front-page publicity in the Los Angeles press in 1961 on the occasion of the Great Gem Robbery. With his enviable flair for showmanship, Dr. Eaton managed to turn the robbery and even the actual worthlessness of the "gems" to good account in a half-page advertisement in which he made one of the most touching appeals ever addressed to a jewel thief: "We feel that you cannot be professional thieves, or you would have known that neither the black opal named 'The Pride of Australia' nor the antique necklace could be marketed commercially. These two are valuable principally for their worth as antiques. . . . The emerald and diamond necklace has small retail value today, because the cut of the stones has been obsolete for many years, and it would be difficult to sell it except as an antique." But it is when he speaks of the need to care for the black opal (named by whom "The Pride of Australia," one wonders) that he is at his most affecting: "We do hope that you bathe it every few weeks in glycerin to prevent it from shattering." Kidnappers! From the bottom of a mother's heart I beg you to give my baby his daily cod-liver oil!

A deeper purpose for the maintenance of a museum in a cemetery is also explained by Dr. Eaton: "It has long been the custom of museums to sell photographs, post cards, mementos, souvenirs, etc." The visitor is summoned to the gift shop ("while waiting for the next showing of the 'Crucifixion' ") by one of those soft, deeply sincere voices that often boom out at one unexpectedly from the Forest Lawn loudspeaker system. Among the wares offered are salt and pepper shakers in the shape of some of the Forest Lawn statuary; the Builder's Creed, printed on a piece of varnished paper and affixed to a rustic-looking piece of wood; paper cutters, cups and saucers, platters decorated with views of the cemetery; view holders with colored views of the main attractions. There is a foldout postcard with a long script message for the visitor rendered inarticulate by the wonders he has seen. It starts: "Dear ———, Forest Lawn Memorial-Park has proved an inspiring experience," and ends: "It was a visit we will long remember." There is a large plastic walnut with a mailing label on which is printed "Forest Lawn Memorial-Park In A Nut Shell! Open me like a real nut . . . squeeze my sides or pry me open with a knife." Inside is a miniature booklet with colored views of Forest Lawn. There is an ashtray of very shiny tin, stamped into the shape of overlapping twin hearts joined by a vermilion arrow. In one of the hearts is a raised picture of the entrance gates, done in brightest bronze and blue. In the other is depicted the Great Mausoleum, in bronze and scarlet with just a suggestion of trees in brilliant green. Atop the hearts is an intricate design of leaves and scrolls, in gold, green, and red; crowning all is a coat of arms, a deer posed against a giant sunflower, and a scroll with the words JAMAIS ARRIÈRE. Never in Arrears, perhaps.

Forest Lawn pioneered the current trend for cemeteries to own their own mortuary and flower shop, for convenient, one-stop shopping. The mortuary "is of English Tudor design, inspired by Compton Wynyates in Warwickshire, England. Its Class I, steel-reinforced concrete construction is finished in stone, half-timber and brick," the guidebook says. There are twenty-one slumber rooms and a palatial casket room, with wares ranging in price from $325 (gray, cloth-covered wood flattop) to $25,000 (48-ounce bronze, protective lock, plush beige velvet interior).

The Forest Lawn board of trustees says of Hubert Eaton, "Today, Forest Lawn stands as an eloquent witness that the Builder kept faith with his soul." It is to the official biography of Eaton, and to his own writings, that we must turn for a closer glimpse of that soul.

If a goal of art is the achievement of a synthesis between style and subject matter, it must be conceded that *First Step, Up Toward Heaven: The Story of Dr. Eaton and Forest Lawn* by Adela Rogers St. Johns is in its own way a work of art. Mrs. St. Johns is best known as one of the original sob sisters, a Hearst reporter in her youth and later editor of *Photoplay,* the first Hollywood fan magazine.

Dr. Eaton, apparently born under whichever star it is that guides a man to seek his fortune below the earth's surface rather than above, started life as a mining engineer, and in short order acquired a gold mine in Nevada. He and his cousin Joe organized the Adaven Mining Company and built a company town named Bob. It was here in Bob that Dr. Eaton ran slap-bang into his first miracle—the first of many, it turns out. One night a group of union organizers (or, in Mrs. St. Johns's words, "a gang of desperadoes bent on murder") came threateningly up the hill towards the mine—no doubt, Eaton thought, armed with dynamite. " 'Unless God takes a hand,' Hubert Eaton said, his voice cracking, 'there'll have to be bloodshed.' The foreman beside him nodded grimly."

Just when all seemed lost, the strains of "Home Sweet Home" suddenly filled the night air. This proved to be too much for the desperadoes; silently they slunk away back down the hill. " 'Looks like He took a hand,' the foreman said grimly, wiping the tears from his cheeks unashamed. 'We'd better give thanks, the way I see it,' Eaton said."

From then on, miracles dogged the footsteps of Hubert Eaton. The next thing that happened to this Child of Destiny was that his mine failed. "That night Hubert Eaton spent longer on his knees, which he had been taught was the proper way to say his prayers, than usual. Since the earth was created for man's use, a man had a right to ask God to help him locate the vein of gold that'd been in his own mine." To no avail, however. Fortunately for Eaton, Destiny had other plans for him this time. He had lost a mere million in the mining venture, a trifle indeed compared with what lay in store for him in future years as he pursued his Dream. And it is to the site of the Dream that we are now led.

The year was 1917; the place, a run-down, weed-infested cemetery called Forest Lawn. Hubert Eaton, as he stood regarding this scene, was trying to make up his mind whether or not to accept a job as manager of Forest Lawn. "If you suggest to Dr. Eaton, in his late seventies, that Destiny led him there, he will give you an I'm-from-Missouri look and say gruffly, 'There doesn't seem to be any other explanation, does there?' " In any event, he went back to his hotel room and there wrote out his vision of a future Forest Lawn: "filled with towering trees, sweeping lawns, splashing fountains, singing birds, beautiful statues, cheerful flowers, noble memorial architecture . . . where memorialization of loved ones—in sculptured marble and pictorial glass—shall be encouraged. . . . This is the Builder's Dream; this is the Builder's Creed."

The Memorial-Park idea was born. Thus it has come about that today Forest Lawn is "a garden that seems next door to Paradise itself, an incredibly beautiful place, a place of infinite loveliness and eternal peace."

Dr. Eaton lived by certain moral precepts learned in childhood at his daddy's knee. They are: Perseverance Conquers All; A Place for Everything and Everything in Its Place; Anything That Is Worth Doing Is Worth Doing Well; and Let the Chips Fall Where They May. In the course of pursuing his Dream, he also developed a sort of informal business partnership with God. For "unless God was with him, this was a pretty lonesome business." As he told a Rotary Club meeting, "Christ in Business is the greatest thing that can happen to business. We must in return give business to carry on for Christ." In his own bluff, Missouri way, he interprets the New Testament, including his Partner in his plans, at every turn: "No, he could not see anything in the Teaching against abundance. . . . Everybody wasn't called upon to don the brown robe and sandals of St. Francis."

Eaton's search for art treasures with which to adorn Forest Lawn led him to Europe on several occasions, and was frequently aided by divine intervention. There was some difficulty getting permission from the Vatican authorities to have a copy made of Michelangelo's *Moses,* but a "Man who could tell the Red Sea to stand still so the Children of Israel could get across ahead of the Egyptians ought not to have any trouble getting his statue reproduced," said Eaton, and "Of course, a lot of it was prayer. But I figure we got at least an assist from Moses." The firing of the stained-glass reproduction of *The Last Supper* gave some trouble, but " 'Nonsense and balderdash,' Hubert Eaton shouted. 'Of course God wants it finished.' " And finished it was.

If much of the Forest Lawn statuary looks like the sort of thing one might win in a shooting gallery, there's a reason for that, too. Some of it was bought at fairs—over the objection of the board of directors—but "as [Eaton] became a benevolent and paternalistic dictator and despot over his Dream Come True, he always met opposition with a gay and somehow endearing determination to win."

While the Builder's soul is something of an open book, facts about the temporal aspects of the Dream—how the "nonprofit" association works, the amount of money involved, how it is distributed—are harder to come by. Forest Lawn executives have shown a marked disinclination to discuss the financial side of the operations. Such reticence, understandable in the world of business, seems not in keeping with the nonprofit, tax-exempt status of Forest Lawn Memorial-Parks, which, declares the Dreamer, "are builded . . . for the living sacredly to enjoy and be benefited and comforted by."

There are some, however, cynical enough to assert that Eaton's cemeteries are builded for profit, and the occasional glimpses of the financial structure of Forest Lawn afforded by disclosures made in legal proceedings in which it is from time to time embroiled support the view that the memorial parks are, for Eaton, a fantastically profitable form of real estate development.

The United States Board of Tax Appeals, in a 1941 decision, describes the advent of Hubert Eaton to Forest Lawn more prosaically than does Mrs. St. Johns. He was hired in 1912 not as manager but as sales agent for "before-need" sales of cemetery lots. Before he arrived, most of the sales had been made at the time of death—"at need"—and total sales had amounted to only $28,000 in the previous year. Eaton's door-to-door selling efforts on behalf of that mean, ugly little cemetery upped sales by 250 percent—and this was five years pre-Dream.

By 1937 annual sales of cemetery space had passed the $1 million mark, and sales of other commodities and services (flowers, postcards, urns, bronze tablets, and undertaking services) added another $800,000. By 1959 annual sales exceeded $7 million, of which over $4 million represented sale of cemetery space.

What happens to all this money? Is it really all plowed back for beautification of the Park? If so, it would pay for an awful lot of fertilizer and statuary.

The Forest Lawn *Art Guide* poses this question: "Again and again people ask: How can Forest Lawn afford to assemble and maintain all of these treasures in such a beautiful place, and open it freely for all to see and enjoy? How can it be that resting places sharing all this loveliness are well within the means of everyone?" The answer is inscribed on a sign by the steps to the Hall of the Crucifixion: "Forest Lawn Memorial-Park is operated by a non-profit association. Excess income, over expenses, must be expended only for the improvement of Forest Lawn."

Well, yes. Only the operative phrase there is "over expenses."

Forest Lawn Memorial-Park Association, Inc., the nonprofit

cemetery corporation, was the sun around which clustered a galaxy of Eaton-controlled commercial corporations and holding companies. One of these, the Forest Lawn Company, a Nevada corporation, was a land company. Another, a holding company, owned over 99 percent of the land company's stock; one was a life insurance company (since sold); one was a mortgage and loan company. To the nonprofit corporation, owning no land, was entrusted the actual operation of the cemetery—the mortuary, the flower shop, the sale of graves, crypts, vaults, statuary, postcards, souvenirs. Discreetly behind the scenes was Eaton's land company, skimming off 50 percent of the proceeds of sales of lots, plots, and graves, and 60 percent of the gross on all sales of niches, crypts, vaults, and other mausoleum space (exclusive of sums collected for endowment care).

It seems curious that the additional land that is needed from time to time for expansion of the existing "Parks" and the development of new ones is not acquired by the cemetery directly. This would save for the beautification of the cemeteries and the ennoblement of mankind the middleman's profit that is now taken by the land company. Direct purchase of land by the cemetery company would result in substantial tax savings as well, since the land which is taxable in the hands of the land company would be tax-exempt if owned by the nonprofit cemetery. More curious still is the fact that the land company buys and develops the land with money which it borrows from the cemetery at only 3 percent interest. As of 1959 Eaton's land company had borrowed over $5 million from the nonprofit company at this exceptionally favorable rate.

All in all, Eaton's commercial companies seem to come off astonishingly well in their dealings with the friendly Memorial-Park company. In a stupendous display of Christ-in-businessmanship, his land company in 1959 sold the Wee Kirk o' the Heather and two other churches to the nonprofit company for eighteen times their depreciated cost, thereby realizing a bonnie profit of over $1 million. To ease the pain of the capital gains tax on this transaction, the Memorial-Park is paying the purchase price, plus 4 percent interest, in installments of $100,000 per year.

As Mrs. St. Johns says of Dr. Hubert Eaton, "He was a businessman-idealist with an inspiration, whose plan's greatness lay in its simplicity."

The Dreamer is not through yet. In 1954 he announced his discovery of the Memorial Impulse. He says he might have called this force of nature the Memorial Instinct, but preferred to defer to "psychologists and scientists" who feel the term "instinct" is imprecise. The Memorial Impulse is a primary urge founded in man's biological nature, and it gives rise to the desire to build (as one might have already guessed) memorials. It is also an indispensable factor in the growth of any civilization.

There are a number of ways to turn the Memorial Impulse, "as old as love and just as deathless," to cash account. "Let every salesman's motto be: *Accent the spiritual!*" says the Dreamer, and, "It is the salesman's duty to measure the force of the Memorial Impulse in his client and to persuade him to live up to that noble urge in accordance with his means. . . . Most important of all, every salesman should understand that if properly inspired the Memorial Impulse will do more for him than he ever did for himself, but let your financial desire be tempered with the morality of the Memorial Impulse."

The Memorial Impulse can also be channeled to remedy what was perhaps a tactical error in the early days of the Dream: insistence upon the use of small, uniform bronze grave markers.

Eaton mused that while there was universal agreement that the elimination of tombstones was a good thing, nevertheless the tombstones did serve a purpose: they were a "great assist" to the Memorial Impulse. The "great assist" that was unwittingly discarded, we learn, is the good old epitaph. There just isn't room for it on the 12-by-24-inch bronze tablets currently in fashion. True, the little markers permit of vast, almost unbroken areas of grass—the "sweeping lawns" of the original Builder's Creed—but since bronze markers are priced by the square inch, more or less, their size also limits the amount that can be charged for them. Now that the Impulse has been discovered, this can be corrected, and the epitaph was slated for a comeback that may radically alter the appearance of the memorial park, transforming its sweeping green lawns into seas of bronze. Eaton suggests that cemetery owners should be thinking in terms of "ever-larger" bronze tablets, big enough, in fact, to contain complete epitaphs and historical data—big enough to cover the entire grave! This, he says, would be a most "convenient outlet" for the client's Memorial Impulse.

10

Cremation

Cremation is not an end in itself, but the process which prepares the human remains for inurnment in a beautiful and everlasting memorial.

—CREMATION ASSOCIATION OF NORTH AMERICA

Nationwide, there has been a phenomenal growth in cremation since *The American Way of Death* was first published. In 1961, 3.75 percent of the American dead were cremated; by 1995, 21 percent and rising.

Preference for cremation varies greatly from region to region. In 1993 (the last date for which a state-by-state breakdown is available) Mississippi had the lowest cremation rate, 2.6 percent; and Nevada the highest, with 58 percent. In general, all the Southern states with the exception of Florida (40 percent) have very low cremation figures. Midwest are medium low; New England, fairly high, West Coast, high.

While national and state statistics show that cremation is gaining ground, a further breakdown by counties is revealing as to who chooses cremation. For example, while 41 percent of Californians are cremated, in the San Francisco Bay Area the figure is 60 percent, and in affluent, trendsetting Marin County, 70 percent. In Sarasota, Florida, an upscale retirement area, the cremation rate is over 70 percent, while for the state as a whole it's 40 percent.

In the 1960s, the Catholic Church lifted its ban against cremation, thus making it permissible for members of most major religious faiths to use this method of disposition.

How to explain this extraordinary increase in the resort to the retort?

A common reaction of people who learn for the first time some of the facts and figures connected with the American way of death is to say, "None of that for me! I'm going to beat this racket. I just want to be cremated, and avoid all the fuss and expense." Cremation is no doubt a simple, tidy solution to the disposal of the dead. It appeals to the nature lover and the poet, who visualize their mortal remains scattered over sunny hillside or remote strand. It is commended by environmentalists and by those who would like to see an end to all the malarkey that surrounds the usual kind of funeral. It has appeal for the economy-minded; logically one would expect the expense to be but a fraction of that incurred for earth burial. And, to continue along that seditious line of thought, why not bypass the undertaker altogether, by taking the corpse directly to a crematory, there to be consigned to the flames—the only expense incurred: a modest crematory charge?

It is true that in most countries where cremation is on the increase, the objectives of economy and simplicity are well served. In England, for example—where there were three cremations in 1885— it is today the mode of disposal for 72 percent of the dead. The average crematory charge of $280 includes amenities such as use of a chapel, not usually available in North American crematories. Specifications for the coffin to be used are the simplest, "easily combustible wood, not painted or varnished"; to facilitate the scattering of the ashes, they are "removed from the cremator, and after cooling, pulverized to a fine texture." The ultimate disposition of 90 percent of cremated remains in England is scattering, or "strewing," as the clergy like to call it. Sometimes the ashes are scattered over the sea or over the countryside; more often, by a crematory attendant in a Garden of Remembrance, consecrated ground specially set aside for the purpose. Most crematoria and cemeteries maintain such a garden; in some there is a nominal charge for the service.

The vogue for cremation is a very recent development in England. The cremation "movement" was initiated there in the nineteenth century. Its adherents included many distinguished physicians, scientists, intellectuals, radicals, and reformers; a few members of the aristocracy. Among the organizers of the first Cremation Society in 1874 were Sir Henry Thompson, Bart., Surgeon to the Queen; Anthony Trollope; Spencer Wells; Millais; and the Dukes of Bedford and Westminister. Naturally, that thorny old critic of the status quo George

Bernard Shaw was strongly in favor of cremation, and he sums up the argument for it with his usual pithiness: "Dead bodies can be cremated. All of them ought to be, for earth burial, a horrible practice, will some day be prohibited by law, not only because it is hideously unaesthetic, but because the dead would crowd the living off the earth if it could be carried out to its end of preserving our bodies for their resurrection on an imaginary day of judgment (in sober fact, every day is a day of judgment)."

There were at first strong objections to cremation from some of the clergy, who thought that it would interfere with the resurrection of the body; this point was neatly disposed of by Lord Shaftesbury when he asked, "What would become in such a case of the Blessed Martyrs?" In the 1870s and 1880s, cremation advocates campaigned on a number of fronts for legality and public acceptance of the practice. They published expository material urging support for their cause; they experimented with various types of furnaces; they went so far as to cremate one another in defiance of the authorities, thus subjecting themselves to public censure and even to criminal prosecution. It was not until 1884 that they won a court decision declaring cremation to be a legal procedure, but there was still much opposition from church and public; police protection was sometimes necessary when a cremation was to take place. In short, acceptance of cremation as a sensible and also respectable disposition of the human dead was only won as the result of a hard-fought, uphill struggle.

The early partisans of cremation, willing to flout the law and risk imprisonment to simplify and rationalize disposal of the dead, would whirl in their urns could they but see what has become of their cause today in America. For cremation, like every other aspect of disposal of the dead, has long since been taken over by the cemetery industry and mortuary interests, which prescribe the procedures to be followed and establish the regulations to which the customer must adhere. Therefore, he who seeks to avoid the purchase of a casket, embalming, and the full treatment will not succeed by the mere fact of choosing cremation rather than burial.

The Cremation Association of North America (CANA) bears no resemblance to its English counterpart. It is in fact merely an association of persons, principally cemetery operators, who are in the cremation business. Simplicity and economy are not their goals; far from it. The philosophical outlook of the association is expounded in its published materials:

Q. Is a funeral director necessary?

A. His services are exactly the same for other forms of care, and his services are needed for the first call, embalming, casket selection and conduct of the service.

Q. What kind of casket is best for cremation?

A. Inasmuch as the casket serves its primary purpose in creating a memory picture at the time of the funeral service, this is a matter for each family to decide. In general, it is recommended that the casket be the same as for any other form of interment.

Administered by the cemetery interests, cremation has become just another way of making a buck, principally through the sale of the niche and urn, plus "perpetual care," for the ashes. Cemetery men are most reluctant to relinquish the ashes for any form of private disposition; one told me rather plaintively, "If everyone wanted to take the ashes away and scatter them or bury them privately, we'd soon be out of business."*

Every state has laws prescribing the procedures for the final disposition of dead human bodies—burial, entombment, donation for medical research, and cremation being the commonly established methods, with the next of kin legally obligated to carry out any expressed wished of the decedent.

But what *is* "final disposition" where cremation has been the choice? And what of Aunt Martha's ashes?

---

*In a remarkable coup for the funeral industry, their lobbyists in California won legislation that prohibits survivors from scattering cremated remains on private or public property—forcing them to go through the cemetery or the funeral director to arrange for the disposition of cremated remains. What few undertakers are likely to acknowledge, however, is that it is perfectly legal for a family to simply take the cremains home with them. After speaking with every law enforcement agency in the state from the FBI to county sheriffs, I learned that no officer is vested with the authority to check up on what happens to Aunt Martha's ashes, nor are they willing to collar culprits caught in the act of "illegal" scattering. Although this law is totally unenforceable, the industry uses it to pressure the family to hand over the cremated remains for more profitable commercial disposition.

CANA would have us believe that "cremation is not an end in itself, but the process which prepares the human remains for inurnment in a beautiful and everlasting memorial."

CANA's view is flatly contradicted by law, which in just about every state defines cremation as a form of "final disposition." Most states likewise make an explicit distinction between bodily and cremated remains. Laws, for example, which prohibit personal ownership of dead bodies do allow family members to retain the ashes, and these are customarily handed over when no other arrangement has been made for their disposition.

So much for the cemetery interests. How might the funeral directors be expected to react to the menace of cremation?

The initial reaction of industry leaders and the trade press was to counsel funeral directors to make all efforts to dissuade the funeral buyer from cremation. The idea was to make the procedure sound as disrespectful of the deceased as possible. One mortician suggested telling the family that if they only knew what went on in the crematory retort, they wouldn't even have a dog cremated. The National Funeral Directors Association advised members to stress the concept of "immediate disposal," implying that the Loved One's remains would be treated as so much garbage. Furthermore, according to the association, the bereaved family should be warned of severe psychological trauma if they choose to flout tradition and forgo the solace of a full-fig funeral with open casket and viewing of the embalmed remains, a time-honored, meaningful ritual with its proven benefit of peace of mind for the survivors.

Slowly, over the years the cruel realization dawned that cremation was not only here to stay but was increasingly the choice of the well-to-do and well-educated—precisely that segment of the population that could easily afford the finest offerings of the mortician. At this point the industry made a U-turn. The emphasis now is on making the best of a bad job.

Essentially, the goal is to sell a "traditional" funeral with all the trimmings as an adjunct to cremation. The Revised Version, as revealed in a spectrum of articles in the trade press, is to "teach the consumer the concept of cremation with service." Some sample headlines: the *American Cemetery,* November 1994, FIGHTING DIRECT CREMATION: Teaching Cremation Customers the Value of Ritual and Memorialization; the *Southern Funeral Director,* September 1993, WHAT IS THE REAL CHALLENGE IN OVERCOMING MINIMAL CREMATION?

According to Ron Hast, editor of *Mortuary Management* (September 1993), "Cremated remains can be a focal point of memorialization. To the far-sighted funeral director, the potential for expanded services and increased profit is unlimited." He cited a case in which several siblings each bought individual urns to hold a portion of Mom's ashes: "There was something of a power struggle to see who would purchase the nicest urn."

A recent book sums it up: *Cremation and the Funeral Director: Successfully Meeting the Challenge,* by Michael W. Kubasak. Described by the author as a "straight-from-the-hip handbook," this 156-page volume instructs the conventional funeral director in the potential profitability of cremation. "The market for cremation urns is usually limited," writes Kubasak. "In my experience the more urns displayed, the more urns sold; the more urns sold, the fewer the scatterings. . . . It is recommended the urn display be as inviting and open as possible." It should surprise no one that Mr. Kubasak when last heard from was an official spokesman for the National Funeral Directors Association.*

Crematoria outside North America are almost universally publicly owned, or, if privately owned, maintained on a not-for-profit basis. Golders Green, Great Britain's oldest crematorium, is located in a London suburb. It is privately owned, but surplus earnings are used for maintenance of the burial grounds, improvement of facilities, and public education. Sixty cremations a week are performed in its four cremators. Three chapels, the largest seating 220, are available for the accommodation of family and invited guests. The cost, $360, which is competitive with crematoria generally in the London area, includes "use of chapel, waiting rooms and all attendances; floral decoration; music (recorded or organ); medical referee's fee ($94); scattering/strewing of ashes."

Children under five years are cremated without charge, those aged six to ten for $90. Choral service is available at a cost of $80 and

---

*And more recently still, an executive officer of Service Corporation International (see chapter 16).

upward for a soloist, $120 for a quartet. The clergy fee, $90, for reading the service is an extra. A rose tree, care and maintenance for five years included, may be purchased for $450.

It is apparent from the foregoing that the role of the undertaker in respect to the 72 percent of the British dead who are cremated is minimal. With the rites of final disposition centered in the crematorium rather than in the funeral parlor, there can be little concern for the elegance and durability of the burial container or for public viewing of the embalmed corpse. A "burping" casket* such as the Batesville Casket Company manufactures, which is warranted to permit noxious gases from the slow decay of the corpse to escape, has yet to be marketed in Great Britain (unless events in that rapidly changing market have caught up with the writer).

A new development in the United States in the early 1970s was the establishment of "direct cremation" firms, commercial ventures offering simple cremation for a fixed fee of around $255, roughly linked to the Social Security death benefit. For an additional $250 survivors could arrange to have the ashes scattered at sea from a plane or boat. The funeral directors poured scorn, labeling the procedure "burn and scatter" or even "bake and shake."

The Neptune Society, founded in Los Angeles by Dr. Charles Denning, a flamboyant character who advertised extensively on radio and TV, was first on the scene, and easily the most successful of the burn-and-scatter outfits, boasting at latest count branches in ten Northern California cities plus locations in New York State and Florida. Neptune's extraordinary success has been due largely to its appropriation of the name "Society," creating thereby the false public impression that it is linked to the nonprofit funeral and memorial societies that have built invaluable goodwill by their consumer protection activities. New York memorial societies, the bona fide consumer organizations, were successful in securing statewide legislation that prevents any mortuary from labeling itself a "society." California's Funeral Board had likewise done surveys to show that the practice is misleading to consumers. The issue was laid to rest, however, when the troublesome board itself was abolished.

Neptune has not hesitated to resort to other dubious practices as

---

*See footnote, page 272.

well. For the last several years it has been embroiled in litigation on every front. Denning sued a rival burn-and-scatter concern in Northern California for using the name Neptune, which he had neglected to trademark and which had by now become a household word for consumers looking for direct cremation. In the mid-1980s, Neptune settled a class action lawsuit involving three hundred families for $22 million plus $5 million costs. . . . In 1988, ashes of 5,342 corpses discovered in remote mountain spot by Neptune pilot. . . . In 1988, out-of-court settlement against Neptune of $12.7 million. . . . A 1991 class action suit for mishandling and commingling thousands of corpses was recently settled for $6.8 million. And most recently, without admitting guilt, three Neptune crematories in California agreed to financial audits and to reimburse the cost of the state's investigation.

Despite such adversity, and a bit of positively bad luck (the uncremated, badly decomposed body of a former mayor of Burbank, California, was discovered after four and a half months in a refrigerator; the case was settled for over $1 million), Neptune continues to flourish like a green bay tree.

Neptune's cremation fees have soared. The minimum charge is now $1,200, up from the original 1970s price of $255. Today there are added charges: "sea scattering without family or friends present," $125; add $395 for family groups of up to eight; there is also an added fee, $295, for "witnessing the beginning of the cremation process."

Neptune's success has not gone unchallenged by the conventional mortuaries. A recent offering of Chapel of the Chimes in Oakland, California, gives these prices:

DIRECT CREMATION WITH CARDBOARD CONTAINER: $1,135
Scattering not provided:
We have found that scattering can be extremely traumatic to the survivors. Family members want to know that their loved one is in a place where they can visit and work out their grief.

In early 1995 the Cremation Association of North America published its long-awaited Special Report on cremation—what goes into the furnace and what comes out. Highlighted was the startling conclusion that 85 percent of the bodies that enter the furnace go in uncoffined—a reassuring affirmation of basic common sense on the part of the funeral buyer in the face of the industry's heavily financed "memoralization" campaign. Why, he persists in asking, spend good money on a casket that will only be burned?

The specter of all those uncoffined bodies going into the retort most directly threatens the casket manufacturers, who as a result have thrown their own considerable resources into the fray. The Batesville Casket Company, "the world's largest," has produced a widely distributed four-color *Cremation Options* brochure. The "options" narrowly defined are two in number: a funeral service to be followed by cremation, or a funeral service after the cremation. Your choice: salad before or salad after the entrée. Casket manufacturers—who recently had regarded the urn business as no more than a sideline—have now gone into it whole hog. Batesville offers a dazzling array of products topped by an "art-urn" line featuring elaborately sculpted pieces such as a seascape with leaping dolphins. Also available are urns crafted in bronze, wood, "semi-precious metals," glass, and "true marble."

A "scattering urn" is offered for those who might wish to, yes, scatter some of the ash as from a saltshaker and preserve the rest for display on the mantelpiece. The wholesale price range for Batesville's art-urn line is $70 to $575, which translates to $450 to $1,695 for the customer making his or her selection in the undertaking parlor.

Funeral directors, facing cruel necessity, are also learning to adapt. Some of the more go-ahead mortuaries will provide a "rental casket" for the temporary display of the embalmed body during visiting hours. According to the CANA Special Report of the cremations performed in 1995 which were preceded by a service with the body on display, no less than 28 percent involved the use of a rented casket. As might be expected, accommodation for the dead is far more costly than for the living. The rental cost for the one or two days' occupancy runs from $600 to $800 a pop, which would pay for an untroubled weekend in a resort hotel.

Since rental caskets are indefinitely reusable—the inert occupant causing no wear and tear, it's in the funeral director's interest to provide merchandise of good quality for the display of the corpse; finished hardwood is a favorite. The removable interiors cost the funeral director less than $100, and—doubling his investment on the very first rental—he can rent the casket again and again.

When in 1995 Massachusetts passed a law permitting rentals,

there was an outcry from the trade that the practice might spread disease, "especially where body fluids are spilled in casket containers." Not to worry, said health officials, because rentals can be fitted with new cloth and cardboard liners each time they are used. Some Massachusetts funeral directors quickly got the picture. With such an extravagant return on inventory kept in perpetual use, they are now urging survivors to consider rental units in preference to low-cost cremation containers.

Not only is cremation discouraged, even hampered, by the funeral industry, but once all impediments have been overcome, the ghouls who had formerly pursued the corpse now lust for the ashes. The natural impulse of survivors to scatter ashes or bury them in a garden or other favored spot has for years been frustrated in California, if not elsewhere, by laws that prohibit the disposition of cremated remains on private or public property. The widespread impact of this cruel restriction is illustrated in a recent (1997) instance where 5,200 boxes of cremated remains, entrusted to a pilot hired to scatter them at sea, were discovered in a storage locker and an airplane hangar.

If you can't sell an urn, why not turn the ashes over to a flying service for sea scattering? Seems fair. But is it? Here again, the byword is follow the money. The dozens of mortuaries that collected $100 to $200 from the survivors for the service paid the poor wretch who was to do the scattering an average of $30 to $60. None of them took the trouble to ascertain whether their instructions were actually carried out. Using median numbers, it will be seen that the mortuaries realized, among them, a profit of $526,000 from this seemingly insignificant sideline. At the same time, preliminary investigation has revealed that the majority of the victims who paid to have their relatives' ashes scattered were never informed that they had the right to take the ashes home with them. Had they known of this option they would not, of course, have paid to have them scattered.

Throughout the industry, cremation today remains the poor, ugly stepchild among the modes of final disposition. Existing state laws, regrettably, serve only to help the industry play havoc with the consumer's desire for a simple, cheap funeral. Funeral people are forever declaiming that cremation is legally more challengeable than burial.

They argue that the reason they so often feel obliged to overrule a decedent's expressed wish for a cheap exit is their desire to avoid being sued by family members who would find such disposition "emotionally damaging." Research, however, has turned up only one case in which such an action was filed, and it was thrown out by the judge on the grounds that the primary right of disposition lies with the decedent if expressed in writing during his lifetime.

After Words

A recent report from CANA issued in December 1996 has spurred cremationists to seek ever more Creative Concepts for the extraction of maximum profitability. According to CANA's projections, 26 percent of Americans who die in the year 2000 will be cremated, and of those who die in 2010, 39.9 percent—three times the number of those who were cremated in 1985—will make their exit in like manner. But not necessarily in the same way. The funeral folk are already looking ahead and have other plans for them.

One such was revealed during a "Keys to Cremation Success" symposium sponsored by the *Funeral Service Insider* in the spring of 1997. The scholars were urged to require "identification viewing" prior to cremation, "to avoid any mix-ups." The title of one presentation, "How to Add $1,400 or More to Each Cremation Call," reveals the larger motive for this tactic. "Seeing Mom in a cardboard box sometimes prompts a family member to ask if we don't have something a little nicer," said the presenter. The ruthlessness of subjecting family members to a forced viewing is something to wonder at until one recalls that it is one of the "keys to cremation success." In one case, where the mother's body had been embalmed before they chose cremation, family members became so distraught from the unwanted experience of an "identification viewing" that they have turned to the Funeral and Memorial Societies of America (FAMSA) to seek an opinion from the FTC on whether consumers can decline this procedure. There is no doubt that they may refuse to pay the fee that some mortuaries are charging.

Another key to cremation success? "When families don't buy an urn, require them to purchase a temporary container to hold the cremains. But make sure you label (or stamp) that box with the words 'temporary container' on all four sides. If you usually give cremains to the family in a box from the crematory, stamp that box with the temporary container label. That makes families most likely to upgrade beyond the temporary container," suggests the *Funeral Service Insider.*

11

What the Public Wants

The funeral service profession exists only because it has received the approval of the public. . . . Present methods, facilities and merchandise exist because the public has found in them values it has been willing to pay for in spite of the necessary sacrifice of other things. . . .

Are these values real? Do they spring from higher and finer motives? Do they lift and inspire? Are they worth what they cost? The answer is found in the reactions of the public. If the public accepts these things, prefers these things, the answer is in the affirmative.

—EDWARD A. MARTIN, B.A., MORTICIAN,
Psychology of Funeral Service

The theme that the American public, rather than the funeral industry, is responsible for our funeral practices—because it demands "the best" in embalming and merchandise for the dead—is one often expounded by funeral men. "We are merely giving the public what it wants," they say.

This is an interesting idea. It is a little hard to conceive of how this public demand is expressed and made known in practice to the seller of funeral service. Does the surviving spouse, for example, go into the funeral establishment and say, "I want to be sure my wife is thoroughly disinfected and preserved. Her casket must be both comfortable and eternally durable. And—oh yes, do be sure her burial footwear is really practical"?

Perhaps it does not often happen just like that. Yet it has been known to happen, and in fairness to the undertaking trade, an example should be given of a case in which the funeral buyer, of sound mind and deeply aware of his own desires, wanted and demanded the best.

The case involves Mr. August Chelini, a fifty-seven-year-old mechanic, sometime scrap dealer and garage owner. His monthly earnings averaged $300 to $400. Mr. Chelini, an only child, lived with his aged mother, who died in 1943 at the age of ninety-nine years and seven months. It then became incumbent upon Mr. Chelini to arrange for the funeral, which he did by calling in Mr. Silvio Nieri, an undertaker and family friend.

What developed is best recounted by quoting from the transcript of the case of August Chelini, plaintiff, versus Silvio Nieri, defendant, in the Superior Court of San Mateo County, California.

Mr. August Chelini comes to life for us in the pages of a court reporter's typescript. We learn his hopes and fears, something of his history, something of his philosophy, his way of life, his motives and methods. He was in some respects an undertaker's dream person, a materialization of that man of sentiment and true feeling for the dead so often encountered in funeral trade magazines. Only the fact that he was suing an undertaker for $50,000 casts a slight shadow.

The case opens with the arrival of Mr. Nieri at the Chelini home. Mr. Melvin Belli, counsel for the plaintiff, is examining:

Q. [Mr. Belli] When he came to the house, did you have a conversation with him?

A. [Mr. Chelini] Well, he come in and he asked me if he should move the body, and I told him I wanted to talk things over with him first.

Q. Did you have a conversation there?

A. So I talked to him out in the kitchen, and explained to him what I wanted, and the conversation was that I told him what my mother requested.

Q. What did you tell him in this regard?

A. Well, I told him that my mother wanted to be buried where there was no ants or any bugs could get at her.

Q. Had your mother made that request?

A. She made that request.

Q. By the way, was your mother of sound mentality at the time?

A. Oh, yes, very sound. Pretty bright.

Q. Did you tell him anything else?

A. Well, I told him that she had $1,500 of her own money, and that I intended to put all that into her funeral, and she had other moneys coming, and I wanted a hermetically sealed casket, because—

Q. You told him that, that you wanted—

A. I told him I wanted the best kind of embalming, and I wanted her put in a hermetically sealed casket.

Q. Did you know what a hermetically sealed casket was at that time?

A. Well, I know that it was a casket that no air or no water could get into.

Q. All right, did you tell him anything else?

A. I told him that is what I wanted. I didn't care what the cost was going to be, but I did have the $1,500 on hand that belonged to her, and these other moneys were coming in that I could put into it later.

Q. All right. Did you tell him anything else at that time?

A. Also told him that I was anticipating making a lead box to eventually put her in, after the war was over; that lead couldn't be had at that time, and I am a mechanic. I intended to construct a lead box.

Q. You were going to do it yourself?

A. Yes, I have a sample of the box, the design of it, and I told him that I was going to figure to put her in a crypt until the war was over, and so that I could get the necessary things and put her away in accordance with her wishes.

Q. By the way, you lived with your mother all her life?

A. There was times she lived out in South City, but we were with her pretty near every day.

Q. So, after you told him that you were going to make this lead coffin, after the war, did you have any further conversation with him?

A. Well, we talked about the embalming, how long he could preserve it, he says, "Practically forever," he says. "We got a new method of embalming that we will put on her, and she will keep almost forever."

Q. Pardon me. Go ahead.

A. I says, "That is a pretty long period, isn't it?" Well, he says, "They embalmed Caruso, and they embalmed Lincoln, that way, and they have these big candles near Caruso, and we have a new method of embalming. We have a new method of embalming. We can do a first-class job, and she will keep almost forever." . . .

Q. Then, the next day, did you have another conversation with him?

A. Then the next day he told me that I would have to come down to his establishment, and pick out a casket. . . .

Q. And you went down there?

A. My wife and I went down there.

Q. And when you got down there, did you have a further conversation with him?

A. Well, yes, he took me down in the basement there where he had all these caskets, and he told me to look them all over, and we picked out what we thought was the best casket in the house. . . . First I looked around, and my wife looked around. We both decided on the same casket. So, I asked him if that was a hermetically sealed job, he says, "Oh, yes, that is the finest thing there is, that is a bronze casket." He told me this was a casket, it was a bronze casket, and was a hermetically sealed casket, and he said that that is the finest thing that is made, and he says, "This is pre-war stuff," and he says, "As a matter of fact, this is—I am going to keep one of these myself, in case anything happens to me, I am going to be buried in one of these myself." . . . He quoted me a price, then he says, "Well, that will be $875, that will include everything, everything in connection with the whole funeral," he says, "That will be completely everything in connection with the whole funeral, $875."*

Q. Yes.

A. So, from what he told me, this casket was the best—it seemed very reasonable, so I told him that we would select that.

*Today such a funeral would cost $8,000 or more. Bronze sealers begin at $4,000 and run up to $25,000 for the heavier gauges.

(Later that day, Chelini's mother was brought back to his house.)

Q. Was there any conversation in the house?

A. Well, by the time I got there, she was up there, the wife and I decided to put her in the dining room, originally, and when I got up there, he had her in the living room.

Q. Did you have some conversation with him at that time?

A. So, he said, "Well, I think it will be better to have her here, because there is a window here, she'll get lots of air." He said he would have to put this body here in the front room on account of the window was here.

Q. Yes.

A. And he said it would be better to have a breeze, a flow of fresh air come in there.

Q. All right, did you have a conversation about the funeral with him to hurry over this?

A. Let's see. I don't think there was very much spoken about the funeral right then. I was feeling pretty bad. He spoke of this new embalming. He picked up her cheeks and skin on her and showed me how nice it was, pliable, it was—

Q. Did he tell you that that was a new method of embalming?

A. Yes, and her cheek was very pliable, her skin was especially.

Q. Is that what he said?

A. Well, that is the way he said that is the way it felt, and he told me that is a new type of embalming that they have, pliable. . . .

Q. All right, then you had a discussion with him at that time about paying him the money?

A. I asked him how much it was. He says, "it was $875." So I says, "Well, I want mother's ring put back on her finger," I says, "when she is removed from the crypt to her final resting place. I want that ring put back on her finger," and I says, "I want some little slippers put on her that I can't get at this time," I says, "I want her all straightened up, and cleaned off nice," and I says, "I will add another $25 for that service, for doing that," so he says, "All right," he says, "if that is the way you want it, we will do it, I would have done it for nothing," so I gave him that extra check for $25. . . . Oh, I also reminded him to be sure that when they put her finally into the cemetery, to see that she was properly secured, and he says, "Don't worry about it," he says, "I will see that everything is done properly." So, he took the check, and I asked him if he would go out and have a little drink with me, which he consented to, and which we did, in the kitchen.

(Probably, a little drink was seldom needed more than at that moment and by these principals. The scene now shifts to Cypress Lawn Cemetery.)

Q. Did you go out there when your mother was taken out there?

A. Yes, I went out to the funeral, and she had the services there. Why, she left here on one of those little roller affairs, and we all walked out. Mr. Nieri—I came out to the car and asked him if he would go in there and see that she was properly adjusted from any shifting, or anything, and make sure that she was well sealed in, so he went in there, and he come out, and I asked him, I says, "Did you get her all sealed in nice? Did you straighten her all up nice?" He says, "Don't be worrying about that, Gus," he says, "I will take care of everything."

Mr. Chelini was, it appears, the exceptional—nay, perfect—funeral customer. Not only did he gladly and freely choose the most expensive funeral available in the Nieri establishment; he also contracted for a $1,100 crypt in the Cypress Lawn mausoleum. He appreciated and endorsed every aspect of the funeral industry's concept of the sort of care that should be accorded the dead. An ardent admirer of the embalmer's art, he insisted on the finest receptacle in which to display it; indeed, he thought $875 a very reasonable price and repeatedly intimated his willingness to go higher.

At first glance, it seems like a frightful stroke of bad luck that Mr. Chelini, of all people, should be in court charging negligence and fraud against his erstwhile friend the undertaker, asserting that "the remains of the said Caroline Chelini were permitted to and did develop into a rotted, decomposed and insect and worm infested mess." Yet the inner logic of the situation is perhaps such that *only* a person of Mr. Chelini's persuasion in these matters would ever find himself in a position to make such a charge; for who else would be interested in ascertaining the condition of a human body after its interment?

It was not until two months after the funeral that Mr. Chelini was first assailed by doubts as to whether all was well within the bronze casket.

Mr. Chelini was in the habit of making frequent trips to his mother's crypt—he was out at the cemetery as many as three, four, or even five times a week. Sometimes he went to pay what he referred to as his vaultage; more often, merely to visit his mother. On one of these visits, he noticed a lot of ants "kind of walking around the crypt." He complained to the cemetery attendants, who promised to use some insect spray; he complained to Mr. Nieri, who assured him there was nothing to worry about.

Over the next year and a half, the ant situation worsened considerably, in spite of the spraying: "I could see more ants than ever, and there is a lot of little hideous black bugs jumping around there. Well, I had seen these hideous black bugs before, like little gnats, instead of flying they seemed to jump like that."

This time, he had a long, heart-to-heart talk with Mr. Nieri. The latter insisted that the body would still be just as perfect as the day it was buried, except for perhaps a little mold on the hands. Ants would never "tackle" an embalmed body, Mr. Nieri said. To prove his point, he produced a bottle of formaldehyde; he averred that he could take a piece of fresh horsemeat of the best kind, or steak, or anything, saturate it with formaldehyde, and "nothing will tackle it."

The idea had evidently been growing in Mr. Chelini's mind that he must investigate the situation at first hand. With his wife, his family doctor, and an embalmer from Nieri's establishment, he went out to Cypress Lawn Cemetery and there caused the casket to be opened; upon which the doctor exclaimed, "Well, this is a hell of a mess, and a hell of a poor job of embalming, in my opinion."

In court, the undertaking fraternity rushed to the defense of their embattled colleague. Defense expert witnesses included several practicing funeral directors and Mr. Donald Ashworth, then dean of the San Francisco College of Mortuary Science. They were in an undeniably difficult position, for in order to build a case for Mr. Nieri they were forced to reveal some truths ordinarily concealed from the public. The defense theory—perhaps the only possible one under the circumstances—was that there is no such thing as "eternal preservation"; that the results of embalming are always unpredictable; that, therefore, Mr. Nieri could not have entered into the alleged agreement with Mr. Chelini. Before the case was over, the theory of "everlasting security for your loved one," an advertising slogan gleefully flung at them by Mr. Belli, was thoroughly exploded by the reluctant experts. They also conceded that the expensive metal "sealer type" caskets, if anything, hasten the process of decomposition. The jury awarded damages to Mr. Chelini in the sum of $10,900.

For another view of what the public wants, let us turn to a man-in-the-street survey conducted by the *San Francisco Chronicle* in 1961. The method of interviewing could hardly claim to be scientific, for it consisted merely of stopping the first eight people to come along the street and posing the question "What kind of funeral for you?" The answers are, however, interesting. All eight spoke up for the minimum: "A very cheap one . . ." "Just a plain Catholic service . . ." "I would like a quiet funeral . . ." "I don't care for pomp and circumstance . . ." were typical responses. One man said, "They can heave me in the Bay and feed the fishes for all I care," and another, "As long as they make sure I'm dead I don't care what they do next. A corpse is like a pair of old shoes. It's ridiculous to put your family in hock over it."

Oddly enough, the funeral men, long aware that these attitudes are more commonly held than that of Mr. Chelini, are not particularly worried. After all, these people will not be around to arrange their own funerals. When the bell tolls for them, the practical essentials—selection of a casket and all the rest—will be in the hands of close relatives who will, it is statistically certain, express their sense of loss in an appropriately costly funeral.

This point was made rather forcefully by a funeral director in the course of a radio interview. The interviewer remarked that it is the law in some states that the express wishes of the deceased as to the mode of his funeral must be observed. What happens then, he then asked, if the deceased has left instructions for a very simple funeral, but the survivors insist on something more elaborate? The funeral director answered with rare candor, "Well, at a time like that, who are you going to listen to?"

Odds are that the undertaker will be the arbiter of what is a "suitable" funeral, that a decedent's own wishes in this regard may not be the final word. Even if he is the President of the United States.

Franklin D. Roosevelt left extremely detailed and explicit instructions for his funeral "in the event of my death in office as President of the United States." The instructions were contained in a four-page penciled document dated December 26, 1937, early in his second term, and were addressed to his eldest son, James.

The instructions included these directions:

- That a service of the utmost simplicity be held in the East Room of the White House.
- That there be no lying in state anywhere.
- That a gun-carriage and not a hearse be used throughout.
- That the casket be of absolute simplicity, dark wood, that the body be not embalmed or hermetically sealed, and
- That the grave be not lined with brick, cement, or stones.

Regarding the latter instruction, James Roosevelt writes, "So far as we can learn, he never had discussed this with anyone. Knowing Father, we can only speculate that he regarded the embalming procedure as a distasteful invasion of privacy, and that perhaps he had an inner yearning to follow the traditional funeral liturgy, 'Earth to earth, ashes to ashes, dust to dust, in sure and certain hope of the Resurrection.'"

Nobody in the Roosevelt household knew of the existence of this document. It was found in his private safe a few days after his burial. It is a common occurrence that when death comes unexpectedly to the ordinary home, burial instructions are found too late tucked away in a safe-deposit box or contained in a will which is not read until after the funeral; it seems ironic that the same mischance could occur in the White House itself. Furthermore, White House aides charged with arranging details of the funeral seem to have been as much at a loss, and as tractable in the hands of the undertaker, as any average citizen faced with the same situation.

News of Roosevelt's death, flashed around the world on April 12, 1945, meant many things to many people. To millions of Americans it signified the sudden and disastrous loss of the most commanding figure of the century and with him the disappearance of an era. To Mr. Fred W. Patterson, Atlanta undertaker, at home enjoying an after-dinner pipe that evening when his phone rang, it was (in the words of the *Southern Funeral Director*) "THE CALL—probably the biggest and most important ever experienced by a contemporary funeral director."

The Call was placed by Mr. William D. Hassett, a White House aide who was with Roosevelt in Warm Springs, Georgia, at the time of his death. He was charged by Mrs. Roosevelt with the task of buying a coffin; being entirely without experience in such matters, he consulted Miss Grace Tully, FDR's secretary, and Dr. Howard G. Bruenn, who had attended the President in his last moments. Both were sure that Mr. Roosevelt would have wanted something simple and dignified, possibly a solid mahogany casket with copper lining similar to the one used for the President's mother.

From accounts of the placing of the order for the solid mahogany casket, it appears there was more than one telephone conversation between Patterson, the undertaker, and the harassed presidential assistants. The following account of Hassett's conversation is given by Bernard Asbell: "Hassett said he wanted a solid mahogany casket with a copper lining. Patterson told him that copper linings had disappeared early in the war. He did have, however, a plain mahogany one, but—Hassett broke in to ask if it were at least six feet four inches long. Patterson said it was—but it was already sold. It was to be shipped the next day to New Jersey to accommodate another undertaker. He added that he had a fine bronze-colored copper model that would—Hassett, in his gentle but most firm Vermont manner, said he wanted the mahogany brought at once to Warm Springs. Patterson asked if he could bring both. Perhaps, on reconsideration, they would choose the bronze-colored copper one. Hassett said he could."

Patterson, writing in the *Southern Funeral Director,* describes a further conversation about the coffin, this time with Dr. Bruenn: "After he [Dr. Bruenn] consulted with William D. Hassett, . . . he requested that only the mahogany be brought; but on my request, in the event a change was desired, we were allowed to bring, in addition, the copper deposit."

Mr. Patterson's very understandable desire to acquit himself creditably and with honor in this situation comes through strongly between the lines. There he was, caught in the spotlight, before his colleagues and before the nation. He must have suffered a nasty moment before permission was granted to bring both caskets to the Little White House.

Patterson and his assistants drove to Warm Springs with two hearses, one containing the plain mahogany casket, the other the "fine bronze-colored copper model," a National Seamless Copper Deposit No. 21200. Patterson relates how the question of which casket to use was finally resolved: "After Mrs. Roosevelt arrived at 11:25 and had seen the President's remains, a conference was held as to funeral arrangements. Dr. Bruenn was asked what they wished to do about the casket. He consulted Admiral McIntire who came with Mrs. Roosevelt. In the conversation, the Admiral was heard to use the word 'bronze' and as the copper deposit had a bronze finish, of course that was the casket to be used."

Did the presidential aides feel that one had been put over on them, albeit discreetly? We do not know.

In one important respect, Mr. Roosevelt's instructions were observed: there was no lying in state. Mrs. Roosevelt felt sure that he would not have wished it. She said, "We have talked often, when there had been a funeral at the Capitol in which a man had lain in state and the crowds had gone by the open coffin, of how much we disliked the practice; and we had made up our minds that we would never allow it."

Failure to carry out certain of his other instructions can only be laid to the unlucky circumstance that they were found too late. It is, however, interesting to compare President Roosevelt's words with accounts given by participants in the funeral:

MR. ROOSEVELT: That the body be not embalmed.
MR. FRED PATTERSON: All three assistants worked incessantly five hours to give the President the proper appearance, and to be certain of proper preservation. . . . We had a difficult case, did our best and believe that we pleased everyone in every

respect. . . . Saturday morning Mr. William Gawler (a Washington undertaker) phoned me stating that the tissues were firm, complexion was fine and those who saw him remarked, "He looks like his old self again and much younger."

MR. ROOSEVELT: That the body be not . . . hermetically sealed.

MR. WILLIAM GAWLER: The casket was closed and the inner top bolted down at 8:30 p.m. Saturday night. The outer top was sealed with cement.

MR. ROOSEVELT: That the grave be not lined with brick, cement, or stones.

MR. JAMES ROOSEVELT: The casket was placed in a cement vault.

MR. ROOSEVELT: That a gun-carriage and not a hearse be used throughout.

MR. PATTERSON: As the caisson did not arrive at the last minute the casket was taken in our Sayers and Scoville Cadillac hearse.

In November 1963, three months after the first edition of this book was published, it became once more the unhappy task of presidential aides to supervise the obsequies of a president. Two writers give particulars of negotiations with undertakers in Dallas and Washington over arrangements for John F. Kennedy's funeral.

In *Robert Kennedy and His Times* (Houghton Mifflin, 1978), Arthur Schlesinger describes RFK's arrival at Bethesda Hospital:

There were so many details. The funeral home wanted to know how grand the coffin should be. "I was influenced by . . . that girl's book on (burial) expenses . . . Jessica Mitford (*The American Way of Death*). . . . I remember making the decision based on Jessica Mitford's book. . . . I remember thinking about it afterward, about whether I was cheap or what I was, and I remembered thinking about how difficult it must be for everybody making that kind of decision."

While Yours Truly was, needless to say, most gratified to learn that her message had been absorbed in high places, further exploration reveals that—much as in the case of FDR's funeral—the best-laid schemes of Robert Kennedy and his assistants went agley. The undertakers prevailed after all.

William Manchester in *The Death of a President* (Harper & Row, 1967) goes into far greater detail when discussing this situation. Of the Dallas undertaker who supplied the coffin in which JFK's body was transported to Washington, he writes:

> Vernon B. Oneal of Oak Lawn funeral home is an interesting figure in the story of John Kennedy. Squat, hairy and professionally doleful, with a thick Texas accent and gray hair parted precisely in the middle and slicked back, he was the proprietor of an establishment which might have been invented by Waugh or Huxley. It had a wall-to-wall carpeted Slumber Room. There was piped religious music, and a coffee bar for hungry relatives of loved ones. . . . (p. 291)

Instructed by a member of JFK's entourage to bring a coffin to Dallas's Parkland Memorial Hospital, Oneal ran into his selection room and

> chose his most expensive coffin, the Elgin Casket Company's "Britannia" model, eight hundred pounds of double-walled, hermetically sealed solid bronze.

The scene now shifts to Washington. Brigadier General Godfrey McHugh told Robert Kennedy that the solid bronze casket had been badly damaged in transit: "It's really shabby. One handle is off, and the ornaments are in bad shape." RFK decided that "he could scarcely permit a state funeral to proceed with a battered casket." Four aides were dispatched to Gawler's, the selfsame old, established Washington firm that had supervised President Roosevelt's funeral. They reported their findings to RFK.

Manchester's description of the casket-price negotiations roughly parallels Schlesinger's, but with elaboration:

> Robert Kennedy had read Miss Mitford's carefully documented exposé of the gouging of bereaved relatives, and so had

Dr. Joseph English, the Peace Corps psychiatrist who stood at Sargent Shriver's elbow Friday afternoon. Robert Kennedy . . . believes he spoke to O'Donnell . . . (special assistant to the President) about price . . . and he has a clear memory of a girl who told him . . . "You can get one for $500, one for $1,400, or one for $2,000." She went on about water-proofing and optional equipment. Influenced by the Mitford book, he shied away from the high figure. He asked for the $1,400 coffin, and afterward he wondered whether he had been cheap; he thought how difficult such choices must be for everyone. . . . (p. 432)

This, as Manchester points out, was already almost twice the average bill for "casket and services" only two years earlier . . . $708 in 1961. But there was worse to come, as he discovered on further investigation.

In the end, Gawler put one over on the White House staff members. He sold them a "Marsellus No. 710, constructed of hand-rubbed, five-hundred-year-old solid African mahogany," for which he charged $2,400. He then slipped in the most expensive vault in the establishment, for a total bill, rendered and paid, of $3,160.

And what about Oneal? His bill to the Kennedy family was finally settled, after some haggling over "services rendered"—spotted by a sharp-eyed CPA—for $3,495. Thus, despite Robert Kennedy's laudable efforts to avoid a price-gouging, he was outmaneuvered; the family ended up paying a total of $6,655 into the coffers of undertakers.

His curiosity piqued by these nefarious transactions, Manchester pursued the subject further, visiting Vernon Oneal in his Dallas establishment:

Actually, as he conceded to this writer, he was hoping for a return of the coffin. He made two trips to Washington in the hope of retrieving it. Word of this reached the right quarters, and to avoid an exhibition he was paid. The wholesale prices of coffins are a closely guarded trade secret, but at the request of the author a licensed funeral director and a cemetery manager made discreet inquiries at the Elgin Casket Company about its Britannia model. Both were quoted an identical figure: $1,150. Thus Oneal's fee represents a markup of $2,345.

Lastly, William Manchester records some reactions to the embalmer's art as practiced by Gawler's:

Arthur Schlesinger and Nancy Tuckerman went in through the Green Room. "It was appalling," Arthur reported. "When I came closer it looked less and less like him. It is too waxen, too made-up." Nancy echoed faintly that the face resembled "the rubber masks stores sell as novelties." He urged Bob to "close the casket." . . . Walton [William Walton, artist, friend of Kennedy's] looked as long as he could, with a growing sense of outrage. He said to Bob, "You mustn't keep it open. It has no resemblance to the President. It's a wax dummy."

And closed the coffin did remain. UPI commented as follows:

When Mrs. Jacqueline Kennedy decided that President Kennedy's casket would remain closed while his body lay in state, she acted as many religious leaders wish that all bereaved families would. . . . They feel that it is pagan rather than Christian to focus attention on the corpse. It is worth noting that in other particulars as well, the conduct of the Kennedy funeral represented a departure from the prevailing funerary practices fostered by the American death industries. There were no flowers, by request of the Kennedy family. At no point did a Cadillac hearse intrude; the coffin, covered by a flag, was transported by gun carriage.

12

Fashions in Funerals

Disposal of the dead falls rather into a class with fashions, than with either customs or folkways on the one hand, or institutions on the other. . . . [S]ocial practices of disposing of the dead are of a kind with fashion of dress, luxury and etiquette.

—A. L. KROEBER, "Disposal of the Dead,"
American Anthropologist, July–September 1927

One of the interesting things about burial practices is that they provide many a clue to the customs and society of the living. The very word "antiquarian" conjures up the picture of a mild-eyed historian groping about amidst old tombstones, copying down epitaphs with their folksy inscriptions and irregular spelling, extrapolating from these a picture of the quaint people and homey ways of yore. There is unconscious wit: the widow's epitaph to her husband, "Rest in peace—until we meet again." There is gay inventiveness:

> Here lie I, Master Elginbrod.
> Have mercy on my soul, O God,
> As I would have if I were God
> And thou wert Master Elginbrod.

There is pathos: "I will awake, O Christ, when thou callest me, but let me sleep awhile—for I am very weary." And bathos: " 'Tis but the casket that lies here; the gem that fills it sparkles yet."

For the study of prehistory, archaeologists rely heavily on what they can find in and around tombs, graves, monuments; and from the tools, jewels, household articles, symbols found with the dead, they reconstruct whole civilizations, infer entire systems of religious and ethical beliefs.

Inevitably, some go-ahead team of thirtieth-century archaeologists will labor to reconstruct our present-day level of civilization from a study of our burial practices. It is depressing to think of them digging and poking about in our new crop of Forest Lawns, the shouts of discovery as they come upon the mass-produced granite horrors, the repetitive flat bronze markers (the legends, like greeting cards and singing telegrams, chosen from an approved list maintained at the cemetery office), and, under the ground, the stamped-out metal casket shells resembling nothing so much as those bronzed and silvered souvenirs for sale at airport gift shops. Prying further, they would find reposing in each of these on a comfortable mattress of innerspring or foam-rubber construction a standardized, rouged, or suntanned specimen of Homo sapiens, USA, attired in business suit or flowing negligee according to sex. Our archaeologists would puzzle exceedingly over the inner meaning of the tenement mausoleums with their six or seven tiers of adjoining crypt spaces. Were the tenants of these, they might wonder, engaged in some ritual act of contemplation, surprised by sudden disaster? Busily scribbling notes, they would describe the companion his-and-her vaults for husband and wife, and the approved inscription on these: TOGETHER FOREVER. For purposes of comparison they might recall the words of Andrew Marvell, a poet from an earlier culture, who thus addressed his coy mistress:

> *The grave's a fine and private place,*
> *But none, I think, do there embrace.*

They might rashly conclude that twentieth-century America was a nation of abjectly imitative conformists, devoted to machine-made gadgetry and mass-produced art of a debased quality; that its dominant theology was a weird mixture of primitive superstitions and superficial attitudes towards death, overlaid with a distinct tendency towards necrophilism.

Where did our burial practices come from? There is little scholarship on the subject. Thousands of books have been written describing, cataloguing, theorizing about the funeral procedures of ancient and modern peoples from the Aztecs to the Zulus; but about contemporary American burial practices almost nothing has been written.

The National Funeral Directors Association, aware of this omission and anxious to correct it, commissioned two writers, Robert W. Habenstein and William M. Lamers, to explore the subject and to come up with some answers. The resulting studies, *The History of American Funeral Directing* and *Funeral Customs the World Over,* bear the imprint of the National Funeral Directors Association and were the subject of a continuing promotion campaign by that organization: "Buy one for each clergyman in your community!" "Place them in your libraries!" are the slogans. The campaign has had some success. In fact, in most libraries these volumes sponsored by the undertaking trade are the only ones to be found on the subject of the American funeral.

The official historians of American undertaking describe the origin of our burial practices as follows: "As a result of a long, slow development, with its roots deep in the history of Western civilization, it is the common American mind today that the dead merit professional funeral services from a lay occupational group. These services include embalming, the preparation of the body for final viewing, a waiting period between death and disposition, the use for everyone of a casket that is attractive and protects the remains, a dignified and ceremonious service with consideration for the feelings of the bereaved, and an expression of the individual and group beliefs. . . ." Elsewhere they assert: "The roots of American funeral behavior extend back in a direct line several thousand years to early Judaeo-Christian beliefs as to the nature of God, man and the hereafter. . . . Despite the antiquity of these roots their importance as regards the treatment of the dead in the world that commonly calls itself Christian today cannot be overemphasized."

In two misinformation-packed paragraphs, we are assured not only that American funerals are based on hallowed custom and tradition, but that they conform to long-held religious doctrine. There is more than a hint of warning in these words for the would-be funeral reformer; he who would be bold enough to make light of or tamper with the fundamental beliefs and ancient traditions of a society in so sensitive an area as behavior towards its dead had better think twice.

A "long, slow development, with its roots deep in the history of

Western civilization," or a short, fast sprint with its roots deep in moneymaking? A brief look backward would seem to establish that there is no resemblance between the funeral practices of today and those of even seventy-five to one hundred years ago, and that there is nothing in the "history of Western civilization" to support the thesis of continuity and gradual development of funeral customs. On the contrary, the salient features of the contemporary American funeral (beautification of the corpse, metal casket and vault, banks of store-bought flowers, the ubiquitous offices of the "funeral director") are all of very recent vintage in this country, and each has been methodically designed and tailored to extract maximum profit for the trade.

Nor can responsibility for the twentieth-century American funeral be laid at the door of "Judaeo-Christian beliefs." The major Western faiths have remarkably little to say about how funerals should be conducted. Such doctrinal statements as have been enunciated concerning disposal of the dead invariably stress simplicity, the equality of all men in death, emphasis on the spiritual aspects rather than on the physical remains.

The Roman Catholic Church requires that the following, simple instructions be observed: "(1) That the body be decently laid out; (2) that lights be placed beside the body; (3) that a cross be laid upon the breast, or failing that, the hands laid on the breast in the form of a cross; (4) that the body be sprinkled with holy water and incense at stated times; (5) that it be buried in consecrated ground." The Jewish religion specifically prohibits display in connection with funerals: "It is strictly ordained that there must be no adornment of the plain wooden coffin used by the Jew, nor may flowers be placed inside or outside. Plumes, velvet palls and the like are strictly prohibited, and all show and display of wealth discouraged; moreover, the synagogue holds itself responsible for the arrangements for burial, dispensing with the services of the Dismal Trade." In Israel today, uncoffined burial is the rule, and the deceased is returned to the earth in a simple shroud. The Church of England's *Book of Common Prayer,* written several centuries before burial receptacles came into general use, makes no mention of coffins in connection with the funeral service, but rather speaks throughout of the corpse or the "body."

What of embalming, the pivotal aspect of the American funeral? The "roots" of this procedure have indeed leaped oceans and traversed centuries in the most unrootlike fashion. It has had a checkered history, the highlights of which deserve some consideration since embalming is (as one mortuary textbook writer puts it) "the very foundation of modern mortuary service—the factor which has made the elaborate funeral home and lucrative funeral service possible."

True, the practice of preserving dead bodies with chemicals, decorating them with paint and powder, and arranging them for a public showing has its origin in antiquity—but not in Judaeo-Christian antiquity. This incongruous behavior towards the human dead originated with the pagan Egyptians and reached its high point in the second millennium B.C. Thereafter, embalming suffered a decline from which it did not recover until it was made part of the standard funeral service in twentieth-century America.

While the actual mode of preservation and the materials used in ancient Egypt differed from those used in contemporary America, there are many striking similarities in the kind of care lavished upon the dead. There, as here, the goal was to outmaneuver the Grim Reaper as far as possible.

The Egyptian method of embalming as described by Herodotus sounds like a rather crude exercise in human taxidermy. The entrails and brain were removed, the body scoured with palm wine and purified with spices. After being soaked for seventy days in a saline solution, the corpse was washed and wrapped in strips of fine linen, then placed in a "wooden case of human shape" which in turn was put in a sepulchral chamber.

Restorative art was by no means unknown in ancient Egypt. The Greek historian Diodorus Siculus wrote: "Having treated [the corpse], they restore it to the relatives with every member of the body preserved so perfectly that even the eyelashes and eyebrows remain, the whole appearance of the body being unchangeable, and the cast of the features recognizable. . . . They present an example of a kind of inverted necromancy." The Egyptians had no Post Mortem Restoration Bra; instead, they stuffed and modeled the breasts, refashioning the nipples from copper buttons. They fixed the body while still plastic in the desired attitude; they painted it with red ochre for men and yellow for women; they emphasized the details of the face with paint; they supplemented the natural hair with a wig; they tinted the nails with henna. A mummy of the XVIIIth Dynasty has even been found wearing some practical burial footwear—sandals made of mud, with metal soles and gilded straps.

Egyptian preoccupation with preservation of the body after death stemmed from the belief that the departed spirit would one day return to inhabit the earthly body; that if the body perished, the soul would eventually perish too. Yet although embalming was available to all who could pay the price, it was by no means so universally employed in ancient Egypt as it is today in the USA. The ordinary peasant was not embalmed at all; yet, curiously enough, his corpse comes down to us through the ages as well preserved as those of his disemboweled and richly aromatic betters, for it has been established that the unusually dry climate and the absence of bacteria in the sand and air, rather than the materials used in embalming, are what account for the Egyptian mummies' marvelous state of preservation. The Greeks, knowing the uses of both, were no more likely to occupy themselves with the preservation of dead flesh than they were to bury good wine for the comfort of dead bodies. They cremated their dead, for the most part, believing in the power of flame to set free the soul. The glorious period that conventional historians call the Golden Age of Greece is for historians of embalming the beginning of the Dark Ages.

The Jews frowned upon embalming, as did the early Christians, who regarded it as a pagan custom. Saint Anthony, in the third century, denounced the practice as sinful. His impassioned plea, recorded by Athanasius, might well be echoed by the American of today who would like to avoid being transformed by the embalmer's art and displayed in a funeral home:

> And if your minds are set upon me, and ye remember me as a father, permit no man to take my body and carry it into Egypt, lest, according to the custom which they have, they embalm me and lay me up in their houses, for it was [to avoid] this that I came into this desert. And ye know that I have continually made exhortation concerning this thing and begged that it should not be done, and ye well know how much I have blamed those who observed this custom. Dig a grave then, and bury me therein, and hide my body under the earth, and let these my words be observed carefully by you, and tell ye no man where ye lay me. . . .

Mummification of the dead in Egypt was gradually abandoned after a large part of the population was converted to Christianity.

The eclipse of embalming was never quite total, however. The death of a monarch, since it is the occasion for a transfer of power, calls for demonstration, and it has throughout history been found politically expedient to provide visible evidence of death by exposing the body to public view. So embalming, of sorts, was used in Rome, and later throughout Europe, but only for the great and near-great, and by the very rich as a form of pretentiousness.

Alexander the Great is said to have been preserved in wax and honey; Charlemagne was embalmed and, dressed in imperial robes, placed in a sitting position in his tomb. Canute, too, was embalmed, and after him many an English monarch. Lord Nelson, as befits a hero, was returned to England from Trafalgar in a barrel of brandy. Queen Elizabeth, by her own wish, was not embalmed. Developments beyond her control caused her sealed, lead-lined coffin to lie in Whitehall for an unconscionable thirty-four days before interment. During this time, reports one of the ladies-in-waiting who sat as watchers, the body "burst with such a crack that it splitted the wood, lead, and cerecloth; whereupon the next day she was fain to be new trimmed up."

Although embalming as a trade or cult was not resumed until this century, there prospered in every age charlatans and eccentrics who claimed to have rediscovered the lost art of the Egyptians or who offered new and improved pickling methods of their own invention. These were joined, in the eighteenth century, by French and English experimenters spurred by a quite different motive—the need for more efficient methods of preserving cadavers for anatomical studies.

The physicians, surgeons, chemists, and apothecaries who engaged in anatomical research were from time to time sought out by private necrophiles who enlisted their services to preserve dead friends and relations. There are many examples of this curious practice, of which perhaps the most interesting is the task performed by Dr. William Hunter, the celebrated eighteenth-century anatomist. Dr. Hunter was anyway something of a card. He once explained his aversion to contradiction by pointing out that, being accustomed to the "passive submission of dead bodies," he could no longer easily tolerate having his will crossed; a sentiment echoed by Evelyn Waugh's mortuary cosmetician: "I was just glad to serve people that couldn't talk back." In 1775 Dr. Hunter and a colleague embalmed the wife of Martin Van Butchell, quack doctor and "super dentist," the point being that Mrs. Van Butchell's marriage settlement stipulated that her husband should have control of her fortune "as long as she remained above ground." The embalming was a great success. The "preserved lady" (as curious sightseers came to call her) was dressed in a fine linen gown, placed in a glass-topped case and kept in the drawing room, where Van Butchell introduced her to all comers as his "Dear Departed." So popular was the preserved lady that Van Butchell was obliged to insert a newspaper notice limiting her visiting hours to "any day between Nine and One, Sundays excepted." When Van Butchell remarried several years later, his new wife raised strong objections to the presence of the Dear Departed in her front parlor and insisted upon her removal. Thereafter the Dear Departed was housed in the museum of the Royal College of Surgeons.*

The two widely divergent interests which spurred the early embalmers—scientific inquiry, and the fascination and financial reward of turning cadavers into a sort of ornamental keepsake— were to achieve a happy union under the guiding hand of a rare nineteenth-century character, "Dr." Thomas Holmes. He was the first to advance from what one funeral trade writer jocularly calls the "Glacier Age"—when preservation on ice was the undertakers' rule—and is often affectionately referred to by present-day funeral men as "the father of American embalming." Holmes was the first to popularize the idea of preserving the dead on a mass scale, and the first American to get rich from this novel occupation.

Holmes developed a passionate interest in cadavers early in life (it was in fact the reason for his expulsion from medical school; he was forever carelessly leaving them around in inappropriate places), and when the Civil War started, he saw his great opportunity. He rushed to the front and started embalming like mad, charging the families of

---

*While on a visit to London, I applied to the Royal College of Surgeons of England for permission to see Mrs. Van Butchell. I received this reply from the office of the curator: "While it is true that the late Mrs. Martin Van Butchell once occupied a place of honour in the historical collection of this College, it is regretted that she was finally cremated with so much valuable material in the destruction of the College in May, 1941, at the height of the London blitz."

the dead soldiers $100 for his labors. Some four years and 4,028 embalmed soldiers later (his own figure), Holmes returned to Brooklyn a rich man.

The "use for everyone of a casket that is attractive and protects the remains" (attractive seems an odd word here) is a new concept in this century, and one that took some ingenuity to put across. Surprisingly enough, even the widespread use of any sort of burial receptacle is a fairly new development in Western culture, dating back less than two hundred years. Until the eighteenth century, few people except the very rich were buried in coffins. The "casket," and particularly the metal casket, is a phenomenon of modern America, unknown in past days and in other parts of the world.

As might be expected with the development of industrial technique in the nineteenth century, coffin designers soared to marvelous heights. They experimented with glass, cement, celluloid, papier-mâché, India rubber; they invented Rube Goldberg contraptions called "life signals"—complicated arrangements of wires and bells designed to set off an alarm if the occupant of the coffin should have inadvertently been buried alive.

The newfangled invention of metal coffins in the nineteenth century did not go unchallenged. An admonition on the subject was delivered by Lord Stowell, judge of the Consistory Court of London, who in 1820 was called upon to decide a case felicitously titled *Gilbert v. Buzzard*. At issue was the right to bury a corpse in a newly patented iron coffin. The church wardens protested that if parishioners were to get into the habit of burying their dead in coffins made proof against normal decay, in a few generations there would be no burial space left.

Said Lord Stowell, "The rule of law which says that a man has a right to be buried in his own churchyard is to be found, most certainly, in many of our authoritative text writers; but it is not quite so easy to find the rule which gives him the rights of burying a large chest or trunk in company with himself." He spoke approvingly of attempts to abolish use of sepulchral chests "on the physical ground that the dissolution of bodies would be accelerated, and the dangerous virulence of the fermentation disarmed by a speedy absorption of the noxious particles into the surrounding soil."

The inexorable upward thrust towards perfection in metal caskets was not, however, destined to be halted by judicial logic. Just one hundred years after the decision in *Gilbert v. Buzzard,* a triumph of the first magnitude was recorded by the D. H. Hill Casket Company of Chicago, and described in their 1920 *Catalogue of Funeral Merchandise:* "A Study in Bronze: When Robert Fulton said he could propel a boat by steam his friends were sure he was mentally deranged—that it could not be done. When Benjamin Franklin said he could draw electricity from the clouds his acquaintances thought he was crazy—that it could not be done. When our designing and manufacturing departments said they could and would produce a CAST BRONZE CASKET that would be the peer of anything yet developed, their friends and associates shook their heads sympathetically, feeling that it would be a hopeless task. All three visions have come to be realities—the steamboat, electricity, and the Hilco Peerless Cast Bronze Burial Receptacle."

The production of ever more solid and durable metal caskets has soared in this century; their long-lasting and even "eternal" qualities have become a matter of pride and self-congratulation throughout the industry—and this in one area of manufacture where built-in obsolescence might seem (as Lord Stowell pointed out) to present certain advantages. As we have seen, the sales of metal caskets now exceed sales of the old-fashioned wooden types. A brand-new tradition has been established; how deep are the roots, Messrs. Habenstein and Lamers?

Mourning symbols have run the gamut. In medieval England and in colonial America, the skull and crossbones was the favored symbol, making its appearance on everything connected with death, from tombstone to funeral pall to coffin maker's sign. Funerary extravagance took the form of elaborate mourning clothes, the hiring of mutes (or paid mourners), tremendous feasting sometimes of many days' duration, and gifts to the living, who were showered with rings, scarves, needlework, books, and, most customarily, gloves.

Funeral flowers, today the major mourning symbol and a huge item of national expenditure, did not make their appearance in England or America until after the middle of the nineteenth century, and only then over the opposition of church leaders.

From colonial days until the nineteenth century, the American funeral was almost exclusively a family affair, in the sense that the family and close friends performed most of the duties in connection with the dead body itself. It was they who washed and laid out the body, draped it in a winding sheet, and ordered the coffin from the local carpenter. It was they who carried the coffin on foot from the home to the church and thence to the graveyard, and who frequently—unless the church sexton was available—dug the grave. Funeral services were held in the church over the pall-covered bier, and a brief committal prayer was said at the graveside. Between the death and the funeral, the body lay in the family parlor, where the mourners took turns watching over it, the practical reason for this being the ever-present possibility that signs of life might be observed. The first undertakers were drawn mainly from three occupations, all concerned with some aspect of burial: the livery-stable keeper, who provided the hearse and funeral carriages; the carpenter or cabinet-maker, who made the coffins; and the sexton, who was generally in charge of bell-tolling and gravedigging. In some of the larger cities, midwives and nurses advertised their services as occupational layers out of the dead, and were so listed in city directories. The under-taker's job was primarily custodial. It included supplying the coffin from a catalogue or from his own establishment, arranging to bring folding chairs (if the service was to be held in the home, which was often the case), taking charge of the pallbearers, supervising the removal of the coffin and loading it into the hearse, and in general doing the necessary chores until the body was finally lowered into the grave.

Shortly before the turn of the century, the undertaker conferred upon himself the title of "funeral director." From that time on, possibly inspired by his own semantics, he began to direct funerals, and quietly to impose a character of his own on the mode of disposal of the dead.

Some of the changes that were in store are foreshadowed in *The Modern Funeral* by W. P. Hohenschuh, published in 1900. Hohenschuh may have been the first to put into words a major assumption that lies behind modern funeral practices: "There is nothing too good for the dead," he declares. He goes on to advise, "The friends want the best that they can afford. . . . A number of manufacturers have set an excellent example by fitting up magnificent showrooms, to which funeral directors can take their customers, and show them the finest goods made. It is an education for all parties concerned. . . . It is to be commended." Hohenschuh's injunctions about funeral salesmanship, although vastly elaborated over the years, remain basic: "Boxes must be shown to sell them. By having an ordinary pine box next to one that is papered, the difference is more readily seen than could be explained, and a better price can be obtained for the latter." And on collections he warns, "Grief soon subsides, and the older the bill gets, the harder it is to collect."

In 1900 embalming was still the exception rather than the rule and was still generally done in the home—although Hohenschuh mentions a new trend making its appearance in California: that of taking the body to the funeral parlor after death for dressing and embalming. He proposes an ingenious approach to selling the public on embalming: "It may be suggested that bodies should be embalmed in winter as well as in summer. It may be a little difficult to have people accept this idea, but after having tried it a few times, and people realize the comfort to themselves in having the body in a warm room, this preventing them against colds, besides the sentimental feeling against having the body in a cold room, it is an easy matter to make the custom general." However, the most profitable aspect of the modern funeral—that of preparing the body for the public gaze—seems to have escaped this astute practitioner, for he opposes the open casket at the funeral service, and remarks, "There is no doubt that people view the dead out of curiosity."

It was still a far cry from these early, hesitant steps of the emerging funeral industry to the full-fledged burlesque it has become.

13

The Newest Profession

Funeral directors are members of an exalted, almost sacred call-
ing. . . . [T]he Executive Committee believed that a cut in prices
would be suicidal, and notified the manufacturers that better
goods, rather than lower prices, were needed. . . . A $1,000 prize
was offered for the best appearing corpse after 60 days. . . . A res-
olution was passed requesting the newspapers in reporting the
proceedings to refrain from flippancy.

—*Sunnyside,* 1885*

These observations are culled from an 1885 report describing the proceedings of one of the earliest National Funeral Directors Association conventions. A century later, the problems they reflect continue to occupy the attention of the undertaking trade: how to be exalted, almost sacred, and at the same time be successful businessmen in a highly competitive situation; how to continually upgrade their peculiar product; how to establish successful relations with press and public.

The special public relations problem that dogs the undertaker has existed for all time, arising out of the very nature of his occupation. It is uphill work to present it attractively, but he tries, perhaps too hard. Of late years he has compounded his built-in dilemma by veering off in his own weird direction towards a cult of the dead unsanctioned by tradition, religion, or common sense. He has painted himself into a difficult corner. His major justifications for his practices fly in the face of reality, but he persists; the fantasy he has created, and in which he by now has so much cash invested, must somehow be made desirable to the buying public. And like every other successful sales-

---

*This journal later merged with *The Casket*. The result: *Casket & Sunnyside*.

man, the funeral salesman must first and foremost believe in himself and his product.

He is in any case not just a funeral salesman. There is the creative aspect of his work, the aesthetically rewarding task of transforming the corpse into a Beautiful Memory Picture. Pride of craftsmanship, fascination with technique, and continuous striving for improvement shine through all that he writes on this subject.

The sort of passionate devotion it is possible to develop for embalming, the true Art for Art's Sake approach, is captured in a testimonial letter published as part of an advertisement for Cosmetic Tru-Lanol Arterial Fluid. Like any other craftsman, the embalmer gets satisfaction from rising to a challenge and often hates to part with his finished product. The letter describes an unusually difficult case: "The subject . . . was a 69-year-old lady, 5'2" tall with 48" bust and 48" hips. Death was a sudden heart attack. She lay 40 hours in a heated apartment prior to being moved." The writer goes on to mention other inauspicious circumstances surrounding the case, such as a series of punctures made in the center of circulation by some bungler in the medical examiner's office. However, Tru-Lanol comes to the rescue: "Surface penetration was slow and even, with excellent cosmetic results. . . . By the fourth day, the swelling in the features was receding in a very uniform manner, and the cosmetic was still excellent. Honestly, I don't know of another fluid that would have done as good a job in this case, all things considered." He adds wistfully, "I wish I could have kept her for four more days." How poignant those last words! And in a way, how very understandable.

Every craft develops its outstanding practitioners, those who seem to live for the sake of their work. Such a one was Elizabeth "Ma" Green, born in 1884, a true zealot of funeral service. *Mortuary Management,* in a tribute to this unusual woman, recalls that "Ma" got her start in a lifelong career of embalming as a teenager: "It was during this early period of her life that she became interested in caring for the dead. As this interest increased, she assisted the village undertaker in the care and preparation of family friends who passed away." "Ma" never looked back. By the early twenties she had become a licensed embalmer, and later took a job as principal of an embalming college. She stayed in this work, girl and woman, some sixty years: "It was obvious she had an almost passionate devotion to the Profession."

Funeral people are always saying that "funerals are for the living," yet there is occasional evidence that they have developed an eerie affection, a genuine solicitude, for the dead, in whose company they spend so much time. It is as though they really attribute feelings to these mute remains of humanity, much as a small child attributes feelings to his teddy bear; as though they are actually concerned with the comfort and well-being of the bodies entrusted to their care. A 1921 issue of *The Casket* describes a chemical which, "when sprayed into the mouth of a cadaver, prevents and stops the development of pyorrhea." And California is one of several states where it is a penal offense to use "profane, indecent or obscene language" in the presence of a dead human body.

When the funeral practitioner puts pen to paper on his favorite subject, the results are truly dreamy flights of rhapsody. Mr. John H. Eckels says in his textbook *Mortuary Science* that "the American method of arterial embalming . . . adds another laurel to the crown of inventiveness, ingenuity, and scientific research which the world universally accords to us. . . . In fact, there is no profession on record which has made such rapid advancement in this country as embalming. . . . In summing up this whole situation, the funeral profession today is one of the most vital callings in the cause of humanity. Funeral directors are the advance guards of civilization. . . ." These vivid metaphors, these laurels, crowns and advance guards, express with peculiar appropriateness the modern undertaker's fond conception of his work and himself. How to generate equal enthusiasm in the minds of the public for the "funeral profession" is a more difficult problem.

Mr. Edward A. Martin, author of *Psychology of Funeral Service,* sees undertakers in a role "similar to that of a school teacher who knows and believes in his subject but who must find attractive ways to impress it indelibly upon his pupils. Our class consists of more than 150 million Americans, and the task of educating them is one that cannot be accomplished overnight." He adds, "Public opinion is based on the education of the public, which believes what it is told."

There is some evidence that while this great pedagogical process has taken hold most strongly among the funeral men themselves, it has left the public either apathetic or downright hostile. In other words, the funeral men live very largely in a dreamworld of their own making about the "acceptance" of their product in the public mind. They seem to feel that saying something often and loudly enough will somehow make it true. "Sentiment alone is the foundation of our profession," they cry. "The new funeral director is a Doctor of Grief, or expert in returning abnormal minds to normal in the shortest possible time!"

But the public goes merrily on its way, thinking (when it thinks of the matter at all) that moneymaking is the foundation of the funeral trade, that the matter of returning abnormal minds to normal is best left in the hands of trained psychiatrists, that it has neither been asked for nor voiced its approval of modern funeral practices. There are really two parts to the particular selling job confronting the funeral industry. The first is that of convincing people of the correctness and essential Americanism of the kind of funeral the industry wants to sell; convincing them, too, that in funerary matters there is an obligation to adhere closely to standards and procedures established by the funeral directors—who, after all, should know best about these things. The second is that of projecting an ever more exalted image of the purveyors of funerals.

Funeral men constantly seek to justify the style and cost of their product on the basis of "tradition," and on the basis of their theory that current funeral practices are a reflection of characteristically high American standards. The "tradition" theory is a hard one to put across, as we have seen; the facts tend to run in the opposite direction. Therefore, certain incantations—Wise Sayings with the power of great inspiration—are frequently invoked to help along the process of indoctrination. There is one in particular which crops up regularly in mortuary circles: a quotation from Gladstone, who is reported to have said, "Show me the manner in which a nation or a community cares for its dead and I will measure with mathematical exactness the tender sympathies of its people, their respect for the law of the land and their loyalty to high ideals."* One could wish he were with us in the twentieth century to apply his handy measuring

---

*Sometime after publication, I met Francis Gladstone, a direct descendant of the erstwhile Prime Minister. When I asked him about his illustrious forebear's comment, he became interested and wrote to scholars of his acquaintance at Oxford. Lengthy correspondence ensued, but no one was able to identify William Gladstone's alleged statement. In the course of their research, one of their number did come up with the dying words of another Gladstone, Sir Joseph, the father of the Prime Minister, who died in Liverpool, aged eighty-seven. His last words—"Bring me my porridge"—while not earth-shattering, have at least the merit of being historically accurate.

tape to a calendar issued by the W. W. Chambers Mortuary. Over the legend "Beautiful Bodies by Chambers" appears an unusually well endowed, and completely naked, young lady. Another favorite sooth-sayer is Benjamin Franklin, who is roped in from time to time and quoted as having said, "To know the character of a community, I need only to visit its cemeteries." Wise old Ben! Could he but visit Forest Lawn today, he would have no need to go on to Los Angeles.

In their constant striving for better public relations, funeral men are hampered by their inability to agree on what they are, what weight should be given the various roles in which they see them-selves, what aspect should be stressed both within the trade and to the public. Is the funeral director primarily merchant, embalmer, lay psychiatrist, or a combination of all these? The pronouncements of his leaders, association heads, writers of trade books and manuals, and other theoreticians of the industry betray the confusion that exists on this point.

"Embalming is the cornerstone upon which the funeral service profession was founded and it has remained so through the years. It is the only facet of service offered by our industry that is not wholly based upon sentiment, with all its attendant weaknesses," editorial-izes the *American Funeral Director*. The authoritative Messrs. Habenstein and Lamers see it differently. They are of the opinion that funeral service rests primarily on "the psychological skills in human relations necessary to the proper handling of the emotions and dispo-sitions of the bereaved." Still another journal sees it this way: "Mer-chandising is the lifeblood of the funeral service business. . . ." And in a laudable effort to reconcile some of these conflicting ideas, there is an article in the *American Funeral Director* headed PRACTICAL IDEALISM IN FUNERAL DIRECTING, which declares, "The highest of ideals are worthless unless they are properly applied. The funeral director who thinks only in terms of serving would very likely find himself out of business in a year or less. . . . And if he were compelled to close up his establishment what possible use would be all his high ideals and his desire to serve?" And so the Practical Idealist comes back full circle to his role as merchant, to "costs, selling methods, the business end of his costs."

Funeral people are always telling one another about the impor-tance of ethics (not just any old ethics but usually "the *highest* ethics"), sentiment, integrity, standards (again, "the highest"), moral responsibility, frankness, cooperation, character. They exhort one another to be sincere, friendly, dignified, prompt, courteous, calm, pleasant, kindly, sympathetic, good listeners; to speak good English; not to be crude; to join the Masons, the Knights of Columbus, the Chamber of Commerce, the Boy Scouts, the PTA; to take part in the Community Chest drive; to be pleasant and fair-dealing with employees and clients alike; not to cuss their competitors; and, it goes without saying, so to conduct themselves that they will be above scandal or slander. In short, they long to be worthy of high regard, to be liked and understood, a most human longing.

Yet, just as one is beginning to think what dears they really are—for the prose is hypnotic by reason of its very repetitiveness—one's eye is caught by this sort of thing in *Mortuary Management:* "You must start treating a child's funeral, from the time of death to the time of burial, as a golden opportunity for building good will and preserving sentiment, without which we wouldn't have any industry at all." Or this in the *National Funeral Service Journal:* "Buying habits are influenced largely by envy and environment. Don't ever overlook the importance of these two factors in estimating the purchasing possibilities or potential of any family. . . . Envy is essentially the same as pride. . . . It is the idea of keeping up with the Joneses. . . . Sometimes it is only necessary to say, '. . . Here is a casket similar to the one the Joneses selected' to insure a selection in a substantially profitable bracket."

Merchants of a rather grubby order, preying on the grief, remorse, and guilt of survivors, or trained professional men with high standards of ethical conduct?

The funeral men really would vastly prefer to fit the latter category. A discussion has raged for many years in funeral circles around this very question of "professionalism" versus a trade or business status, and the side that contends that undertaking is a profession is winning out in the National Funeral Directors Association.

Once again, it is apparently expected that the mere repetition of the statement will invest it with validity. Sample speeches are prepared and circulated among association members: "I am not an undertaker. He served his purpose and passed out of the picture. I am a funeral director. I am a Doctor of Services. We are members of a profession, just as truly as the lawyer, the doctor or the minister."

In 1951 *Mortuary Management* reported another example of successful pioneering on this front by National Selected Morticians: "Leave it to NSM to come out with new names for old things. We've passed through the period of the 'back room,' the 'show room,' the 'sales room,' the 'casket display room,' the 'casket room.' Now NSM offers you the 'selection room.' "

A 1949 press release issued by the NFDA on a survey of public attitudes towards the funeral business hopefully asks, "Please Do Not Use the Term 'Undertaker' at the Head of This Story." As late as 1962, the *American Funeral Director* was moved to chide the *New York Times* for its "continued insistence upon using the relatively obsolete and meaningless words 'undertaker' and 'coffin' to the exclusion of the more generally accepted and meaningful ones, 'funeral director' and 'casket.' "

Funeralese has had its ups and downs. The word "mortician"—first used in *Embalmers Monthly* for February 1895—was barred by the *Chicago Times* in 1932, "not for lack of sympathy with the ambition of undertakers to be well regarded, but because of it. If they haven't the sense to save themselves from their own lexicographers, we shall not be guilty of abetting them in their folly." "Casket," dating from Civil War days, was denounced by Hawthorne: "a vile modern phrase which compels a person to shrink from the idea of being buried at all." Emily Post uses it, albeit reluctantly: "In spite of the fact that the word coffin is preferred by all people of fastidious taste and that the word casket is never under any circumstances used in the spoken language of these same people, it seems best to follow present-day commercial usage and admit the word casket to these pages."

A network of trade associations reflects the complexity of ambitions and viewpoints within the industry. While one undertaker may (and often does) belong to more than one association, and while the various associations may (and often do) join forces on a specific issue, the associations are not always in accord, for on many questions they represent conflicting economic interests.

The names of the associations are in some cases merely descriptive of the membership they represent: National Funeral Directors Association, Jewish Funeral Directors Association, National Funeral

Directors & Morticians Association. Others have chosen more imaginative and even lyrical names: International Order of the Golden Rule and National Selected Morticians.

The associations with the high-sounding names generally limit membership to one funeral establishment to a community, to enable members to display the insignia on their advertising material and letterheads. To the public, it might seem that to be "Selected" denotes some sort of official certification by an outside agency; actually the members Select one another.

National Selected Morticians is a go-ahead concern numbering among its members some of the largest and most successful firms in the country. "You have to be sponsored by a member and you join by invitation," one of them explained to me.

While all the trade associations like to refer to undertaking as "the Profession," their understanding of that term varies widely. NSM seems to use it because it sounds nice, rather than for its full implications. The NSM emphasis is on merchandising, sound business methods. They are in favor of prearranged, prefinanced funerals, and price advertising because their member establishments depend primarily on big volume.

Mr. Wilber Krieger, managing director of NSM, was also the director of the National Foundation of Funeral Service in Evanston. Here a school of management is maintained, where courses are offered in advertising, market analysis, credit and collection, ethical practice, letter writing, sales techniques in funeral service, and so on. The Foundation is housed in a two-story ersatz-Colonial mansion. Among its facilities is a "selection room for Merchandising Research to improve merchandising, to demonstrate lighting (more than five different types in the room), to show arrangements and decoration through the twenty-five-unit balanced line of caskets." The Avenue of Approach and Aisles of Resistance, Mr. Krieger's own brainchildren, are here laid out for all to see. There is also a vault selection room aimed at helping the funeral director "create a 'Quality' atmosphere, conducive to better vault sales," and at showing him how to "increase his burial vault profits by encouraging better sales through better merchandising."

The oldest, largest, and most influential of the funeral trade associations is the National Funeral Directors Association, founded in the

1880s. From the beginning, the NFDA has campaigned for professional status; from the beginning, their dilemma, still unresolved after the passage of years, was evident. The first code of ethics, adopted in 1884, says, "There is, perhaps, no profession, after that of the sacred ministry, in which a high-toned morality is more imperatively necessary than that of a funeral director's. High moral principles are his only safe guide." But a corollary objective of the organization—that of keeping prices pegged as high as possible—was expressed in a resolution passed in the previous year: "Resolved, that we, as funeral directors, condemn the manufacture of covered caskets at a price less than fifteen dollars for an adult size."

The National Funeral Directors Association serves its affiliated state groups through bulletins, keeping watch on legislative developments, lobbying activities, advising member firms on methods of cost accounting, and other business procedures. It conducts an annual convention at which casket manufacturers, burial-clothing firms, vault men and embalming-fluid supply houses exhibit their wares. It sends speakers to state conventions. It conducts surveys among its members on operating expenses, income, etc., as well as on such apparently far-afield subjects as reading habits—a 1958 survey reveals with pride that 56.7 percent of funeral service personnel read "newspapers, trade journals, magazines and books," compared with only 40 percent for the population as a whole.

The NFDA concerns itself deeply with public relations. It has produced a couple of films: *Funeral Service—A Part of the American Way* and *To Serve the Living*, prepared in conjunction with the Association of Better Business Bureaus, Inc. Two of the most important public relations aids, the use of which have been constantly urged upon its members by the NFDA, are a pamphlet, *Facts Every Family Should Know About Funerals and Interments*, issued by the Association of Better Business Bureaus, and *Funeral Service Facts and Figures*, issued annually by the NFDA.

The Association of Better Business Bureaus is held in high esteem by many people, who regard it as a watchdog organization designed to protect the public from unscrupulous and crooked businessmen. Its stamp of approval on the line of conduct of any enterprise is bound to allay doubts and suspend criticism. I was surprised to find how many of the "facts" every family should know had the familiar ring of NFDA propaganda, and that the pamphlet, which has been distributed by funeral directors in the hundreds of thousands, closely follows the NFDA line in all important respects. I asked the BBB where they got the "facts" for the pamphlet; they replied, from the National Funeral Directors Association and other (unidentified) sources. For example, the "fact" given in the pamphlet that "there is an adequate service available in every funeral establishment for every purse and taste" is given "on the basis of information furnished by the NFDA." The "fact" that "most funeral directors do not consider it ethical to advertise prices . . . and [that] this view is shared by a majority of the public" is again reported as "the official position of the NFDA."

By the mid-1990s, the most persistent advertisers, to the consternation of the conventional mortuaries that maintain elaborate establishments on Main Street, were the low-cost, low-overhead cremation providers. The majority of funeral homes still refrain from public disclosure of their prices—let alone price advertising—although FTC rules require them to make price information available when asked.

In recent years, the NFDA and other trade associations have provided their members with annual estimates of "average prices" currently charged for mortuary services and vaults. The estimates of the NFDA and FFDA (Federated Funeral Directors of America) vary very little. FFDA's average for 1995 was $4,211 for "services plus casket," plus $770 for outside container. Industry observers have no doubt that the dissemination of these numbers within the trade serves to establish uniform price minimums, in violation of the antitrust laws. Hence the caveat, "The NFDA sponsored this study to give you statistics with which you can compare data from your funeral service operation. However, you should not take any or all of the findings as a suggestion for funeral service pricing in your establishment." This caveat is reminiscent of a legend printed in prominent letters on the wine bricks sold for a time during Prohibition: "Do not under any circumstances place this brick in one gallon of water and let it stand at room temperature for one week, since this will cause it to turn into wine, an alcoholic beverage, the manufacture or possession of which is illegal."

In 1930 the NFDA established an academy of funerary erudition with the scholarly-sounding name Institute of Mortuary Research—the actual function of which was, according to the NFDA's official historians, "to disseminate information favorable to organized funeral directing to the various media of communication . . . and to 'trouble-shoot' points of hostility and attacks on the occupation."

Throughout its history, the NFDA has generally acted to boost the educational requirements for the licensing of embalmers. The time required for completion of an embalming—or mortuary science—course has crept up by stages from six weeks in 1910 to about two years. At such lofty-sounding institutions as Carl Sandburg College, Malcolm X College, or Vincennes University, one may earn an Associate in Applied Sciences degree.

Or one may get a diploma in funeral service in just forty weeks at the National Education Institute of New England; among the sixteen ten-week courses one must take there are "Issues and Concerns for Modern Professionals," "Marketing and Merchandising in Funeral Service," and "Restorative Art."

But the educational requirements vary from state to state. The qualifications for licensing an embalmer—who is, after all, usually an underling, an employee of the funeral establishment—are generally more stringent than those for the funeral director who employs him. Wyoming has no educational requirements for a funeral director's license. Six states require only a high school diploma and a year or two of apprenticeship. Just what meaning the term "profession" can have when applied to this calling is hard to conceive.

The NFDA itself sets no educational, moral, or ethical standards for membership. In fact, the only qualifications appear to be the payment of dues and a state license.

A major reason for the existence of most professional organizations is the maintenance of standards of ethical practice among its members, and the disciplining of members who deviate from these standards. Here the NFDA is in some difficulty, because the practices that have led to the severest public criticism—tricky selling methods and overcharging—are nowhere condemned in its official policy pronouncements. *Mortuary Management* commented on this difficulty: "[The NFDA] has little or no control over who belongs. It has to accept any member of an affiliated state association, and that includes everyone from the desk and telephone curbstoner to the 5,000 case a year corporation. . . . True, NFDA has a Code of Ethics. But there are no minimum standards for membership. . . . There is no restriction whatever on the curbstoner."

The NFDA, not to be deterred by a little thing like the realities of a situation, in 1961 issued a ringing cry for professional status: "Before this decade is completed, professionalism will be a standard for funeral service." There was more behind this yearning than just the desire for gentility and recognition. The achievement by undertakers of professional status would, it was hoped, be a convenient way to secure legal sanction for a ban on price advertising, long an objective of the NFDA. Restrictions on advertising by professions as well as by businesses have long since gone by the boards, invalidated by the courts on constitutional grounds. Members of the learned professions, on the other hand, have codes of ethics, at one time enforced by law, which prohibit advertising.

Possibly the vast gap between desire and reality on this question of professionalism—the contradiction between the high-flown talk of Ethical Values and vexatious commercial necessities—accounts in good measure for the painful sensitivity to criticism evidenced by the funeral men. The slightest suggestion of opposition to any part of their operation, the slightest questioning of their sincerity, virtue, and general uprightness, produces howls of anguish and brings them running like so many Brave Little Dutch Boys to plug the holes in the dike.

It is as though generations of music-hall jokes, ribald cartoons, literary bons mots of which the undertaker is the butt had produced a deep-seated persecution complex, sometimes bordering on an industry-wide paranoia. The very titles of their speeches reveal this uneasy state of mind. Topics for addresses at one convention were: "What Are They Doing to Us?" and "You Are Probably Being Talked About Right Now."

In their relations with the community as a whole, the funeral men carry on a sort of weird shadowboxing, frequently wildly off the mark. There is an old act—possibly originated by W. C. Fields?—in which a bartender is trying to get rid of a bothersome fly. He goes after it with his bar towel, knocking down bottles as he swings; soon the bar is a shambles. Finally the fly settles on his nose and the bartender takes a last swipe, this time with a full bottle, and succeeds in knocking himself out while the fly unconcernedly buzzes off. The funeral industry's approach to public relations is frequently reminiscent of that bartender.

Enemies seem to lurk everywhere—among competitors, of course, but also among the clergy, the medical profession, the tissue banks, the cemetery people, the press. There is hardly an issue of the many funeral trade publications that does not reflect some aspect of this sense of bitter persecution, of being deeply misunderstood and cruelly maligned.

14

The Nosy Clergy

"To the avaricious churchman there must be provided proof that a funeral investment does not deprive either the church or its pastor of revenue." This extraordinary statement appeared in the *National Funeral Service Journal* for April 1961, together with the opinion that the three most important reasons for the mounting rash of criticism of funeral service are "religion, avarice, and a burning desire for social reform."

The same idea is expressed a little more fully in another issue of the same magazine: "The minister is perhaps our most serious problem, but the one most easily solved. Most religious leaders avoid interference. There are some, however . . . who feel that they must protect their parishioners' financial resources and direct them to a more 'worthy' cause. Some of these men, after finding more dimes than dollars in the collection plate, reach the point of frustration where they vent their unholy anger on the supposedly affluent funeral director."

These are salvos fired in a rather one-sided battle which rages from time to time between some of the clergy and some sections of the funeral industry—one-sided because, while the funeral men are always ready with dukes up to go on the offensive, the average minister is generally unaware that war has been declared.

The issue boils down to this: The morticians resent the intrusion into their business of clergy who take it upon themselves to steer parishioners in the direction of moderation in choice of casket and other matters pertaining to the production of the funeral. Many of the clergy, for their part, deplore what they regard as the growing usurpation of their role as counselors in a time of grief and need, and the growing distortion of what they view as an extremely important, solemn religious rite.

Not infrequently, the controversy spills over into print. There is a considerable body of church literature on the subject: pamphlets, booklets, and ecclesiastical-magazine articles which explain the religious significance of the funeral as an expression of faith. These stress the importance of ministerial counsel at the time of death, the spiritual nature of the funeral service, the need to face realistically the facts of life and death, the advisability of giving some thought to the type of funeral desired before the need arises.

Sometimes the advice is taken a step further: "Consider the cost in the context of your stewardship. Thoughts of preservation of a body, coupled with the inflationary pressures of our time, have led some people to excessive expenditures for burial vaults and caskets. Yet, we know that the body shall return to the elements from which it came. . . . This means that we will be conservative in the purchase of casket, burial, and additional services, conserving frequently limited funds to meet the needs of the living. Let us recognize that ordinarily this would also be the desire of the deceased. . . ."

From the funeral director's point of view, these are fighting words; bad enough on paper, but when followed up by the corporeal presence of a clergyman with the family at the crucial moment of the selection of a casket, they constitute a call to arms. "The man who has the clergyman making the selection for his families does have a nasty problem," wrote an undertaker.

The posing of this nasty problem in the pages of *Mortuary Management* produced some very down-to-earth advice, best relayed by quoting from the correspondence of the funeral directors who participated in the discussion:

There is one possible solution to the problem of ministers accompanying families to the casket display room in an attempt to persuade them to purchase a minimum funeral service. . . . The funeral director should do a little "pre-selling." . . . Then take the family into the showroom, introduce them to a few caskets, showing them the price card, and say that you realize that the selection of a funeral service is a very intimate and personal thing which the family alone can do and that you want them to be able to do this without the influence of others. *At this time, invite the minister to join you in your office* while the family discusses the selection.*

The scheme of separating the minister from the selecting group by "invit[ing him] to join you in your office" is discussed more explicitly by the next writer:

We tell the family to go ahead and look over the caskets in the display room and that the minister, if he has come with them, will join them later. We tell the minister that we have something we would like to talk to him about privately, and we've found that if we have some questions to ask him, he seems to be flattered that his advice is being sought, and we can keep him in the private office until the family has actually made its selection.

Just in case the point has not been thoroughly clarified, a third writer describes in further detail how best to lure the unsuspecting man of God from the side of his parishioners:

Ministers seem to be getting into the act more and more, and, in general, becoming more and more inimical to us. . . . We make a point of emphasizing, during our pre-selection period, the idea that making the selection is something that only the family can do. . . . We emphasize this very strongly, particularly if there is a minister around. Also, we make it a point to think up something to talk about, if the minister comes with the family . . . such as the new addition to the church property, their parking problem, the local Boys' Club in which they are interested, their golf game, politics (a red-hot subject in this part of the country right now!) or anything else that will keep them occupied and happy while the family goes ahead with the selection.

A fourth writer throws in the sponge:

*Italics in the original.

We have this same problem of nosy clergymen in our town, and I am convinced that there is nothing that can be done about the situation. We tried!

Compared with these views, those expressed by most clergy themselves are moderate and even tolerant. Their occasional criticism is mild and reserved. Some of the clergymen with whom I discussed the matter confessed to having been sorely tried from time to time in their dealings with the funeral people. Most of them—including the most outspoken foes of high-priced, showy funerals—made a sharp differentiation between the funeral price-gouger and the "honest, ethical mortician." Others felt that the funeral director is in a sense the prisoner of his own wall-to-wall carpeting; that, having installed all the expensive gadgetry and luxurious fittings, he is obliged to charge high prices in order to pay for the upkeep of his fancy establishment.

I sought to learn from a number of churchmen of different faiths something of ecclesiastic attitudes towards the funeral service. What are the actual ritualistic requirements; what is the status of the dead body; what is the position on "viewing the remains," on the willing of the body for medical research? How closely does the sort of funeral generally provided today conform with the traditions of the church? What, if any, criticisms are there of today's typical funeral service? Should the clergyman participate with the family in making the actual arrangements for the funeral—should he go with them into the selection room? These were some of the questions I had.

The Right Reverend James A. Pike, bishop of the Episcopal Diocese of California at the time, came out foursquare in favor of the "nosy" clergy. He urged that the pastor be called in *first*—that is, before the funeral director is consulted—when death occurs. The clergyman should accompany the family to the funeral parlor for the specific purpose of helping them to resist the pressures towards overspending. In any event, the casket, whether pine box or magnificent solid bronze, is, in the Episcopal Church, covered with a funeral pall during the service—"the point being to minimize the showpiece aspects. We feel that earthly remains are not to be made that much of." Although the clergy strongly favor moderation in funeral expense and simplicity of decor, individual freedom in the choice of a coffin is respected: "If people insist on doing something foolish in the matter of funeral expense, that's up to them, of course. What's sometimes wrong is the element of pride, apparently fostered in the advertising approach of some funeral directors. In terms of a remedy, a lot of teaching in advance is needed—the use and purpose of the funeral pall, and why it is our position that the casket should be closed during the service."

What about the practice of displaying the body in a slumber room at the mortuary before the funeral? "This might bring some comfort and peace to the relatives; one can see that the widow might wish a final glance at the deceased. This is a private affair, up to the family to decide." While Bishop Pike was neutral on the matter of the "open casket" beforehand, he was definitely opposed to it during and after the service. "This is not merely my personal view," he said. "Our tradition does not favor the 'viewing of the remains' after the service by those who have come. In other words, when the casket is closed after the preliminary period, it remains closed."

Theologically, Bishop Pike explained, the body has served its sacramental purpose, that of housing the personality of the individual, "which in life to come receives a new, appropriate means of expression and relationship." The remains are not the person; they are rather like discarded clothing. Nevertheless, as the outward and visible sign of personality, they are to be treated with respect and reverence. In the same way, the presence of the casket at the funeral service has a symbolic function, much like that of a flag in a parade. There is no objection to cremation; on the contrary, most Protestant clergy think it a very good idea. The memorial service, at which the coffin is not present, is also quite permissible, and this practice is, in fact, on the increase.

Is there any contradiction between the reverent treatment of human remains and the bequeathing of those remains to medical schools for research purposes? "No, a positive, constructive use of the body for medical research is by no means irreverent. It is in fact a noble and fine thing for a person to make such provision in his will. We believe in the Resurrection and the continuous personal life of the individual spirit, not of the earthly remains."

Speaking of the use of flowers at funerals, Bishop Pike explained that while people are free to have flowers sent, this is not encouraged.

More and more frequently, donations to charity in memory of the deceased are in order. "When many flowers are in fact sent, in many churches they are placed in the narthex or in the transept—except for flowers in the two vases at the altar."

Lastly, Bishop Pike emphasized that the proper place for a religious funeral service is in church—and *not* in the "chapel" of a mortuary. Protestant ministers will officiate at the funerals of non–church members if asked to do so. Most churches make no charge whatsoever; some churches in the East do make a small charge to those who are not contributing members, "but it's chicken feed compared to the overall cost of the funeral." The family may want to make a small payment to the verger ("That's up to them"), and the organist generally makes a charge.

In all of this, there is cold comfort indeed for the funeral director, who is most anxious to put his entire range of goods and services fully at the disposal of the mourners. For, to what avail the art of the embalmer if his handiwork is to be concealed in a closed coffin? Of what use is the "copper casket of SEAMLESS construction, made without joints or seams of any kind," if its seamlessness and freedom from joints are hidden beneath a funeral pall? What is to become of the "chapel" with its rheostat-controlled lighting, deep-piled wall-to-wall carpeting, cushioned pews, soft, cold color scheme, and Pilcher organ if funeral services are to be conducted in—of all things—a *church*? And, if the family so desires, with no casket present at all? Lastly, if the minister will be counseling and comforting the bereaved family, what is then left of the funeral director's "professional" role of grief therapist?

Many of the views expressed by Bishop Pike were echoed by a Jewish religious leader, Rabbi Sidney Akselrad of Temple Beth El in Berkeley, California: "In Jewish practice, simplicity is the rule. There's no need to go into debt over a funeral. The Jewish tradition emphasizes a very simple coffin." He spoke with approval of a Jewish custom in pre-Hitler Germany; simple, identical coffins were stored up for rich and poor alike "that there might be no competition in death." Rabbi Akselrad advised: "Ask the cost; don't be embarrassed to put the question to them." But he found that people on the whole do not like to go through this kind of survey.

Although the Jewish faith requires the presence of the coffin during the funeral service, Rabbi Akselrad did not approve of the open-casket ceremony: "I don't like the display. It's not very Jewish. I don't like the parade to view the handiwork of the funeral director, especially after the service, which should attempt in some small way to bridge the gulf between life and death; the viewing of the remains tends to reopen the wound." However, like Bishop Pike, the rabbi felt that in some cases the immediate family might derive comfort from looking on the face of the dead.

Of slumber-room visiting, he thought this was something of a social experience, where people gather for a reunion—"So glad to see you" said all around—but "sometimes the deceased is overlooked."

Rabbi Akselrad related one embarrassing experience in which a widow begged him to accompany her to the funeral establishment to help negotiate the price of the funeral. The funeral director quoted one price as the least expensive funeral he offered. The rabbi demurred, saying that he had told the woman she could purchase one for less, upon which the funeral director quickly relented. Since that time, Rabbi Akselrad has been loath to get involved in the financial end of the funeral.

Not so Reverend Laurance Cross, pastor of the Berkeley Community Church. As one who has officiated at more than six thousand funerals, Reverend Cross was a veteran in dealing with undertakers of every kind.

He placed great emphasis on the importance of distinguishing between the fair-minded, ethical undertaker with a conscience and those who use "psychological pressure" to force up the price of a service. "You can't damn them all," he said. "It's not true to portray them as all of a kind." He told of several in his own community—"decent, sincere people who pursue their work according to the highest ideals." Many of these would like to see far-reaching changes in the approach and practices of the industry; one almost suffered a nervous breakdown because of the sharp business dealings of his partner. "Unfortunately, though, of the two kinds of undertaker, the expensive kind dominates," Reverend Cross said.

In relating one of his selection-room skirmishes, he took on aspects of an avenging angel with an Alabama accent—for he hailed originally from that state. The selection-room arrangement described by Reverend Cross had none of the subtleties of the Triangle Plan or the Keystone Approach. "First you come to a magnificent casket—it's like a pink show window. You'd think it was the Queen's jewels on display. The inside is made of beautiful satin, and it's set out on a thick white carpet. You walk along and come to the next one. That's another beauty, maybe in a different pastel shade. You see a few more, and then you come to the absolute end. There aren't any more. Those you have seen are priced very high. At this point, most people say, 'Well, that's more than I can afford, but he doesn't have any others—I guess I'll have to settle for one of these.' However, if the customer is mean enough to say, 'I haven't got that much. We'll have to take the body elsewhere,' then the funeral director opens a door you *never knew existed*."

Shifting angrily in his chair, Reverend Cross warmed to his theme. "You go into another room where there are maybe half a dozen caskets—in less attractive colors than the other beauties—and at somewhat lower prices. That's where psychology comes in. The average person who has managed to avoid the more expensive caskets now feels that at least he has saved several hundred dollars. But if you're as mean as the devil, you may still insist that the caskets you've seen are more than you were prepared to pay. So you go through the same procedure. The funeral director opens *yet another door* you never knew existed, and here are some for even less. If you are so mean that you still won't spend that much, you are led into the last room. The funeral director pulls down a thing that looks like an ironing board, and shows you an ugly casket, maybe purple in color. The cheap ones are purposely made up in hideous colors, and they have no handles, no lining. If you still won't buy that, you are taken from there through a concrete alleyway as dark as Egypt. You come to a garage where all the funeral cars are parked. There he pulls out a box. It's just six pieces of redwood nailed together."

"How much does he charge for that one?"

"He'll charge anything he can get out of you for it," said Reverend Cross, giving that avenging-angel look.

Those in the funeral trade who had looked upon the mild and occasional interventions of the clergy as yet another "menace" have more recently been confronted by a threat of honest-to-God authenticity. It has cropped up in various parts of the country, and has been led, unexpectedly, by Catholic clerics, who have come out foursquare to denounce not the occasional undertaker but the business as a whole.

One such is Father James Connolly, pastor of St. Blaise Church in Bellingham Center, Massachusetts. In a broadside attack on funeral directors published in the *National Catholic Reporter* (August 1995), Father Connolly called into question the legitimacy of the funeral director's participation in Catholic funerals.

Defining the Church's view of the funeral Mass as a celebration of the believing community in which members should be active participants in the rituals of death, he expressed deep concern over the extent to which mortuary personnel seek to supplant the role of the parishioners.

In a statement deplored by *Mortuary Management* as "bold," Father Connolly went on to say:

> Funeral directors have greater power over the bereaved who put themselves in their hands. It is so sad to see this power turn into manipulation. Attempts to undermine what we are doing, it seems, involve more than the individual funeral director on duty. It seems that Americans have been rendered powerless by the funeral industry. Bright, independent people permit themselves to be moved as if they were mechanical.
>
> They are led to their automobiles, from their automobiles, to the church, down the aisle to their seat and to the open grave as if they wouldn't otherwise see it.

The parish decided the time had come to take matters in hand. "We announced to them that they would no longer lead the entrance procession at funerals in our church. We meet them at the front door and the community receives the body and returns it after Mass to the funeral directors at the front door," said Father Connolly. He goes on to describe the shocked and incredulous reaction of the mortuary brethren:

> Among all the uncertainties of life there is one constant. Funeral directors smile, exude friendliness, purr compassion and have great respect for the priest. I never thought of these sweet folks as anything but gentle and deferential. Then I

saw them transfigured before me. . . . Something akin to guer-rilla war broke out in our church. . . . The funeral industry is big business. Maybe they own the parish church and nobody told us.

Mortuary Management soon had reason to bewail an even more egregious instance of clerical meddlesomeness. The setting is Phoenix, Arizona, where a parish priest has likewise barred mortuary personnel from the church, asserting that "there is no need for deliv-ery men unaccustomed to Catholic liturgy and not members of the family or the parish to insert themselves into our sacred liturgy and procession when they are not needed and are not requested to do so by the priest." The latter voice is unmistakably that of Father Henry Wasielewski.

Fifteen years ago, outraged by the high cost of dying, Father Henry felt called upon to do something about it. Aware that the key to any solution lay in consumer education and in penetrating the highly secret wholesale price of coffins, he organized the Interfaith Funeral Information Committee (IFIC), an ecumenical task force consisting of local clergy, social workers, and community leaders to study the industry. Starting modestly, the committee opened an infor-mation hot line. Two telephone lines were installed, one for taped messages in Spanish and one in English. Callers were given the names of five funeral homes which offered complete funerals for $650. Sur-veys by the committee disclosed that some mortuaries in the area were charging as much as $1,800 for the identical product.

Since those early days, Father Henry, with extraordinary dedica-tion and energy, has gone on-line, extending his information network to a nationwide audience.

An example of the facts and figures he offers includes a mind-bogglingly exhaustive price survey of 120 funeral homes in the Hous-ton, Texas, area. To establish a basis for comparison, he uses the following guidelines:

- a retail casket price of $428 to $600—metal, with a choice of three colors—(the wholesale cost is $285; a markup of 50 percent to 100 percent is reasonable, he says)
- a reasonable service charge for a "traditional" funeral—$800 to $1,400

- a reasonable price range for a complete funeral including metal casket, choice of colors, embalming, and viewing— $1,450 to $2,500.

Father Henry has found sixteen mortuaries in the area that will provide a complete funeral for the recommended maximum sum of $2,500 or less, and lists them in his report. Also listed are three casket retailers that will deliver a designated casket to the mortuary as priced above.

There follow price lists for the next hundred Houston-area establishments, whose charges for the same products and services run from $3,000 to $9,910. The casket markup for some of these is more than five times the wholesale cost.

The establishments in the highest bracket—$7,000 to $9,910 for the same services and commodities—are:

Forest Park Westheimer	$7,020
Waltrip Funeral Directors	$7,133
Settegast-Kopf	$7,161
Memorial Oaks	$7,595
Forest Park Lawndale	$8,309
Settegast-Kopf-Kirby	$8,420
George Lewis Funeral Directors	$9,910

These are of interest because all seven are owned by the giant conglomerate Service Corporation International (SCI). Robert Waltrip is founder and chairman of the board of SCI.

Close on the heels of SCI is the Loewen Group, second-largest corporate consolidator in North America, represented by five Houston-area mortuaries, all quoting a uniform minimum price of $5,990.

Although the major consolidators have in the past shown a preference for high-end sales and have invested money to better attract high-end consumers by improving the appearance of the physical plant, it should by no means be assumed that the low-end public is being neglected. Low-end mortuaries are being acquired, in some cases to close them down and thereby reduce competition, more often to gouge low-end consumers. That the poor pay more is a truism that has not been disregarded by the conglomerates. Our investigator has ascertained that in a Denver mortuary fronting for SCI, a gray-cloth-covered coffin, the likes of which would create consternation if found befouling the premises of one of their high-end establishments, was being retailed to its customers for $1,995. The standard wholesale cost of this box is $140. SCI's cost is even lower because of its volume discounts.

Also included in this survey are the names of twenty mortuaries in the area that will provide direct cremations for less than $700, cremation container and crematory fee included. The funeral homes owned by SCI and Loewen quote prices of $2,745 to $3,985 for the identical service. For more information, Father Henry's Web site is: www.xroads.com/~funerals.

No one, not even fellow members of the ministry, has escaped the righteous wrath of this avenging angel who has chosen as his special target malfeasance in the funeral industry. The IFIC also uncovered what it regards as a pattern of mortuary manipulation of the clergy. According to the panel, some clergymen have relationships with morticians that entail receiving gratuities or inflated stipends for funeral services. The committee's findings were the subject of a feature story in the *Arizona Republic,* which reported a pattern of offers—gifts to clergymen of country club memberships, trips on mortuary airplanes, and tickets to sporting events.

In Montana, one mortician makes it a practice to buy a side of beef at the 4-H fair and put it in a freezer for the local minister. Another keeps an RV available—for the local preacher to use for his vacation, and yet another provides the pastor with a "beeper."

Then, of course, there's the ubiquitous and somewhat more subtle calendar. Mortuaries supply churches with these for distribution to parishioners. The calendars prominently display the name of the funeral home, which is frequently thanked from the pulpit for its contribution.

In yet another instance, Green Acres Mortuary donated several kegs of helpful beer for a picnic at Our Lady of Perpetual Help Catholic Church in Scottsdale. When asked about this, the pastor said that such donations do make him uncomfortable. There is no question but that such a donation is a form of advertising, he said. "We want to receive the gifts, but at the same time I don't want to bite the hand that gives it." The mortuary's spokesman saw things very much the same way. "Donations from mortuaries are a legitimate business practice to solicit recommendations," he is reported as saying. "Am I out there hustling business? You're damn right I am. . . . You always hope you will get recommended when you make a donation. That's why you do it. You expect your associations and friendships with priests and ministers will bring you some business."

15

The Federal Trade Commission

In 1975, after an intensive two-year study, the Federal Trade Commission's Consumer Protection Bureau announced with much fanfare a proposed "trade rule" on funeral industry practices. The rule produced a flurry of articles in newspapers and magazines across the country, hailing it as a significant victory for consumer rights. At the heart of the original proposal were these requirements:

The Consumer's Right to Choose. Existing industry practice was to quote a package price based on a multiple of the cost of the casket, stating that "this includes our full range of services." The FTC rule would require itemization so that the purchaser could choose or refuse such services as embalming, use of slumber room, or grief counseling (!), with a corresponding reduction in price for unwanted items.

Prices must be quoted over the telephone. The undertakers had theretofore routinely refused to quote prices over the phone on the ground that this information was "too sensitive" to discuss by telephone. Come into my parlor, said the spider to the fly; and once there, there is little hope of escape.

Undertakers would be prohibited from misstating the law specifically with reference to embalming. They must inform the buyer that this dubious and expensive procedure (the "financial foundation of the funeral profession," as one industry spokesman put it) is nowhere required by law. They must not tell the buyer that a casket is "required by law," likewise untrue.

The cheapest casket must be displayed with the others. Typically, the cheapest casket would be discreetly tucked away in a closet or in the basement, where only the most persistent buyer might discover its existence.

Funeral providers would be prohibited from telling the customer that the "eternal sealer" casket will preserve the embalmed corpse for a long or indefinite time.

Arthur Angel, an FTC lawyer from 1972 to 1978 who was the main author of the rule, gave me a mini-history of its genesis. "For many years, during the fifties and sixties, the FTC had been a quiescent bureaucracy largely populated by hack lawyers from second-rate schools, and cronies recommended by politicians, mostly Southern," he said. "This changed dramatically around 1970 or 1971 as a result of the Ralph Nader report on the FTC which roundly criticized the agency for failing to carry out its mission as watchdog in the marketplace, and the protection of consumers from abusive practices."

It so happened that President Nixon's son-in-law Ed Cox was a "Nader's Raider." He brought the report to the President, who said somewhat testily that he could not take any action on the basis of a report by Ralph Nader, but he did agree to appoint a blue-ribbon panel of American Bar Association lawyers to examine the FTC's performance.

The panel confirmed Nader's findings, whereupon Miles Kilpatrick, head of the panel, was appointed chairman of the FTC and its counsel, Robert Pitofsky, director of the Bureau of Consumer Protection, with the mandate to revitalize the agency.

"Beginning around 1970, and over the next four years or so, the FTC began hiring lots of new lawyers, activists from the top law schools in the country," Angel said. "I was hired in 1972 as part of that effort."

His description of the newcomers—"young, aggressive, disdainful of and removed from political and lobbying pressures"—was to me reminiscent of the New Dealers of the 1930s, as was the dedicated way they set about doing battle for the beleaguered consumer. First, they tried to identify especially vulnerable groups, which included the poor, the bereaved, the handicapped, the elderly. The next step was to devise projects responsive to the abuses that affected them. "One item on the list was the word 'funerals,' " Angel told me. "We then read your book, Ruth Mulvey Harmer's *The High Cost of Dying*, trade journals, and the like." Out of this emerged a pilot survey of funeral prices in the District of Columbia, which led eventually to the trade-regulation rule.

To the average reader, the FTC's proposed rule might seem mild and unobjectionable; all it sought to do was to bring the funeral transaction into line with standard fair-business practices, and to require undertakers to refrain from lying about the law concerning embalming and caskets. But the industry responded with characteristic belligerence, as to a call to arms. IT WILL BE A COSTLY WAR, declared the *American Funeral Director,* which described the FTC hearings as "a Soviet-style set piece staged by FTC." The rhetoric got pretty wild. Howard C. Raether, at the time the industry's most influential spokesman, writing in the house organ of the National Funeral Directors Association, lambasted the proposed rule as "a veiled attempt by the FTC staff to reverse the philosophy of American funeral customs, which have been historically developed within our society by the American public to effectively meet their needs when confronted by a death in the family. . . . There is an implication that these rules may bring about that which will be revolutionary."

Mr. John C. Curran, past president of the New York State Funeral Directors Association, went him one better: testifying at the New York FTC hearing, he called the rule "a threat to the American way of life" and accused the FTC of "tampering with the soul of America." The same thought was voiced in *Mortuary Management:* "FTC staff are trying to force their agnostic, atheistic ways on the God-fearing, traditional family-oriented America. . . ."

As required by law, the FTC held hearings on the proposed rule in six cities across the nation, at which spokesmen for each side—consumer and industry—testified, and were then subject to cross-examination by the opposing side. I was asked to testify in favor of the rule at the hearing in Los Angeles, where, to my surprise and pleasure, the industry spokesman chosen to cross-examine me was none other than Howard C. Raether himself.

The hearing room was packed with partisans for and against: members of the Los Angeles Memorial Society, Unitarians, Quakers cheek by jowl with black-suited CEOs of the finest Los Angeles mortuaries, with plenty of press on hand to record the event. I spoke my piece, a brief rundown of how the Funeral Rule would serve to curb some of the worst excesses of undertakers, then sat back, agog for Mr. Raether's questions.

Seeking to demonstrate that the undertaker does indeed have an obligation as "grief counselor" to guide the funeral purchaser in his choice of an aesthetically pleasing casket, he asked some hypothetical questions, and I found myself led on a merry chase into the fantasy world of the mortuary:

> RAETHER: John Jones dies of a kidney disease. He is jaundiced. His wife is looking at a casket with an interior which will bring out the jaundiced condition. Should he [funeral director] suggest other caskets which would make a more aesthetic picture for the wife and members of the family?
>
> MITFORD: Well, I like the idea of the matching casket, the jaundice-colored one. I mean, if *I* died of jaundice I would rather have a jaundice-colored casket for myself. Just so with scarlet fever, I should have a red one.

There was a gratifying clatter of laughter from the pro-rule members of the audience; the black suits sat stony-faced. But Mr. Raether, not to be deterred, continued doggedly:

> RAETHER: Joanna Smith is a heavy person.
> MITFORD: We are all getting a little stout.
> RAETHER: Her husband is looking at a casket in which the funeral director knows she will not look proper because of the size and the nature of the casket. Should he so advise the husband?
> MITFORD: Well, maybe the husband is trying to guy her up a bit. Perhaps he was always saying to her, "You should go on a diet," and now he is just getting even. Who knows?

While on the surface the outlook for successful adoption of the rule appeared bright, behind the scenes the mortuary interests were having some success. Industry leaders exhorted rank-and-file undertakers to bring pressure on their elected representatives, and were able to report occasional victories, as when Mr. Thomas H. Clark, counsel for the National Funeral Directors Association, congratulated one industry group for its lobbying efforts: "Many of you were instrumental and helpful in trying to get to the various Congressmen of the United States. . . . You know, we got seventy-three Congressmen and thirteen Senators who signed resolutions condemning the FTC."

Arthur Angel and his colleagues at the Federal Trade Commission soon began to feel the impact of this activity. He told me, "By 1976 the FTC's activism and aggressive actions against many powerful interests had galvanized escalating lobbying efforts. Lobbyists for various groups swarmed over Capitol Hill complaining about youthful zealots who were running amok and who could not be reasoned with. The FTC began to feel the pressure. To try to placate its foes, some of the FTC's leadership began trying to moderate or weaken various projects. The attempts to weaken the Funeral Rule were part of that effort."

By 1978 two components of the rule had already been dropped: the requirement to display the cheapest caskets with the others, and the prohibition against trying to influence the buyer in his choice of funeral. Frustrated and foreseeing correctly, as it turned out, that the rule would be further gutted, Arthur Angel resigned.

The mills of the FTC grind slowly, yet (in terms of results) exceedingly small. To those involved, the process seemed interminable— from 1973, when Arthur Angel and colleagues had begun researching the funeral industry, to announcement of the proposed trade rule in 1975, on through the public hearings to final adoption of the rule in 1984.

By 1985 it would seem that all was now in place for at least some minimal protection for the funeral buyer as provided in the rule.

However, that year I had a letter from a Mr. H., a seventy-six-year-old resident of Palo Alto, California, who was thinking about his funeral. Wishing to spare his daughter the job of arranging it, he telephoned a funeral home and asked their price for a simple cremation. About $300, said the funeral home. Mr. H.'s next step was to ask the funeral home for a written quotation. When it eventually arrived, the listed price came to $525.

Mr. H. knew all about the FTC "Funeral Rule"; he had made quite a study of it. So he wrote a letter of complaint to the San Francisco regional office. He sent me a copy of his letter together with the reply from an FTC staff member:

> We have only limited resources to take formal actions against possible violators. Our actions are designed to correct those violations which affect a significant number of consumers.

That seemed to me ridiculous, for is not Mr. H. a member of the general public? And was not the funeral home's misrepresentation exactly what the FTC rule was supposed to prevent?

My conversation with a lawyer in the same regional office, with whom I discussed this correspondence, was not reassuring. "We don't represent individuals. This is an isolated case," he told me. What, I asked, is considered to be "a significant number of consumers"? There is no set number, he answered. Would it be three? Six? A hundred? "I couldn't say," he said.

Frustrated, I telephoned FTC commissioner Patricia Bailey in Washington. She immediately saw the point; after that, things happened quickly. The director of the regional office, informed of the facts of this matter by Commissioner Bailey, promptly investigated and determined that Mr. H.'s case was "completely mishandled." He assured me that the staff member who wrote the letter and the lawyer with whom I spoke had been "appropriately admonished."

At the time, I thought this incident did raise some troubling questions: How many potential funeral shoppers would have the gumption of Mr. H., the tenacity to make a complaint to a government agency, and to a writer whom he had never met? Should one have to go to the expense of a phone call to Washington, D.C., to resolve the difficulty? But at least, thanks to the intervention of Commissioner Bailey, there was every reason to believe that the FTC staff members would never again treat a correspondent with a legitimate complaint in this patronizing and dismissive manner. Not so, as it turned out.

I remember once asking an editor at *Life* magazine what happens when the subject of an article complains that he or she has been misquoted, maligned, or otherwise unfairly treated by the mag. "Well, the first thing we do is to fire Murphy, and this usually satisfies the aggrieved party," he explained. Murphy, of course, doesn't exist except for the purpose of getting fired to placate an irate reader.

Ten years after our efforts on behalf of Mr. H., I discovered that Commissioner Bailey and I had been victims of a similar stratagem: evidently the alleged "appropriate admonishment" of some imaginary staff member was a convenient fiction adopted to shut us up.

In February 1995 I sought out Gerald Wright, the attorney responsible for enforcing the Funeral Rule in the San Francisco regional office of the FTC. What would happen today, I asked him, if an individual wrote to his office with a complaint like that of my long-ago Palo Alto correspondent? Mr. Wright produced a form letter, dated February 3, 1995, which read:

> Unfortunately, we have only limited resources to take formal action against possible violators. Our actions are taken only on behalf of the general public and are designed to correct those violations which affect a significant number of consumers.

Plus ça change . . .

Further on enforcement, Mr. Wright told me that from 1984 to February 1995 there had been a total of thirty-eight cases "formally filed" against funeral directors; of those, only two had gone to trial. Fines imposed for violations range from $10,000 to $100,000; the average is about $30,000.

He estimated that it takes eight months to a year to finish a case. An average of a little over three cases a year for eleven years seemed very slim pickings. I asked Mr. Wright how the assignments for any given FTC project are handled—how much staff time would be allotted to enforcing the rule? Reverting to the bureaucratic idiom of his calling, he explained that the FTC employs some six hundred attorneys nationwide and three hundred economists; "about half of them will cover consumer protection measures. When you get down to enforcing the Funeral Rule, maybe two work years out of six hundred will be delegated to covering that particular rule," but he was unable to estimate how much time he personally devoted to enforcing the Funeral Rule.

In 1990 the FTC, after a review by its Bureau of Economics Analysis, concluded—to no one's surprise—that "the Rule has not contributed to a general reduction in the price of funerals." By a subsequent series of capitulations to industry lobbyists, the agency has abandoned any pretense of consumer protection and has cleared the way for an era of unprecedented profitability.

In June 1994 the commission adopted an amendment to the rule to permit sellers to add their overhead to a nondeclinable fee, to cover a laundry list of items such as insurance, taxes, staff salaries, maintenance of common areas including the parking lot, and, not least, an unrestricted allowance for profit. The FTC thereby, in a single stroke, obliterated the import of itemization and the consumer's right to choose established only a decade earlier. Package pricing, under the guise of the now FTC-endorsed nonnegotiable fee, has come back with a vengeance, and with it, for the funeral director, an exhilarating upward spiral of prices and profits.

The added fee is another device to enable the funeral seller to further confuse his already befuddled customer. In the bad old days—before there was any FTC rule and when package pricing was the norm—the consumer at least knew that the price of the casket was the cost of the entire funeral. Now, however, the standard general price list looks like this:

Pumphrey Funeral Home
General Price List

Basic services of funeral director and staff	$1,525
Transfer of remains to the funeral home	$ 255
Embalming, or	$ 370
No embalming, refrigeration	$ 375
Dressing, cosmetics, casketing	$ 215
Use of facilities for Viewing, per day	$ 290
Use of facilities for Funeral Ceremony	$ 315
Hearse	$ 235
Flower Car	$ 85
Sedan	$ 115
Limo	$ 120
Total for services and use of premises	$3,375

To this must be added the cost of the casket—quoted by this mortuary in the $500 to $25,000 range—and the cost of the outside burial container or vault (required now by almost all cemeteries)—quoted range, $525 to $6,500.

The price list of the Pumphrey Funeral Home, Washington, D.C., is taken as an example because its prices fall within the middle range nationwide.

If the price of the cheapest steel casket—$2,000—is added, the funeral director's bill comes to $5,375—exclusive of cemetery and outer container costs.

In the Houston, Texas, area, for example, the identical goods and services (cemetery and vault charges not included) can be had for as little as $1,585 or as much as $8,420.

The FTC makes no effort to ascertain whether funeral establishments are complying with the rule, Mr. Wright told me. However, in scattered parts of the country there are stalwart souls, mostly unpaid volunteers, who for some reason—often a firsthand run-in with an undertaker—have become obsessed with righting the wrongs inflicted by the industry. Such a one is Lisa Carlson, longtime consumer advocate on funeral issues and active in the nonprofit Vermont Memorial Society.

Vermont, with about five thousand deaths a year, is blessed or afflicted—depending on one's point of view—with seventy funeral homes to handle these, meaning that each "home" averages just under 1.4 customers a week. In 1994 Lisa Carlson conducted a price survey covering 87 percent of the state's funeral establishments: she found that *none* were in full compliance with the FTC's Funeral Rule. After the FTC announced its new watered-down rules, the price situation deteriorated fast. In 1995 Ms. Carlson wrote a furious letter to the FTC saying that "the changes have left consumers at serious risk" and had "effectively gutted consumer protection," since the new Funeral Rule now permits "bundling" of charges that the original rule had banned. Statewide, the already bloated nondeclinable fee had increased 28 percent in the year after the rule was amended. She cited the case of a Swanton woman whose mother's funeral in 1993 cost $2,900. When her father died in June 1995, the identical funeral was billed at $7,100.

Five months after Gerald Wright had assured me that the FTC makes no systematic effort to discover whether funeral establishments are complying with the rule, suddenly—surprise, surprise—on July 6, 1995, the FTC came out with guns ablazing in the form of a press release headlined NATIONWIDE CRACKDOWN ON FUNERAL HOMES THAT FAIL TO PROVIDE REQUIRED CUSTOMER INFORMATION LAUNCHED BY FTC WITH STATE ATTORNEYS GENERAL. Jodie Bernstein, director of the FTC's Bureau of Consumer Protection, is quoted as saying that "the Commission has joined forces with state Attorneys General to switch from targeting violators based on complaints to a proactive approach designed to send a no-tolerance message and follow it up with quick and sure enforcement action."

The proactive approach, it develops, was to send "test shoppers into funeral homes in a given area to determine whether the homes provide consumers with copies of itemized price lists." This, of course, is precisely what Lisa Carlson and memorial society colleagues around the country had been doing for years while the FTC was soundly sleeping (in fact, of the thirty-eight actions against violators resulting in fines since promulgation of the Funeral Rule fourteen years ago, over half had been turned in by members of the consumer funeral watchdog group).

So far so good, although when one reads further it turns out that the crackdown wasn't all that nationwide, since it involved only seven of Tennessee's 436 funeral homes, all in Nashville; nor was it all that much of a crackdown, as only three were fined, ranging from a measly $4,000 to $16,000—sums that could handily be recouped by the funeral homes from the profits of a funeral or two.

For the next six months the FTC, perhaps exhausted from its efforts in Tennessee, lay low and said nothing. On January 16, 1996, there came another press release stating that five of Florida's 794 funeral homes—all in Tampa—were the latest to be identified in the FTC's response to low compliance: a nationwide "crackdown." Four of these received fines ranging from $4,000 to $35,000; one escaped any penalty by pleading poverty. The next episode in the great nationwide crackdown came shortly thereafter, when the FTC announced a "sweep" conducted in the Delaware area. This netted five violators, four of whom were fined from $3,200 to $7,700, and the fifth again let off because of the defendant's "financial situation."

This, then, was the sum total of the "nationwide crackdown," which in the course of a full year had managed to miss forty-seven states altogether, had discovered no more than seventeen of the nation's funeral homes in violation (although the FTC had reported in 1990 that less than 30 percent of all mortuaries nationwide were in compliance), and had recovered a total of $104,000 in fines.

The question remains: Why, after years of inactivity, was the "nationwide crackdown" suddenly announced in 1995? Whose idea was it?

According to Tom Cohn, one of the FTC lawyers in charge of the "sweeps," these questions cannot be answered: "That is not public information," he said. One could, of course, speculate that somebody—or bodies—in the FTC had begun to feel a wee bit nervous about renewed public scrutiny: Lisa Carlson and her assiduous surveys; parallel activity in many parts of the country by other consumer advocates; a documentary about funerals on "20/20"; my interview with Gerald Wright, plus numerous calls to the FTC by Karen Leonard, my persistent research assistant. . . .

Was the FTC's tepid burst of activity intended to assure Congress and the consumer watchdogs generally that the commission was in the arena protecting the public interest? Or was it nothing more than a maneuver to distract attention from the agency's shameful failure to take even a single step to curb the fraud and criminal misconduct that have become endemic in an industry engaged in fixing prices at ever higher levels and profiteering at the expense of bereaved families, and that has misappropriated hundreds of millions of dollars in funds entrusted for prepayment of funerals and cemetery property?

Here, for once, was government action which produced no outcry from the industry. The reason became clear when the *Funeral Monitor,* a privately circulated offshoot of *Mortuary Management,* in its January 29, 1996, issue reported:

NATIONAL FUNERAL DIRECTORS ASSN. AND FTC STRIKE UP A DEAL:
Funeral professionals will be pleased to know that the only national organization with the size and clout to make a deal with the federal government has negotiated a bold and innovative agreement regarding enforcement of the Funeral Rule. The old confrontational enforcement approach wasn't a notable success, so somebody said let's try something new.

Apparently that somebody was none other than the NFDA itself, for an FTC release of January 19, 1996, announcing the plan, says:

The programs were developed by the National Funeral Directors Association and will be implemented jointly by the NFDA and the FTC. . . . [T]hrough these programs, the funeral industry will be working together with the FTC in a committed way to resolve low compliance with the Rule's price disclosure requirements.

Under the new plan, no longer will funeral homes be subject to a fine for violating the rule. The FTC release states that "funeral homes that failed to give test shoppers the general price lists may have the option to enter the Funeral Rule Offenders Program. Under the program, the funeral home will make a voluntary payment to the U.S. Treasury that is lower than the civil penalty the FTC can obtain for Rule violations. . . . Funeral home participants will benefit from reduced legal fees, reduced and tax-deductible payments to the Treasury, and free training."

So much for the FTC's official concession. The *Funeral Monitor*'s account is a far better read, and it includes some significant items omitted from the FTC's announcement for public consumption. Here we learn that

> specifics of the FTC offenders program include: The FTC will no longer publicize the names of funeral homes accused of violating the rule. Funeral homes which violate the rule will be able to avoid a complaint filed in federal court, as well as an injunction against the funeral home and owner. And to top it off, violators will receive an emblem telling consumers that the establishment is a program participant and has voluntarily agreed to comply with the provisions of the Funeral Rule.

No wonder that NFDA executive director Robert Harden exultantly told the *Monitor*, "These programs create a win-win situation!"

But will the FTC be able to assure the anonymity of its favored offenders—known now only as "FROPees"—under its Funeral Rule Offenders Program? Not if the ever-troublesome band of "Memorialites"—as one industry writer has dubbed them—has its way. Exercising rights under the Freedom of Information Act to obtain the names of FROPees, the Funeral and Memorial Societies of America (FAMSA) is posting the names of offending funeral homes on its Web site: www.funerals.org/famsa/frop.htm.

But that is a small gesture compared with the current goal of FAMSA—the umbrella organization for the 125 nonprofit funeral and memorial societies in the U.S.—which is nothing less than to recast the FTC rule altogether to make it truly, in the FTC's own words, "proactive" on behalf of the long-neglected consumer. High on the list of changes being sought are elimination of the nondeclinable fee and bringing cemeteries under coverage of the rule.

16

A Global Village of the Dead

O
f all the changes in the funeral scene over the last decades, easily the most significant is the emergence of monopolies in what the trade is pleased to call the "death care" industry. Leaders in the drive to upgrade and up-price funerals, the principal beneficiaries of the Federal Trade Commission's ignoble retreat, are the multinational corporations that have put their imprint on every facet of the business. Of the three publicly traded major players— Service Corporation International (SCI), the Loewen Group, and Stewart Enterprises—SCI, incorporated in 1984, is the undisputed giant.

To trace its brilliant trajectory, a good starting point is its 1995 annual report to stockholders, which vibrates with pride of accomplishments: "SCI experienced the most dynamic year in its history in 1994, reaching new milestones in revenue and net incomes while establishing a solid presence in the European funeral industry." Revenues exceeded the $1 billion mark for the first time. Its crowning achievement was the takeover of some 15 percent of British funeral establishments added to its existing 9 percent in the U.S. and 25 percent in Australia.

Ever on the prowl, by mid-1995 SCI had devoured yet another large U.S. holding, Gibraltar Mausoleum Corporation, with its 23 funeral homes and 54 cemeteries, and had obtained a foothold in Europe with the acquisition of France's largest funeral chain, Lyonnaise des Eaux, comprising 950 funeral homes in France and others in Switzerland, Italy, Belgium, the Czech Republic, and Singapore.

SCI's annual revenue for 1995 exceeded $1.5 billion. By 1996 its prearranged funeral revenue surpassed $2.3 billion and its prepaid cemetery sales accounted for an additional $251 million.

Given these outstanding accomplishments, much now depends on the level of performance of the Grim Reaper. Can he be counted on to do the job? *Mortuary Management* was gloomy on this score, noting that due to medical advances in the treatment of cancer and heart disease, the death rate was bound to decline.

Not so the brokerage houses and investment analysts, who are showing much interest in the new "consolidations," as they are called. The Goldman, Sachs brokerage house, analyzing their prospects, predicts a rosy future:

> Aggregate deaths have increased at roughly 1.1 percent on a compound basis since 1940. . . . Going forward, the continued aging of the baby-boomers, coupled with an increasing proportion of people over age 65, should keep aggregate deaths rising. . . . The aging of America should enable the death care industry to experience extremely stable demand in the future.

The Chicago Corporation is equally sanguine. "The addition of well-chosen death care stocks to an investment portfolio can increase the value of that portfolio nicely." One advantage cited: "Consumers rarely comparison shop due to the infrequency of purchase, which averages once in every 14 years. In many instances, a deceased's survivors will trade up for more expensive options than what may have already been prearranged." There is also a word of caution:

> Cremation, which is becoming an increasingly popular option, is seen as the biggest risk to the industry. We agree that it is a risk, but do not believe that it is as great as perceived—and it may even yield some opportunities. Moreover, there are risks inherent in the aggressive strategies and tactics favored by industry participants. Industry pricing practices could be subject to greater scrutiny.

In February 1996 Merrill Lynch noted that

> operating results were strong in the fourth quarter. . . . However, the year-over-year increase was below our 51% estimate.

The shortfall is attributable to continued softness in the U.S. death rate.

J. P. Morgan in February 1996 carries an optimistic headline: SERVICE CORP. INTERNATIONAL: A STRONG 1995 AND POSITIONED FOR 1996. Here also the continued softness in the death rate is perceived as a bit of a problem:

Throughout 1995, the death rate in North America was lower than the historical trend. Case volume was down 3% year to year. . . .

But there was a silver lining. As John Betjeman wrote in his poem "For Nineteenth Century Burials," "This cold weather / Carries so many old people away." The J. P. Morgan bulletin continues:

With extremely cold weather in North America during the first two months of 1996, the first quarter death rate should be closer to the historical trend of approximately 8.8 deaths per thousand. It is our understanding that where extreme weather conditions have been experienced in Europe and North America, volume did, in fact, increase during the first five weeks of 1996, and Europe appears well on its way to meeting or exceeding its plan for the first quarter.

The twin strategies that go far to account for SCI's phenomenal success, both concepts entirely new to the funeral industry, are "clustering" and anonymity.

Of the twenty-two thousand funeral homes in the United States, the vast majority are small operations doing somewhere between fifty and one hundred funerals a year. Critics of the industry attribute high prices to this factor; they point out that the owner who performs one or two funerals a week must nevertheless maintain a full complement of embalmers, equipment, hearses, funeral cars, and sales personnel to serve these few customers. "It's full-time pay for part-time work," as one analyst put it.

SCI entered this picture with the force of a hurricane, swept away the antiquated methods of the old-timers, and substituted "clustering," the latest in streamlined mass production. Borrowing from the successful techniques of McDonald's, where food preparation and management functions are centralized, SCI first buys up a carefully chosen selection of funeral homes, cemeteries, flower shops, and crematoria in a given metropolitan area.

The next step is to move the essential elements of the trade to a central depot. "Clustered" in this hive of activity are the hearses, limousines, utility cars, drivers, dispatchers, embalmers, and a spectrum of office workers from accountants to data processors, who are kept constantly busy servicing, at vast savings, the needs of a half dozen or more erstwhile independent funeral homes. Needless to say, the savings obtained via the cluster approach are not passed on to the consumer. SCI prices have risen sharply, with a targeted increase of 30 percent. In markets like Houston, where SCI with its 20 funeral and cemetery businesses has a predominant position (75 percent of the market), its prices—according to a recent survey—average 60 percent higher than those of independents in the area; in Washington D.C., 40 percent higher. Prices of Loewen Group mortuaries tend to parallel those of SCI.

Although the consolidators own only about 10 percent of the nation's funeral homes, these tend to be prime properties in key markets and account for 20 percent of the country's funerals. The funeral customer is totally unaware of the strategy of clustering because of the immensely successful SCI policy of anonymity. In general, the plan is to acquire Johnson's Chapel of Eternal Rest and keep not only the name but also Johnson himself, now installed as salaried manager, thus ensuring continuity of recognition and goodwill. When the occasion arises, you think of dear old Mr. J., honest old chap that your family had dealt with over the years, and so you go to Johnson's, where Mr. J. greets you and leads you through the casket-selection room and signs you up for the funeral. Little do you know that the Dear Departed has been whisked off for embalming elsewhere, to reappear looking twenty years younger, nicely made up, and elegantly dressed in Johnson's "slumber room," where friends and family may gather to say their last farewells. Nor do you know that Johnson's Chapel is now a highly predatory outfit where nothing's the same—particularly the prices.

As a customer following Mr. Johnson into the casket-selection room, you may think you are being shown some randomly placed caskets, with nary a clue to the strategy carefully plotted by SCI, Johnson's employers, as he leads you through your paces. An SCI directive to its Australian employees reads like a TV miniseries script, complete with stage directions:

As your arrangement comes to the casket selection stage, we would like you to use the following approach:

"Mr. and Mrs. _____, I would now like to assist you in selecting a suitable coffin or casket for _____."

ENTER SELECTION ROOM AND PROCEED TO STAND BEHIND THE CLASSIC ROYAL IN THE MIDDLE OF THE ROOM. GUIDE THE FAMILY TO STANDING IN FRONT OF THE CLASSIC.

"I would like to introduce you to our Classic Royal. This design is that of a European contemporary coffin. It is elegant [sic] finished in Rose Mahogany gloss with fine line gold engraving on the sides. This unit combines expert craftsmanship with a fully satin lined interior. It is priced at $1,595."

NOW MOVE TO YOUR RIGHT AND STAND BEHIND THE CLASSIC REGAL.

"Here to the right, we have our most recent design and we call this the Classic Regal. It combines the shape of both a coffin and a casket to give us the very popular wider shape with a Rose Mahogany gloss finish. This item combines the versatility of Australian native timber and craftwood. It is priced at $1,995."

MOVE TO THE WHITE PEARL ON THE STAND TO YOUR LEFT.

"This is our White Pearl. . . . It has been designed in the traditional coffin shape. . . . [T]he material from which it is made is craftwood. It is priced at $995."

NOW PROCEED TO THE HANOVER IN YOUR RIGHT BACK
CORNER AND STAND BESIDE IT.

There follows a glowing description of the Hanover, which is
priced at $2,995. Doe or counterpart then tells the family:

"I will be just over here (move to near the top of the stairs) if
you have any questions."

The final stage direction:

ALLOW YOUR FAMILY AS MUCH TIME AS THEY NEED BUT
ENSURE THAT YOU DO NOT LEAVE THEM IN THE ROOM.
READ THEIR BODY LANGUAGE.

The casket prices quoted for Australia may be increased by a factor of three or more for their U.S. equivalent. Note, too, the use of
the word "coffin," a definite no-no in the lexicon of the American
funeral trade. But Down Under, the word "casket" may mean—as
elsewhere in the English speaking world except for the United
States—an ornate box for jewels and other valuables. Australians are
just now being indoctrinated by SCI into its undertaker-bestowed
meaning of burial receptacles.

SCI has improved upon the somewhat primitive list of okay
words (see chapter 5) in its recent manual for the use of its cemetery
salespeople (emphasis as in the original text):

Terminology of SCI Cemeteries

A SPECIAL TERMINOLOGY has been developed at all SCI cemeteries in keeping with the memorial park plan. Just as well-
designed tablets, flower gardens and statuary of genuine merit
have taken the place of bleak and often garish tombstones,
so words that are pleasing in their suggestion of BEAUTY
AND DIGNITY are used in place of those that are HARSH and
linked with depressing ideas. CERTAIN WORDS AND PHRASES
long associated with cemeteries sometimes increase sales resistance because they suggest images of a negative, morbid and

depressing nature. The following is a list of POSITIVE-ACTION words and phrases in contrast to those that are negative. The latter should, as far as possible, be eliminated from all sales vocabulary.

Herewith a partial list of SCI's deathless words:

Casket Coach	not	Hearse
Display Area	not	Casket Room
Interment Space	not	Grave
Opening Interment Space	not	Digging Grave
Closing Interment Space	not	Filling Up Grave

The gravedigger has a problem. He may not fill the grave with Dirt, he must fill it with Earth. His task will be preceded not by a Funeral, but by a Memorial Service. The decedent was not Sick, he was Ill. And he didn't Die, he Passed On. His remains were not Embalmed, they were Prepared. There were no Mourners present for the Service, only Relatives and Friends.

Mortuaries acquired by the Loewen Group have their own method of boosting casket prices, known in-house as "Third Unit Target Merchandising." It capitalizes on the propensity of the muddled survivors to avoid the cheapest caskets and choose the next one up in price. This means chucking a newly acquired mortuary's usual lowest-priced offerings and replacing them with more expensive substitutes, so that when the customer picks that third-unit target he ends up choosing a casket that yields a much sweeter profit. A similar practice is in general use among consolidators; who refer to it simply as "remerchandising."

The buccaneering tactics introduced by the consolidators have paid off in enviable profit margins. The Loewen Group in a recent filing with the Securities and Exchange Commission (SEC) reported a stunning gross profit margin of 41 percent from its funeral operations. SCI's profit margin for funerals for the same period was a still robust 25.3 percent.

According to a survey by the nonprofit Memorial Society of North Texas, mortuaries owned by SCI, Loewen, and Stewart Enterprises, the three largest consolidators, were consistently more expensive than the independents in the area. A Loewen-owned mortuary in Amarillo, Texas, charged a "basic services fee" (the nondeclinable fee allowed by the FTC) of $1,638. The other three Amarillo funeral homes in the survey charged an average of $863.

A *Time* magazine price survey found that Amarillo's Boxwell Brothers, an independent, charged $185 for embalming, but the Loewen's N. S. Griggs charged $425.

It is numbers like these that account for the complacency of Loewen's recent report to the SEC pointing to "lack of price sensitivity" on the part of the consumer as one of the "attractive industry fundamentals" of the funeral business.

The stockholder owners of the corporate consolidators have reason to be pleased by the reports of soaring profits. But what of their consumer victims?

The painful and humiliating experience of Mrs. Ann R. Merchant, as reported in her letter to the Funeral and Memorial Societies of America (FAMSA), may be seen as representative:

My husband died very unexpectedly 6 weeks ago in Cleveland, TX. at 43 yrs. of age. There are only 2 funeral homes here, both owned by the same huge corporation. We have 2 small children that heard him fall when he had his heart attack, therefore you can see what kind of state I was in when I went to the funeral home the next morning to make arrangements. I thought the arrangements would take approx. 30 min., instead of the 3-1/2 hrs. it took, by which time I was begging them to let me go home. But no, I had to go out to physically pick a cemetery plot because of state law (so they said, I would really be interested in knowing if Texas has such a law).

I only have one receipt the funeral home gave me. The first charge on it is for professional services of $1990. Embalming was $525, dressing & cosmetology $225, visitation $255, funeral ceremony $425 (this was held at the church we attend, but the funeral home said the price was the same whether it was held there or elsewhere, that doesn't sound right, does it?), transfer remains to funeral home $125 (they told me that the county paid for transportation and autopsy fees, doesn't that sound like a double charge?), hearse driver $275, Flower van

& driver $95, casket-18 g. Ocean Blue steel crepe lining $2095 (it was one of the least expensive in the casket room they just threw the doors open and told me to browse and find what I wanted, luckily my brother was there to catch me before I hit the floor from the shock of being thrust in the midst of a room full of caskets), concrete box $425, memorial register $25 (the little book visitors sign in), memorial cards $25 per 100 (I could have done a much better job on my computer if I had been able to at the time), death certificates $18, for a grand total of $6503. But that is not all, I signed an insurance assignment to them for $9097, so apparently there is $2594 worth of cemetery expenses. I know the plot was $895 and I bought two apparently. I don't know what the rest is for since I received no copy of a receipt or price list on this portion of the bill.

I bought these plots next to a friend of mine that bought hers less than 2 yrs. ago for $395 ea. All the cemeteries and funeral homes in a large surrounding area have been bought out by some huge corporation (I need to find out the name of it) that has apparently more than doubled all prices. The cemetery said the only way to get a plot cheaper is to buy pre-need and save $200. They didn't seem to understand that I am not dead yet, therefore mine is pre-need and I want it for $695. I asked them to just take the $895 for my plot off the bill because I did not want it, but in a couple of weeks I may buy one pre-need for $695. They said I couldn't do that because they knew who I was now.

The cemetery sales mgr. and a sales rep. came out $2\frac{1}{2}$ weeks after the funeral for a "condolence" call, but which was actually to sell a headstone. They called me the next week with a price for what I wanted of $2700. They called back the next week to tell me they had gotten a new price list in and all the prices had gone up. That was basically the final straw, I proceeded to tell them exactly what I thought of their rip-off ways when people couldn't think about what they were doing, or signing. The lady hung up on me and I haven't heard from the people again.

I just received their check from the life ins. 2 days ago, made out to me and Pace-Stancil Funeral Home. I haven't taken it by there yet, because I want to know what my legal rights are and if I am entitled to some kind of refund. These folks are legally robbing people while they are speaking so softly to you like they actually care, which is a crock.

I am going to ask for a refund of $2200, the $2000 rip-off professional fee and the $200 off of my plot. I think that is more than fair, they made plenty of money from all the other overcharges, don't you agree?

Please e-mail me back with answers or opinions, as I really need to take this check in to them next week before they dig up my husband and cremate him (that's what the cemetery rules say will happen for non-payment).

Ann R. Merchant

Tucked into SCI's annual financial report is a conveniently detachable card addressed "To our valued SCI shareholders, directed toward the more personal side of funeral service." The message:

As an owner of shares in SCI, you are probably aware that the company's name does not appear on any of our family homes or cemeteries. If you, your family, or your friends are ever in the need of the services we provide, or would like to investigate the advantages of preplanning, the 800 number below has been enclosed to help you find the SCI firm most convenient to you.

As we work to help your company grow and prosper, we are also here to help you when you have suffered a personal loss.

The socko ending, as a journalist friend of mine would call it: "Please accept our sincere apologies if this message reaches you at a time of loss." On the other hand, what could be a more propitious time for the message to arrive, enabling the shareholder to kill two birds with one stone, as it were: making an expeditious decision about how and where to dispose of the departed, and at the same time enhancing the value of his stock?

I rang the number, 1-800-9CARING, and obtained the names of SCI mortuaries in a number of cities across the country. Eventually I got the price lists from a dozen or so. These are several pages long, covering a dizzying variety of "services" and merchandise: caskets, vaults, burial clothing. The accompanying explanatory text is virtually identical for all SCI establishments, and it is to this that one must look for clarification, if any. And here is where the full import of the Federal Trade Commission's 1994 revision of the Funeral Rule becomes apparent.

First comes the FTC-required statement, *"The goods and services shown below are those we can provide to our customers. You may choose only the items you desire. However, any funeral arrangements you select will include a charge for our basic services and overhead."*

The crunch is in that "however." It means that whether or not you "choose" or "desire" any of the listed "basic services," you will have to pay for all of them willy-nilly. And here they are, set forth in bold type: "MINIMUM SERVICES OF THE FUNERAL DIRECTOR AND STAFF. This fee for our basic services and overhead will be added to the total cost of the funeral arrangements you select."

"Personnel available 24 hours a day, 365 days a year to respond to initial call." That is, somebody will answer the phone, most likely an office worker trained for the purpose and stationed at the central clustering point.

"Arrangement Conference." Mortuary-speak for clinching the sale.

"Coordinating service plans with cemetery, crematory, and/or other parties involved in the final disposition of the deceased." This would be akin to what your travel agent does when she arranges your schedule involving plane, rental car, hotel, etc.

"Securing and recording the death certificate and disposition permit." The doctor or coroner supplies the death certificate. The non-medical death-certificate information must be supplied by the family. Permit-for-disposition forms are simple and routine, and are often signed by the morticians themselves, then dropped in the mail.

"Clerical assistance in the completion of various forms associated with a funeral." These forms are needed to apply for monies due from insurance policies, Social Security, Veterans Administration, trade union death benefits, and the like. The principal information needed? Name, address, Social Security number, date and place of death.

"Also covers overhead, such as facility maintenance, equipment and inventory costs, insurance and administrative expenses, and general governmental compliance." Curiouser and curiouser. Here the buyer is assessed for everything from upkeep of the parking lot to dusting the office furniture, and, on top of that, under "government compliance" must pay for the funeral parlor to refrain from breaking the law.

Most of these "services" could be performed by the deceased's family and would, in any event, take up a minimal amount of funeral home staff time. This is a prime example of the Federal Trade Commission's craven capitulation to industry lobbyists.

What the FTC now calls a "minimum service charge" or "nondeclinable" fee is known in the trade less elegantly as the "cover charge." Although the chain-owned mortuaries are not the only ones guilty of abusing this fee, they are the most conspicuous:

Phoenix, Ariz.	A. L. Moore & Sons, Inc. (SCI)	$1,295
Phoenix, Ariz.	Shadow Mountain Mortuary (SCI)	$1,295
Sacramento, Calif.	Harry A. Nauman & Son (SCI)	$1,145
San Diego, Calif.	Clairemont Mortuary (SCI)	$1,145
Washington, D.C.	Joseph Gawler's Sons, Inc. (SCI)	$1,870
Springfield, Mass.	Byron's (Loewen)	$2,465
New York, N.Y.	Frank E. Campbell (SCI)	$1,395

Forest Park Westheimer Funeral Home in Houston, Texas, where SCI's world headquarters are located, charges $1,682 for "Minimum Services" (or basic service fee), about average for the twenty SCI-owned homes in that city. Forest Park's cheapest "traditional" funeral is $7,020. It includes a metal casket in a choice of three colors (the wholesale cost of which is under $400). Forest Park also boasts a cemetery, a mausoleum with additional crypts now under construction, and an innovation—"lawn crypts," crypts beneath the sod. Thanks to the dogged determination of a live and feisty Marcia Carter, longtime resident of Houston who spent days unraveling Forest Lawn Westheimer prices, a fully developed picture emerges.

Marcia happens to be the owner of two FPW crypts, bought by her parents in 1960 for $1,705. When her parents died they were cremated elsewhere, and over the years Marcia had made sporadic efforts to unload the crypts. FPW declined to buy them back; "I was told they had very little value because they were in the 'old, outdoor' section of the mausoleum." She told me, "The desirable crypts are now in the new air-conditioned section." Marcia next proposed to donate the crypts to a local church or nursing home for the use of a destitute family. "The cemetery told me that transfers of the crypts to 'unknown persons' is prohibited. I asked if that didn't infringe on my rights as the legal owner. But they said that the cemetery reserved the right to have the final say as to who would be buried there. At this point I lost interest in the problem, bouncing between the comical absurdity of the whole thing and righteous indignation."

In the spring of 1995, I had arranged an interview with Robert Waltrip, SCI founder and CEO, in Houston about these matters. I had many extremely friendly phone conversations with Bill Barrett, whose full title is "director of corporate communications of SCI Management Corporation," in Houston. Just when a date for our meeting had been set, I got a fax from Mr. Barrett: "I regret to report that Mr. Waltrip's travel and business commitments over the next couple of months are going to make it impossible to schedule time to visit you."

This was sad news indeed. I had been most keenly looking forward to a long, informative chat with Mr. Waltrip. But the reason for canceling the interview could be glimpsed in an article written by Mr. Barrett for "Inside SCI: A Publication for SCI Employees and Affiliates" slipped to me by a disaffected former SCI employee. Mr. Barrett warns his readers: "An interview with the media is serious business. The image and reputation of your business is at stake. If the preparation leads you to conclude it is not in your best interest to do the interview, don't."

An address given by Mr. Barrett at the Conference of the American Cemetery Association in April 1995 on "how to identify and respond to a crisis situation" elaborates. Some excerpts:

1. *Define the problem.* Is it life threatening or simply a corporate embarrassment? . . .
2. *Control the information being released.* Assign a single spokesperson when possible. . . . If you have to have more than

one, it is important that everyone sing from the same song-book. . . .

3. *Select a crisis team.* Your lawyer should either be a part of that team, or at least have the opportunity to review the strategy. . . .

4. *Know where you are going.* Before agreeing to do an interview, you have the right to know the name of the reporter you will be talking with and whether or not the reporter has already drawn a conclusion from the information he or she has. . . .

5. *Be prepared.* No amount of work you do in preparation for a media interview is wasted. And sometimes this work leads you to the conclusion that it is not in your best interest to do the interview. If that is the case, don't! I was asked once to have someone appear on the Phil Donahue show to defend the industry against allegations by some members of the clergy and grieving families. No Way!

How could I hope to succeed where Donahue failed? I decided to try another tack and metamorphose into Marcia Carter's beloved old Aunt Jessie from England.

Aunt Jessie seemed like the perfect solution. Alone in the world, her British contemporaries long dead, she would welcome the idea of Houston as a final resting place, close to her niece's family. Marcia phoned for an appointment, and together we repaired to Forest Park Westheimer on May 26, 1995. (Dates are important in this line of work; Forest Park's general price list notes that "these prices are effective as of March 10, 1995, but are subject to change without notice.")

A stylish young "pre-need counselor" named Sandy showed us around. Marcia said she was keen to see everything, since she might want to do some advance planning for her own family. Very sensible, Sandy said. And she should decide soon, as the prices for crypts would be going up on June 1. "You mean six days from now? That doesn't give us much time . . . and how much more would they cost?" Sandy didn't know the actual cost; that's up to the head office, which hasn't yet announced the new prices. But the prices of crypts nor-mally double about every five years, she said. (Mulling this over later,

Aunt Jessie and Marcia reckoned that at this rate Marcia's existing crypts must now be worth $217,600.)

Sandy showed us everything. As Aunt Jessie, I was especially interested in the crypts, so unlike the ones in Westminister Abbey. More like mini-mini high-rise condos, I said. These coffin-sized concrete boxes, six to a tier, were variously priced from $7,395 to $8,895. Why the $1,500 difference, inasmuch as they appear to be identical? The more expensive ones are at heart level, Sandy explained, adding, "Oh, by the way, there's an opening and closing charge of $660 per vault."

The following day Marcia phoned the SCI headquarters to inquire about the June 1 price increase for the crypts. There was a certain amount of foot-dragging, during which she was shunted from executive to executive; eventually Mr. Pat Geary, manager of Memorial Oaks, yet another SCI mortuary-cemetery combination, rang back to say that there was no increase planned for the crypts, Sandy was mistaken. (Or was she merely following suggestions given in sales courses? Marcia wondered.)

For some days thereafter, Marcia strove to sort out what the total cost would be for Forest Park's cheapest plan—first, if one of the crypts was used; second, for a "direct burial" or a "direct cremation," meaning no "viewing" of the body and no religious service.

"Well, I must say, these people really don't like to talk prices!" she said. David Dettling, funeral director at Forest Park, was less than forthcoming about the first item, "Minimum Services." "He could not/would not break it down," Marcia told me. "There's no way of avoiding that charge, even if we are able to perform most of the things enumerated ourselves."

Next on the price list: PREPARATION OF THE BODY. Embalming, $425. Refrigeration, $425. "They get their $425 either way," said Marcia. "If you choose not to be embalmed, then you have to be refrigerated, even if you have direct cremation. Mr. Dettling also told me that an unembalmed body can only be viewed by the legal next of kin, and then only for a few moments. This has to do with liability of the funeral home for 'blood-borne pathogens'!!" (One of the more dazzling flights of fancy; as any pathologist will tell you, a dead body presents no risk whatsoever of infecting the living when there's no contagious disease.)

After many telephone discussions with various SCI personnel, Marcia got some figures.

First, direct cremation:

"Minimum Services" for direct cremation (SCI has magnanimously reduced the price from $1,682)	$1,252
Transportation of the body from place of death	$ 355
Refrigeration	$ 425
Cardboard box	$ 275
Crematory charge	$ 475
Vehicle for picking up certificates	$ 100
Total	$2,882

Next, assuming that Aunt Jessie breathes her last in Houston and ends up in one of Marcia's already paid for crypts, the cost would be:

"Minimum Services"	$1,682
Transportation of body from place of death to funeral home	$ 355
Refrigeration/embalming	$ 425
Minimum sealed (gasketed) casket	$2,598
Transferring body from funeral home to crypt	$ 275
Open/close crypt (removing and replacing the faceplate)	$ 660
Vehicle for picking up permits	$ 100
Total	$6,095

(Opening/closing crypt charges rise to $685 on Saturday, $780 on Saturday afternoon, $975 on holidays. Never on Sunday.)

I asked why they charge $275 to take the body the two hundred yards from the funeral home out to the crypt. "That seemed exorbitant," said Marcia. "He said it's a fixed fee within a fifty-mile radius. Even so close, it's the same because of the 'cost of maintaining the vehicles, their insurance, and so forth.' Outrageous! Also, I asked why the minimum service fee of $1,682 couldn't be discounted for immediate burial the same as it was for cremation, and he said, 'Well, they do that to make cremation a little cheaper than burial.'"

These arrangements may be all very well for Marcia; she's obviously not your typical Houston funeral buyer. She's going to dump Aunt Jessie in an old, unair-conditioned crypt in the cheapest casket, no opportunity for neighbors to come and visit her, no religious service or memorial gathering. Those who are inclined to even a modicum of ceremony would have to add a few items from the FPW price list to the above rock-bottom minimum:

Use of facilities and staff services for visitation (per day)	$ 98
Funeral service in FWP chapel, or	$725
Staff and services in other facility, or	$725
Chapel for memorial service without remains present	$725
Equipment and staff services for service at graveside	$515
Additional charge for use of facilities/staff on Sunday or holiday	$600
Caskets from $2,598 to $25,145	
Copper vault (resists the entrance of outside elements)	$20,378

There is lots more—clothing up to $192, flowers up to $2,000, memorial booklet, commemorative flag case—but why go on? Readers can check out the SCI facilities in their own communities via 1-800-9CARING.*

What happens to all that money? According to Graef S. Crystal, corporate-compensation expert, SCI is one of ten companies out of a total of 414 that he studied in 1995 whose directors and chief executives were most overpaid (*New York Times*, June 27, 1995). The directors, he reckons, are overpaid by 95 percent, and CEO Robert Waltrip, founder and brains behind the company, by 62 percent.

I asked Mr. Crystal how much the SCI directors get. A total package, comprising annual retainers, meeting fees, stock options, pension benefits, and deferred compensation, of $102,000 maybe more, he said. "Fair pay, considering the size and performance of the company, would be $49,700," And the CEO? "He gets a total value of $4,321,000. Using the same factors, a fair package would be

---

*The FAMSA Web site, www.funerals.org/famsa/chains.htm, posts a listing of chain-owned mortuaries, although the rapid rate of acquisitions makes it hard to keep up with the latest on who owns what.

$2,670,000." He added that the CEO's performance has been "unremarkable, neither very good nor very bad, for the past ten years; but it has improved recently."

Heading the list of these high-priced directors is Anthony L. Coelho, president and CEO of Wertheim Schroder Investment Services, Inc., better known as Tony Coelho, former Democratic congressman from California. In 1989, under a cloud of scandal, he resigned from the House of Representatives, relinquishing his powerful position as majority whip, just one step ahead of a Justice Department and House Ethics Committee investigation involving his personal investment in a junk bond that was completed with the help of a savings and loan executive (*Wall Street Journal,* March 29, 1994).

As chairman of the Democratic Congressional Campaign Committee from 1981 through 1986, according to the *Washington Post* (January 8, 1995), Coelho, some say, "sold his party's soul by vastly expanding contributions of business PACs and the expectations those contributors felt in return."

In 1994, rehabilitated by the passage of time, he joined President Clinton's inner circle of advisors. But like the Grim Reaper himself, Mr. Coelho is a bipartisan sort of fellow: "I love Bob Dole!" he told the *Washington Post* in an interview. "I have great friends on the Republican side. [Lobbyist] Jim Lake and I are as close as brothers!"

All of which bodes exceedingly well for the future of SCI's global village of the dead.

17

Funerals in England Then and Now

A public exhibition of an embalmed body, as that of Lenin in Moscow, would [in England] presumably be dealt with as a revolting spectacle and therefore a public nuisance.

— ALFRED FELLOWS, *The Law of Burial*

In order to appreciate the changes in the funeral landscape that are currently taking place in England, it will be useful to revisit the scene as it existed thirty years ago.

Funerals in England Then

American funeral directors often say, "England is about fifty years behinds us." To the English, this might sound like a veiled note of warning: does it mean, for example, that fifty years from now much of England's green and pleasant land will have been converted into Memorial Gardens of Eternal Peace? From Sherwood Forest to Forest Lawn in one easy step? It requires more than a little imagination to visualize a bluff English squire and his hard-riding, rugged-faced lady transformed into Beautiful Memory Pictures, their erstwhile stony and disapproving features remolded by the hand of a Restorative Artist into unfamiliar expressions of benign sweetness. Would their caskets be named (like the American "Valley Forge") after famous battles—the "Battle of Britain," in delectable shades of Royal Air Force blue, or "Flodden Field," with an archery motif? Or perhaps (like the American "Colonial Classic") after periods in English history: the Restoration Rolick, the Crusader, Knighthood in Flower, the Victorian Voluptuous with overstuffed horsehair interior made expressly to simulate the finest drawing-room furniture of the period? Would the squire and his wife be decked out as for the Royal Enclosure at Ascot, he in top hat and cutaway, she in trailing flowered chiffon, or more simply in Harris tweeds complemented by Practical Burial Gum Boots?

There has been heard in America a singing radio commercial whose words, set to the tune of "Rock of Ages," go like this:

> *Chambers' caskets are just fine,*
> *Made of sandalwood and pine.*
> *If your loved ones have to go,*
> *Call Columbus 690.*
> *If your loved ones pass away,*
> *Have them pass the Chambers way.*
> *Chambers' customers all sing:*
> *"Death, oh death, where is thy sting?"*

This might be going a little too far for England, but it would be rash to underestimate the penetrating power of American enterprise.

Jingles like this may one day be beamed on commercial telly and adorn billboards in the countryside: "Repose with your mate / Near the bones of the great / By appointment, I ween / To H.M. the Queen."—Westminster Memory Gardens, Ltd. Or, "Your Heart in the Highlands-Forever!"—Happy Hebridean Haven, Ltd.

Fanciful, perhaps, yet perhaps also the English would be well advised to note that American missionary schemes to "civilize" English funerals are already under way, and some headway has been recorded.

As early as 1926, a member of National Selected Morticians reported to his colleagues on what had most impressed him on a visit to England: "I spent a day in Liverpool with a fine gentleman, one of the very best. They know very little about embalming in any other part of the world, outside of America. They are going to. England has been agitating the matter. I take one of their journals, and they commenced agitating a couple of years ago. I think if we could send some missionaries over there, we would do them a world of good. . . ."

It took a long time for our missionaries to show tangible results for their efforts. The Brits seemed to *like* being fifty years behind their Yank counterparts.

It is of little use to ask English friends to describe the procedures in a typical funeral, because so few have been to one. Whereas Americans flock to the funeral of a coworker, a neighbor, or a casual acquaintance, in England only the closest relations go; consequently many people, even those of middle age, have never actually seen a funeral. Some are, perhaps understandably, reluctant to make inquiries. One friend wrote, "I have not yet been to call at _____ Undertakers, although I walk past there every day; I fear I have the superstitious feeling of an old horse passing the knacker's yard."

Another friend spent some time with a country undertaker and sent a full report: "First and foremost, he said—and this is borne out by my own feelings and the experience of everybody I have asked— that we aren't even on the fringe of imitating Americans yet, and there will have to be a big change in the psychology of everybody concerned before we do. This at least is one area where there's no attempt to produce a milk-and-water copy of the American original. The undertaker is quite definitely regarded as a tradesman—no cachet attached to the job whatsoever; and in the country he is almost invariably the local builder as well. About embalming, the local man said he's only had to embalm one corpse in ten years (the family was abroad and the funeral had to be delayed ten days), and there's not the slightest indication that it is likely to grow in popularity. The whole mentality of burying here is that the dead should be disposed of with quiet respectability and the minimum of fuss and publicity. Decent and quiet, you might say."

Further investigation convinced me that there were contradictory forces at work. There are those within the trade who are envious of their American counterparts, who would love nothing better than to transplant the American way to England's unreceptive soil. They find themselves, however, up against the relentless English common sense and preference for the ordinary way of doing things. An English undertaker, speaking at a Dallas meeting of National Selected Morticians, explained the difficulty: "The chief reason why our average is low is the very fact that I have tried to tell you about British character—their desire for moderation. In our own selection room we display a full range of hardwood caskets, oak, walnut, and mahogany. Yet of the clients who can afford the best, 90 percent would choose the traditional coffin. They would say of the caskets, 'Very beautiful, but too big, too elaborate! We will have an oak coffin like we had for grandfather!' This is a problem that has concerned us for many years. . . . I must tell you, also, that our presentation must be accomplished without the use of cosmetics. Heavy cosmetizing would bring the strongest complaints from our clients. They tell us quite firmly, 'I don't want Mother touched up!' " He does, however, mention "an aspect of American funeral service which appears to be more readily accepted by our British public. All over the country funeral directors are building funeral homes, putting in private chapels and rest rooms.* They are not comparable with the beautiful buildings I have already seen this last week, but nevertheless, our men have recognized the need and are now beginning to provide the facilities."

The English trade publications the *Funeral Director* and *Funeral Service Journal* reflect in their pages a predominantly traditional approach, with occasional revealing flashes of possible changes on the way. Their very titles, which must have, to the English ear, an unfamiliar transatlantic ring, tell us something; yet unlike the American funeral magazines, they are modest in format and sparsely illustrated.

The advertisements for the most part call a coffin a coffin, a hearse a hearse, and a shroud a shroud; there is "Coffinex Aqueous Emulsion, [which] supersedes the old method of applying boiling pitch and wax, which was both laborious and uneconomical" (an improvement we can surely applaud); but "casket" is by no means unknown; there is Casketite Bitum Emulsion, "for simpler, more economical sealing of caskets and coffins." Social events for English undertakers as reported in these journals have not reached the Vaultburger Barbecue stage; they adhere rather to traditional English ideas of what constitutes jolly good entertainment; we are told that "in April a number of members and their ladies attended a performance of 'The Iron Hand' given at H.M. Prison, Sudbury." The editorial writers tend towards conservatism. One of them, describing an American funeral director who distributes "packs of quite good-quality playing cards which, on the back, carry an advertisement for

---

*Semantics Note: In England, "rest room" means a room in which to rest.

so-and-so's funeral home," comments that he "would not like to see such advertising in this country." Yet there are also reprints from American magazines: how to use the telephone ("never use the personal pronoun 'I,' always use 'we'; speak with warmth in your voice, clearly and with sincere friendliness"); how to set up a casket-selection room, and the like—but they did not seem to have altered the basically English character of these journals.

There was a study course available, a fairly comprehensive text of some seventy-five mimeographed pages, prepared by members of the trade for the "voluntary examination in funeral directing." Since there is no law in England requiring licensing of undertakers, the study course and examination are in effect an exercise in self-improvement rather than, as in America, a legal requirement.

The study course, like the trade publications, is a strange mixture of old and new concepts about the disposal of the dead, English and American terminology, the traditional English approach combined with aspects of the American Way.

How refreshing to read, for example, that "it is not the function of the funeral director to become the family sympathiser but rather to offer helpful advice." And that while it is permissible to let the family know that a private chapel is available on the premises for the service, it is "very wrong to be over-persuasive in this matter"; that if they are regular church attenders, "it is certainly good practice to suggest that the Service be held in their own church. This is appreciated by the family and the Clergy." Equally permissive—in contrast to the attitude of the American burial industry—is the position on cremated remains ("cremains" has not yet found its way across the Atlantic); this is a "matter for the family to decide. The majority seem to prefer the scattering of the cremated remains in the Garden of Remembrance attached to all Crematoria" or at some other spot of their choice. Sentimentality is positively discouraged. Discussing obituary notices, the study course cautions: "In some cases, one is requested to insert over-sentimental verses, and all the Funeral Director's tact is called upon to dissuade them in their own interest."

Some agreeably down-to-earth advice was offered about the proper treatment of the corpse itself: "Dress in clean clothing—pyjamas, shirt or nightdress, etc. . . . Insert the laying out board under the body. . . . DO NOT TIE THE BIG TOES TOGETHER. . . . IN NO CIR-

CUMSTANCES WHATSOEVER SHOULD THE ARMS AND HANDS BE SECURED BY POSITIONING THEM UNDER THE BUTTOCKS. . . . DO NOT PLACE PENNIES OR WET PACKS OVER THE EYES."

However, there are indications that a new day may soon dawn for the dead in England. A large portion of the course is devoted to the importance of embalming and how to sell it to a reluctant client, apparently best accomplished by not being frank. The words "hygienic treatment," it is suggested, should be used in discussing the subject with the client: "By this, of course, you mean modern arterial embalming, but funeral directors are generally agreed that in the early stages of the arrangement, the use of the word 'embalming' is best avoided. . . . Although some funeral directors boldly speak of embalming, the majority consider it preferable to describe the treatment by some such term as 'Temporary Preservation,' 'Sanitary Treatment,' or 'Hygienic Treatment.' In this way it is felt that there is less likelihood of associating the modern science with that of the ancient Egyptians."

The familiar justifications are offered for what one English authority has called "the meaningless practice of embalming": it delays decomposition, it promotes public health, it restores a lifelike appearance. "The change effected is truly remarkable—gone is the deathly pallor . . . instead the family sees a life-like presentation of their loved one appearing as though peacefully sleeping. This result is a source of great comfort and has a decided psychological value." Furthermore, the family may have "open casket or coffin at all times until closed for the Funeral."

It is to the growing army of embalmers that we must turn for enlightenment on progress in introducing American funeral practices in England. Most English people are astonished to learn that embalming is sharply on the increase there. The British Institute of Embalmers claims over one thousand members. The uphill nature of their efforts to ply their trade can be inferred from an official statement issued by the institute: "Two primary factors have retarded progress. Primarily the fact that customs die hard in this country and in no case is this more evident than in funerals. The introduction of any new methods, apparatus or merchandise was treated with suspicion, not only by the mourners but often by the priest or minister conducting the funeral service. . . . Up to the present moment there has been little governmental support or recognition of the science. With exceptions, the medical profession ignore it. . . ."

Hard is the lot of the really go-ahead embalmer in England. There is the unaccommodating English law, which requires that a death certificate be obtained and the death properly registered before the embalmer can get going. No chance there of getting started before life is completely extinct.

An English contributor to the *American Professional Embalmer* describes some of the roadblocks he has encountered. The main trouble seems to be that "the open-casket is unknown in this country. . . . The coffin is invariably closed at the funeral service proper and, more important still, the funeral director is frequently instructed at the first call to close the coffin immediately when the remains are placed in it. This lack of acceptance by the public of a fundamental American concept produces more than one difficulty for British embalmers; with no demand there can be no practice."

English doctors, we learn, are most uncooperative: "The medical profession in Great Britain exercise a power second to none. Despite the National Health Service, and statements to the contrary, as a pressure group they are supreme . . . [T]hey would oppose with all the power at their command any attempt to limit autopsies. Indeed, no group can show more rooted opposition to modern funeral service and embalming in particular than this one. They stand squarely behind the cremation movement here, actively campaigning for it, doing all they can to reduce funeral service to little more than simple rubbish disposal." Not only that, but the doctors are often unkind to the embalmers: "Except between friends and request by a funeral director or an embalmer, cooperation on the part of an examining surgeon will be wasted; if anything more than an ill-mannered rebuff is received it will be calculated obstruction carried even to the lengths of deliberate mutilation."

With true British grit, the author ends on a note of hope for the future: "There can be no argument about it; in England the embalmer is out on his own and any progress he makes is over hard ground. That does not mean he is a quitter, however; far from it. At the moment satisfactory restoration is almost impossible to achieve but it will be achieved in the end, with help or without it, and no matter how far distant that end may be!" Rather bravely spoken, considering that achievement of the distant end apparently depends upon a complete reversal of the law, of public attitudes, and of views of the medical profession.

Some months after I had read about the ups and downs in the English undertaking trade, I had a chance to visit an English funeral establishment to check the vision against the reality. The very location of the one I visited, in changeless South London, seemed to foreshadow the attitudes I would find there. The West End may present a new façade from year to year—here an unfamiliar skyscraper under construction, there a block of service flats where before had stood the London mansion of some Scottish laird, everywhere the bright awnings and colored tablecloths of the newly imported espresso houses. South London remains the same: the haberdashery and furniture display in shopwindows might have been there for generations; the very buns in the cafés have a prewar flavor. "Clapham Road?" said the corner newspaper vendor whom I asked for directions. "Not far, just a nice twenty-minute walk; it's just round from where my aunt's lived for fifty years." Not the sort of place, I thought, where people would be amenable to newfangled methods in any phase of life, let alone death; and in a way I believe I was right.

Mr. Ashton, whose establishment in Clapham Road is easily the most imposing building in the vicinity, is in some respects far from being a typical English undertaker. Whereas most of his colleagues are very small operators indeed, and generally perform this work as a sideline to some other trade, Mr. Ashton is the owner of nine London branches with a total volume of around twelve hundred funerals a year. Few English establishments could compare with this. Furthermore, he is among the tiny minority in England who routinely embalm all comers, and who might therefore have been expected to have absorbed at least some of the concomitant American approaches to the funeral. For these reasons, he seemed the ideal person from whom to seek clarification about likely trends in English funeral practices.

Mr. Ashton was a charming host. He led me through his entrance hall, conservatively decorated with neutral wallpaper and wine-red upholstered furniture, up the stairs to his private office, where we chatted over a cup of tea. I wanted to know about his own firm; something about the funeral trade as a whole; and, above all, the steps taken and procedures followed in the average English funeral.

Like a great many English undertaking concerns, Mr. Ashton's is an old established family firm. It has been in existence for a hundred and fifty years, and he is of the fourth generation in the business. There is a growing tendency, he explained, for large firms to take over smaller ones, and this is how he acquired the nine establishments, all located in South London. The smallest of these averages about fifty funerals a year, the largest, three hundred. The clientele is mostly middle and lower class, and comes from South London. He runs his own coffin factory, in which he employs twelve factory hands, woodworkers who make the coffins. He also employs nine managers, nine drivers, an office staff of five, and three full-time embalmers. It takes four months to learn embalming, he told me; the minimum embalmer's wage is 12 pounds a week (about $34) and "perks"—use of the car, etc. The managers do no embalming; their function is entirely separate.

There are in all Great Britain perhaps ten firms the size of Mr. Ashton's, in the larger cities such as Edinburgh, Glasgow, Cardiff, London. In London, there are some 350 major firms, compared with 800 in New York, serving a population of about the same size. The larger firms all make their own coffins. There are a few wholesale coffin companies, which in many circumstances also furnish cars, embalmers, and all services for the smaller establishments.

Discussing the routines that follow between death and the funeral, Mr. Ashton positively exuded the no-nonsense, humbug-free attitudes so prized by this "nation of shopkeepers" in all their dealings, and in this particular calling so reassuring to find. I asked him what happens when a person dies in the middle of the night. American undertakers, to a man, take the greatest pride in rushing to the scene at no matter what hour; in fact, high on their list of "essential services"—and a major justification for their high charges—is maintenance of a twenty-four-hour operation, their ability to remove the deceased any time of the day or night within minutes of death. "I'd send along in the morning," said Mr. Ashton. "Well, I mean unless the chap dies in the lavatory, or something, which did happen once, and then I had to go along at once, you see." He explained that they are prepared to come in the night if necessary, "but we certainly don't encourage it as long as the family is under control. Personally, I'm all for a quiet life and a little peace, and anyway people are more intelligent about such things these days. They realize that nothing can be done until the morning." Death at home is anyway the exception. Eighty percent of deaths occur in hospitals. In that case, a relative goes to the hospital and procures the death certificate, which the registrar must have before burial can be authorized. The practice of keeping the body at home until the funeral is losing favor. Before World War II, this was done in 90 percent of cases, now in less than 10 percent. The minority who prefer to keep their dead at home tend to be at the opposite ends of the social scale: the very poor ("poorer people are far more traditional") and the very rich, who are not only traditional but have more room in their houses. "The middle classes say, 'It's all unpleasant, let's get it over.' "

We went to look at Mr. Ashton's stock of caskets and coffins, which are kept in two small rooms. The caskets are styled somewhat after the American ones, only far less elaborate; all are made of wood. The use of metal for this purpose is almost unheard of. In fact, the only difference between an English "casket" and a "coffin" is in the shape, the former being rectangular, and the latter, tapered or "kite-shaped." The lids of all were shut. Feeling that I ought to make some remark, I murmured, "Lovely, lovely," which would have done nicely in America, where the funeral men take enormous pride in their stock. "I think they're perfectly awful-looking things," commented Mr. Ashton cheerfully. He opened one: "Look at that frightful lacy stuff, and all that ghastly satin." He told me that there is practically no demand for the caskets; not more than a dozen a year are sold. We proceeded to another small room, containing five or six coffins. The cheapest are made of imported African hardwood or English elm, chosen by the majority of Mr. Ashton's clients. Next in price is the English oak, and most expensive, mahogany. Vaults, in the American sense of a metal or concrete container for the individual coffin, do not exist ("Quite unnecessary," said Mr. Ashton), although sometimes a family vault of brick may be built to accommodate six or eight coffins. I asked whether without a vault, earth might tend to cave in as the coffin disintegrates. This apparently is not a problem, although it is customary to wait six months for the ground to settle before putting up a gravestone, which is generally erected upon a concrete slab laid over the grave.

The majority of Mr. Ashton's funerals average about 50 pounds ($140), to which must be added about half as much again for the additional expense of cemetery or crematorium fee, memorial stone, and the like. The most expensive funeral offered in the ordinary course of his business is 100 pounds ($280), and the most expensive one he remembers doing came to 300 pounds. Cremation costs about 4 pounds, and graves are from 15 pounds up—"London-wise, that is," said Mr. Ashton. Away from London the cost is lower. The great majority of cemeteries and many of the crematoria are municipally owned.

I noticed that the minimum-priced coffin was not displayed with the others, and here I thought I detected the introduction of a particularly obnoxious American practice; was the cheapest coffin being deliberately concealed from the public gaze? I asked where the coffin for the 33-pound funeral was kept, and Mr. Ashton said there were plenty of them in the factory. Hidden there from the customers? I asked. Of course not! The customers never come up here; very very rarely does a person ask to see the coffins in the course of arranging a funeral. "You mean this isn't a selection room in the American sense—you don't bring them up here to choose?" "Good Lord, no!" said Mr. Ashton rather reprovingly, as though the very suggestion was in violation of decency and good taste. "People don't want to look at these dreadful things. I mean, why should they? All that is settled when we talk to the family in the office."

We next proceeded to the "rest rooms" where the deceased is laid out until the day of the funeral. They looked like cozy little sitting rooms, comfortably furnished with chairs and curtains. While they did not begin to approach the elegance of slumber rooms I had seen in the States, they were, I was told, exceptionally well appointed for England. I was curious to know to what extent survivors make use of these rooms. This varies quite a bit. A fair number never come at all. Generally, one or two of the immediate relatives, perhaps the widow supported by her grown-up son, come once to see the deceased. "It's a sort of identification. Having looked, and presumably approved, that's probably that." Occasionally the reverse is true; a small percentage come daily with fresh flowers. Among the poorest classes, the neighbors sometimes come.

The funeral is usually held in the crematorium or cemetery chapel.

("They all have these horrid little chapels nowadays," said Mr. Ashton.) The Ashton premises have a large room which he was intending to convert into use as a funeral chapel, but he found that there was so little demand for it that, instead, he uses it as a rest room. On an average, a "car and a half"—six to seven people—attend the funeral, although attendance varies tremendously; between two and three hundred may show up for the funeral of a prominent person. As in America, mourning is no longer worn except by the very old, who still think it proper to go out and buy "a bit of black" for the funeral. "Flowerwise," said Mr. Ashton (once more springing this incongruous Americanism), he estimates that there would be an average of twenty floral pieces at an ordinary funeral. Workers spend a lot more on funeral flowers than do the middle classes; in fact, the latter tend to be more moderate in all ways.

If a country dweller happens to die in London, his body is generally taken back to his home parish for burial. A private motor hearse may be used, or the body may go back by rail. They fetch the coffin and take it to the station in a hearse. I asked whether embalming is required when a body is to be shipped. "If it's to go by air, it's got to be embalmed, but British Railways don't require it; they're not particularly fussy."

An open-casket funeral is almost unheard of, said Mr. Ashton. Such a thing would be considered so absolutely weird, so contrary to good taste and proper behavior, so shocking to the sensibilities of all concerned, that he thinks it could never become a practice in England. He recalled the funeral of a Polish worker whose family requested an open casket: "The gravediggers objected very much to this. Rather absurd of them, when you come down to think of what their job is, don't you know, but still they didn't see why they should stand for having the thing *opened*. Cosmetics are never used. That sort of thing might go over in America, but really, I mean I don't think you could get the people here to use it. If I had to say, 'Come and see your *loved one*,' I honestly don't think I could keep a straight face." Mr. Ashton added that Evelyn Waugh's book *The Loved One* is one of his favorite novels, and that when it first came out he bought four copies for the amusement of his staff. But nevertheless, what about the adoption of certain American euphemisms—"funeral director" instead of "undertaker," for example? Mr. Ashton thought that was originally instituted to stop the music-hall jokes about the trade, and because "the word 'undertaker' doesn't mean anything." He said that doctors and officials continue to use "undertaker," although the telephone directory has recognized the new term and now has a listing for "funeral directors." He added that some practitioners prefer "funeral director" simply because "it sounds more chichi, but personally I don't mind." As to other euphemisms—avoidance of words which connote death, "space" for "grave," "expire" for "die," "Mr. Jones" for "corpse," and so on—he did not think these would catch on in England. "The attitude of the general public is, it's a practical thing—if you don't want to say anything about it, just don't mention it."

All this led directly to the subject of embalming; if there is to be no viewing, why then embalm? Mainly, for the convenience of the funeral establishment personnel. There is an average lapse of four to six days in London between death and the funeral (it takes one full day to get a grave dug), and, said Mr. Ashton, "the unpleasantness can be simply appalling."

There is no restorative work done at Mr. Ashton's place, and no cosmetics are used. Although he embalms routinely, without seeking permission of the family, he has not had any complaints. Over the past ten years, there have been perhaps three people who have specifically requested that there be no embalming. "When there's been a long series of operations before death, somebody may say, 'I don't want 'er cut apaht anymore," he explained. He agreed that the argument that embalming benefits the public health by preventing disease is not well founded: "We've tried to prove the disease factor, but we just can't—we'll have to accept the pathologists' view on that."

The complicated procedures required by English law relating to obtaining the death certificate have often been condemned; I wondered whether there were any efforts afoot to get the law changed. Quite abortively, said Mr. Ashton, there are attempts in that direction; in fact, he himself is a member of a Home Office "working party" initiated by the cremation authorities to simplify the law and speed up the process of getting a death certificate. "But I'm absolutely outnumbered on that," he said cheerfully. "The doctors are dead against it, because the embalming process can hide certain poisons, make crime detection very difficult."

Having in mind the "do-it-yourself" efforts of certain American funeral reform groups, I asked whether in England it would be possible for a survivor to bypass the funeral establishment altogether and take the deceased directly to the crematorium. Such a thing actually did happen once in Mr. Ashton's experience. Two young men drove up in a Bedford van and said they wanted to buy a coffin. Mr. Ashton told them he didn't sell coffins, he sold funerals. The young men insisted they did not wish a funeral; their mother had died, they had procured a properly issued death certificate, they had been out to the Enfield Crematorium to make arrangements, they intended to buy a coffin and take the mother out there themselves. "We chatted and chatted," Mr. Ashton recalled. "Finally I was convinced they were on the level, so I sold them a coffin. What could I do? They weren't doing anything wrong, there was nothing to stop them. But it really shook me. Afterwards I rang up the chap at the crematorium. I said, 'Did that shake you? It shook me.' "

My final question was about "pre-need" arrangements; is there much buying and selling of graves and funeral services to those in the prime of life? Practically none, it seems. You can reserve a grave space, but it is almost never done. Once in a great while, said Mr. Ashton, some old lady may come round to the establishment, explain she is all alone in the world and feeling poorly, and ask him to care for all arrangements when her day comes. "We just put her name in our NDY file," he said. "Meaning?" "Not Dead Yet, don't you know. But nine times out of ten she'll start feeling much better, might live another twenty years."

Throughout our discussion Mr. Ashton impressed me as a realistic businessman, a kindly and responsible person, straightforward and practical in his approach to his work, with a good dash of wit in his makeup. One cannot even quarrel with the innovations he has introduced; the pleasant appearance of his premises is undoubtedly an improvement over years ago. It reflects concern for the comfort of those he must deal with, but does not remotely approach the plush palaces of death to be found everywhere in America. Whatever one may think of his practice of embalming all comers, at least he advanced truthful and comprehensive reasons for doing so.

If Mr. Ashton is a typical representative of the English undertaking trade, traditional English attitudes towards the disposal of the dead may after all be safe from the innovators for some time to come.*

Funerals in England Now

A cartoon depicts a group of sorrowing goldfish gathered round a lavatory bowl in which one of their number floats belly-up. The caption: "He always wanted an open casket." Another shows two somberly suited pallbearers shouldering a casket, each wearing an outsize button inscribed HAVE A NICE DAY. One exclaims, "Always dreaded an American takeover." Thus with a mixture of groans and ridicule was the advent of SCI greeted in the British press in 1994, the year in which SCI acquired two of the largest British funeral chains, the felicitously named Plantsbrook Group and the Great Southern Group, comprising more than five hundred undertaking establishments, cemeteries, and crematoria:

> *The Independent,* June 12, 1994—
> GRAVE UNDERTAKING: GROUP THAT BURIED ELVIS WANTS TO TAKE OVER U.K. FIRM. "I'm here to do a deal, and I'm here for the duration," said Bill Heiligbrodt, SCI's Texan president.... Mr. Heiligbrodt has been called a cowboy but he loves the term. "I gather it's not such a compliment in Britain, but I am a cowboy.... I just love being competitive," he said.

> *The Telegraph,* August 11, 1994—
> The Texas-based Service Corporation International is plotting a takeover of Britain's third-biggest undertaker, Great South-

---

*When the above was written some thirty years ago, it seems likely that the writer was more than slightly enamored of "Mr. Ashton," who is treated with such respect that his first name is never revealed. But as the calendar leaves float by, and with them the members of the Ashton family as they depart, their nine mortuaries are, in the mid-1980s, scooped up by none other than Howard Hodgson, the "yuppie undertaker," and in turn by Plantsbrook, and then in 1994 by SCI. Ashton prices are now the highest in the relatively downscale areas in which they do business; they have run afoul of the Monopolies and Mergers Commission, which has ordered them to divest two of their eight mortuaries. *O tempora! O mores!* Which translates roughly to "What a falling off was there!"

ern. However sensitively it approaches the British market, inevitably any U.S. involvement is bound to raise here the spectre of the American way of death. Across the Atlantic, death has long meant big money.

The Tqqwelegraph, August 13, 1994—
TEXANS OUT TO MAKE ANOTHER KILLING. The Texas funerals group Service Corporation International has become trigger-happy. . . . These Texan undertakers have mastered taking-over rather quickly. . . .

The Guardian, September 3, 1994—
Last night SCI president, Bill Heiligbrodt, was jubilant about the success of his lightning campaign, which started on May 30 when he landed in the U.K. with the fixed intention of building a major business in the U.K. "I'm having a lot of fun now," he said. . . . "We are here now for the rest of time."

Across the pond, the funeral trade press was in a celebratory mood. The *Southern Funeral Director* (September 1994) offered some predictions about the future of British funerals now that SCI was on the scene:

The British cremation rate runs about 75 percent. This is not necessarily by choice, but because nobody markets "Americanized funerals" to them. The British aren't real big on selling the casketed service. But leave it to SCI to educate them. SCI will establish yet another stronghold market for caskets.

Resistance to SCI's pedagogical incursion was soon apparent. *Pharos,* organ of the British Cremation Society, called its account of the takeover INVASION OF THE BODY SNATCHERS. It warned of "possible price rise and the arrival of U.S.-style high-pressure sales methods." Imported American coffins, it noted, may have a markup of up to 900 percent.

Unkindest of all was a prizewinning television documentary deriding the SCI takeover, scathingly titled "Over My Dead Body," unanimously praised by the television critics and chosen as "Pick of the Week" by the *Times*. It was broadcast on November 27, 1994, just three months after SCI had consummated its U.K. transaction.

Set forth for British viewers to gape at in wonder are a funeral directors' trade fair at which are displayed a gruesome array of embalming fluids, tools for removing the innards, cosmetics for corpses, and a dazzling assortment of caskets, culminating in "our top-of-the-line" item priced at $85,000. Jerry Pullin, SCI's man in London, explains:

> We feel the opportunities are greatest in offering a broader range of merchandise and services which will enhance our revenue base by offering enhanced consumer choices.

L. William Heiligbrodt, president of SCI, tells the viewing audience why the average price of Australian funerals rose by 40 percent after his company entered that market:

> We have found in Australia in the short time we've been there that people have chosen to spend more on funerals. I want again to emphasize "chosen." It's been their choice. The fact that our revenues per funeral have grown in Australia is because the Australian public have demanded it. In the U.K., that's our goal, as well.

There is a segment on SCI's immediate predecessor, one Howard Hodgson, known as the "yuppie undertaker," a great fan of Mrs. Thatcher and one of the entrepreneurial stars of the Iron Lady's regime. He describes how he achieved economies of scale via the "clustering" strategy, refurbishing funeral parlors, buying new hearses, and adding services like embalming, in fact, preparing the ground for SCI, to whom he eventually sold.

According to "Over My Dead Body," 50 percent of the British dead were embalmed in the Hodgson era; yet the *Independent* of January 7, 1992, quoted Peter Hall, general secretary of the British Institute of Embalming, as saying that "a quarter of all corpses in this country are now embalmed." He voiced the unappetizing suggestion that "the difference between a well-embalmed body and an untreated one is the difference between a plum and a prune." If these figures are

accurate, Mr. Hodgson had succeeded in less than three years in dou-
bling the number of British dead transformed from prune to plum, an
encouraging portent for the newly arrived SCI.

I was fortunate to be given what is known in the trade as a
"cameo appearance" in the video. This took place in a large and
well-appointed undertaker's showroom where Derek Gibbs, owner
of the London Casket Company, explained the offerings. He oblig-
ingly raised the casket lids to display a variety of beauteous linings in
"luxury velvet" or "high-quality crepe." Best of all was "The Last
Supper," described in the catalogue as "mahogany finished poplar
timber, cream madeira crepe interior. Scene of The Last Supper
colour insert in lid. Swing bar handles and adjustable bed. Angel corner pieces supplied on request at no extra cost."

"Oh, how absolutely smashing," I said. "I think they're lovely,
they're absolutely top-quality," replied Mr. Gibbs. "We do not hard
sell them at all. They really just sell themselves." We had the following conversation:

JM: But they must cost a fortune. First off, how much is the
wholesale cost?
DG: Well, we supply purely to the trade, so what funeral directors do in this country is they buy the casket from us, and then
they add it to the cost of their traditional funeral service.
JM: How much do you charge them for this, for example? You
charge them how much?
DG: Well, I would be loath to say, because as I say we supply
to the trade and they would actually add this to their traditional funeral.
JM: That's why I wanted to find out. How much do you pay
for it?
DG: I don't really want to discuss what we pay—is this a
rehearsal?

Long accustomed to the reticence of American funeral directors
on the sensitive subject of the wholesale cost of caskets—one of the
best-kept trade secrets—I was not surprised by Mr. Gibbs's reluc-
tance to disclose prices. But as it turned out, this was by no means the
end of the matter. Some weeks later, on January 30, 1995, Mr. Gibbs

wrote to the Broadcasting Complaints Commission, which is responsible for maintaining standards of fairness and privacy. (Its function is roughly parallel to that of the U.S. Federal Communications Commission.) His letter was full of anguish:

> Apart from one small moment, I thought that I handled myself well and gave sensible and reasonable answers. I accepted that my products are very foreign and extravagant but explained that there was a demand for elaborate high quality burial caskets.
>
> It was to be my first appearance on television and so I told all my customers, friends and family to be sure to watch it. You can therefore imagine my acute embarrassment when the program turned out to be a complete hatchet job on the industry that I serve. . . .
>
> At the time, I tried to laugh it off. . . . As time goes on, I felt increasingly angered by the whole affair. Every customer that I visit taunts me with the phrase, "This is only a rehearsal, isn't it?" . . .

Reading this letter, I could not fail to be impressed by the poignancy of Mr. Gibbs's experience. However, it hasn't hurt his business. In April 1996 he told an interviewer that his casket sales for 1994–95 had been 312—up from 242 the year before. "It was slow going to begin with," he said, "but our sales have grown steadily over the years. This last quarter, January, February, March, has been our busiest quarter ever. So it's getting better. People like the idea of preservation. That is the point of the sale."

Fast-forward to 1996. SCI has now held sway in this scepter'd isle for two years, long enough for a preliminary estimate of its impact on the British funeral scene. The *Guardian* led off February 27, 1996, with the headline HAVE A NICE DEATH:

> The Americans pioneered a fast-food, hard-sell approach to death. It is not the British Way. Sarah Bosely and Peter Godwin investigate creeping disneyfication—and soaring prices—in the British funeral industry.
>
> It's the ultimate commercialisation—the final tastelessness. McDeath is on its way to a funeral parlour near you. The

Americans are here, although you may not yet have noticed it. We British don't talk about these things. But there they are . . . gearing up to effect a huge change in the British way of death.

The BBC's "Public Eye" obliged with a documentary broadcast on February 17 entitled "Pay Now, Die Later." Unsurprisingly, the presenter tells us that SCI refused to be interviewed for the program. But as is often the case, some of the best copy was mined from "internal documents" procured by some light-fingered sleuth on the "Public Eye" team.

For example, we are treated to "notes" issued to "SCI funeral directors in Britain to help them to overcome their 'difficulty combining their helping role with that of a business role' when helping a client to choose a coffin." And here are the notes, eerily reminiscent of SCI's directive to its Australian employees (see chapter 16, "A Global Village of the Dead"). It's a small, small world.

Present the coffin range to its best advantage.
Direct the attention of the family to the highest quality item on
    display (perhaps the Regal).
Next present the Crown.
Then present the Classic Royal, and so on in descending price
    order.
Know how to respond to objections: Respond with empathy,
    not defensiveness or aggression or impatience. For exam-
    ple, "I can understand your concern about the price but
    let me explain the difference in design and manufac-
    ture again." Or for example, "Yes, I can see your point
    about them just going into the ground, but we need to pro-
    vide an extensive range like this in order to suit everyone's
    taste."

So far so good, but that's only for starters. Through more internal documents, "Public Eye" discovered that SCI was disappointed with the low income from "memorial sales,"* which, according to a

---

*"Memorial," in the trade, means merchandise for sale—for instance, a head-stone or plaque, a rose tree ($450), or other remembrance.

memo to its general managers, is "without a doubt the single most important area of our activity to be improved." To remedy the situation, SCI launched a new sales program, its details spelled out in the memo:

> All families that we have conducted a cremation [for] in 1995 but who have not purchased a memorial from us . . . to be contacted by letter with a phone contact follow-up where possible . . .
>
> In the case of some of our larger volume locations, this will require our contacting upwards of 1,000 to 1,500 families. . . . Do not be overwhelmed if there are large numbers of families to be contacted. Large numbers only mean big opportunities! If all you do is post 100 letters a week, this is 100 possible sales that you would otherwise not have.

The unfortunate inclination of many survivors to scatter cremated ashes over sea, land, or in the Gardens of Remembrance adjacent to British crematoria has long been a major headache for the funeral industry, resulting as it does in the loss of lucrative niche and urn sales. In England, with its soaring cremation rate, the problem is particularly acute. SCI's solution is to meet it head-on by sending a lavish memorial brochure with color pictures of available offerings, accompanied by the following poem:

> *Scatter me not to restless winds*
> *Nor toss my ashes to the sea.*
> *Remember now those years gone by*
> *When living gifts I gave to thee.*
>
> *Remember now the happy times,*
> *The family ties we shared;*
> *Don't leave my resting place unmarked,*
> *As though you never cared.*
>
> *Deny me not one final gift*
> *For all who come to see,*
> *A single lasting proof that says*
> *I loved, and you loved me.*

Who could resist this admonishment, at once stern and loving, delivered as a direct order by a voice from the Great Beyond? Apparently quite a few people, such as Helen Lewis, who, according to "Public Eye," was "particularly incensed" when the poem and brochure were sent to her from SCI's Chichester crematorium where her father had been cremated. "I realize that that was just another ploy to get you to spend some money and do something with the person's ashes," she said. "It's so awful when I think of that poem, because it's so manipulative, really."

There is more in store for the grieving family—SCI is not quite through with them yet, for now is the optimum moment to get them thinking about future funerals. It is, in fact, "pre-need" time. "Public Eye" has obtained a report written by a senior British SCI manager sent to the U.S. to study the company's operation there. Fresh from this illuminating experience, he tells colleagues how to canvas families who have used an SCI funeral home in the weeks after the bereavement. Some pointers:

> Immediate service follow-up is based on the somewhat harsh premise that you've got to get 'em before the tears are dry. Engaging the emotions of the client is the key to a successful sale. "Freezing the cost tells them why, but emotion makes them buy."

SCI was predictably none too pleased with the "Public Eye" effort. On February 29, less than two weeks after the broadcast, CEO Peter Hindley produced yet another internal memo addressed to "All Staff," designed to deflect the blow:

> By now many of you will have seen the "Public Eye" programme which was based on changes in the funeral industry in the U.K. and in particular changes that SCI, in the programme's opinion, could introduce. I wanted you to know that SCI is firmly committed to improving standards and services and client choice with the highest regard and respect for traditions that exist in the U.K. We will clearly be innovative and through better service we will increase our market share.

The programme, in my opinion, was motivated by some of

our competitors who are probably concerned that they will not be able to provide the same level of service as ourselves. . . .

You can be proud of being a member of SCI, and I would not wish you to allow either the media or our competitors to distract you from the task of providing our families with the best possible service.

That not "All Staff" were receptive to this appeal to their loyalty is evidenced by some extremely salty comments made to my London researcher by former SCI employees who quit around the time of the "Public Eye" program and others who still have an SCI connection.

Some SCI defectors, finding themselves in a fairly dicey position vis à vis the industry, spoke on condition of anonymity. Mr. A, as I will call him, who had worked first as "arranger" then as "director" at Plantsbrook, stayed the course for a scant two weeks after SCI bought up his firm.

"I didn't like the way it was run," he said. "We sold set packages—a major rip-off. We were given about an hour with each client to find out what they could afford, then had to sell within this range or slightly above. We were not allowed to offer cheap funerals unless we had permission.

"It's all about high-powered selling. The average member of the public only gets an inkling that the funeral home is American-owned when the final bill is sent out. The Americans are just like a lot of parasites eating away at the country." He emphasized that "the main message to get through to everyone is, one, ask if the funeral director is independent, and, two, get an estimate from at least two different funeral directors."

Green Undertakings, where Mr. A is now working, is far more to his liking. "We don't offer packages. We ask a client what part of the funeral arrangements they want us to do," he said. "There is no need to say good-bye by spending a lot of money. We encourage families to provide their own bearers. As to embalming, I haven't embalmed a single body at Green Undertakings, though I would if asked."

Mr. B, as I will call him, had been employed for four years by a Plantsbrook funeral parlor; several months after SCI took over, he resigned. "I was very unhappy with them," he said. "I left because I couldn't stand it. SCI just chases the buck; their commercialism is going to ruin them in the end."

SCI has its own canny method of gradually softening up the new British employees, a form of behavior modification designed to ease them into acceptance of the American Way. For the first six months or so, Mr. B said, nothing really changed. Then, all employees were summoned to a meeting in a smart Kensington hotel where a new range of coffins was unveiled, amid assurance by the SCI mentors that they were not going to promote high-pressure sales techniques. "The old Plantsbrook range was made up of typically English-looking, pleasant coffins," said Mr. B. But the new lot was proof to him that despite their protestations, "the Americans are committed to a very subtle form of high pressure."

Here is how it works: The cheapest available is not displayed in the showroom, and there are no photos of it in the brochure. The only time it is ever mentioned is if somebody telephones to inquire about prices, the assumption being that "if they are the type of customer who is phoning, they will phone everybody to compare prices." Total price of the rock-bottom funeral is $1,016* (which does not include "disbursements," embalming, or complimentary car).

Those who come into the funeral parlor looking for a bargain will not be told of this option—"We were not allowed to mention it face-to-face with somebody in the shop," said Mr. B. Instead, they are told the cheapest is "The Fundamental," which Mr. B says looks like cardboard—and moreover, "it is specifically designed to look like cardboard." The price of a funeral using "The Fundamental:" over $1,760—not including disbursements. $1,340 of this sum is for "professional services," a hearse, and limo.

There are two more in the bottom range: "The Primary," which "looks like a hi-fi unit that someone has dismantled and then put together to look like a coffin," and "The White Pearl." "They really look cheap," said Mr. B. "It's really bloody painfully obvious. The first three in the range are so awful. I wouldn't bury or cremate your dog in the first two, let alone a member of your family. The cardboard ones really look super-cheap." The fourth coffin is "The Consort," which is "the nearest to the traditional English coffin," but costs $760! To which, of course is added the $1,340 fee for "professional services" and the rest of the paraphernalia.

---

*635 pounds at the exchange rate of $1.60.

"Every single funeral director in every single shop complained about the coffins," said Mr. B.

The above prices are in any event only meant for the serious bargain hunter, the rare hard-nosed individual whose main concern is keeping down the cost. For the average customer, "funeral directors are instructed to work from the top of the range down, and to keep the family in the coffin showroom for forty minutes. We are pushed to sell the more expensive coffins." And here come the carrots and sticks: at the beginning of each year, each funeral parlor is assigned a target figure and a target budget. This is further refined as a breakdown of the number of funerals each is expected to perform each month and how much should be earned per funeral. "Some funeral directors have to sell a Consort or above to reach the budget figure," Mr. B explained. Those who fail to achieve the budget figure get a letter or phone call expressing disappointment; Somebody Up There is watching, namely SCI's control department. Mr. B had such a phone call last January, saying that he was down 12 pounds from the sales of the previous January. Conversely, two thousand overachievers are singled out each year for a "loyalty or productivity" bonus.

The SCI bigwigs were inclined to shrug off adverse comments from any quarter. Eric Spencer, an Englishman whose SCI title is senior director of corporate development, was chief executive of the Great Southern Group before the takeover. His primary responsibility, he said, is in Europe, although he does also look after some of the British acquisitions.

"This anti-American hysteria is quite laughable," he said. "Although SCI is owned by Americans, there are only two American executives permanently in the U.K. Everyone below them is English." He explained that SCI intended to maintain a low profile; it refused to get into a shouting match with its detractors in the media, which is why they declined the invitation to appear in the "Public Eye" documentary. He now thinks that decision might have been a mistake, and said that "we'll see a more active response from SCI in the future."

Peter Hindley, the English chief executive of SCI in the U.K., is the author of many an in-house directive to "All Staff." Accusations of hard sell? "Absolute rubbish," he said. "We do not have hard-sell tactics. What we have is people offering client choices, informed choice. We offer a much wider range of coffins than other funeral directors. We will offer a much greater range of ashes caskets [cremation urns]. We will offer memorial books, and a much wider range of graveside memorials. We will offer a better range of flowers." Echoing his memo to "All Staff" in the wake of the "Public Eye" documentary (in his opinion, the program was "motivated by some of our competitors"), he declared that "small-minded funeral businesses spend their life trying to sling mud at SCI."

Of far greater moment than the slings and arrows of the media to SCI's plans for achieving its goal of "enhancing its revenues by enhancing consumer choices" is the May 1995 report of the Monopolies and Mergers Commission presented to Parliament by the secretary of trade and industry by command of Her Majesty. The MMC is the British counterpart of the Federal Trade Commission, but the approach of the two agencies to their mandated job of consumer protection couldn't be more different.

The FTC does not normally concern itself with so-called market share until it becomes formidable enough to threaten competition in wide regional areas. SCI's national market share in the U.S., measured in terms of its own undertaking establishments, is about 10 percent. Not to worry, says the FTC. But what of Houston, Texas, where SCI's market share, measured by its share of the funeral business, is no less than 70 percent?

The MMC, recognizing that competition in the funeral trade is of local rather than national concern, has taken a different view of SCI's recent acquisitions in the U.K. It has condemned the merger on the ground that "it may be expected to operate against the public interest." Its reasons stated with typically British reserve, the report castigates the merger in terms which would equally apply to SCI's operations in the U.S. and Australia:

> Our investigation indicates that although funeral directors do compete on price the competition is muted. The market is a long way from functioning effectively. Entry is likely to be particularly difficult where a powerful, well-run supplier has a large share of the market. . . . We also have concerns about the degree of transparency of funeral directors' charges, the lack of transparency of ownership of funeral directing outlets and the ability of funeral directors unduly to influence the choice of funeral arrangements.

The report identifies ten localities where the merged companies' share of funerals performed range from 29 percent to 51 percent. Consequently, the report continues, "SCI may be expected . . . to raise prices excessively . . . to the detriment of consumers in these localities." While the Federal Trade Commission has turned a blind eye to SCI's practice of concealing from the public its ownership and control of its hundreds of funeral homes by the fictitious use of their pre-purchase names, this practice is a matter of concern to the MMC:

> SCI's failure to disclose to consumers the ownership of its branches will add significantly to the inability of consumers . . . to make informed decisions.

The report recommends that SCI be ordered to sell off enough of its funeral business in the ten Greater London markets to reduce its market share to not more than 25 percent, and that it be ordered to make no further acquisitions in those areas without prior approval.

The report notes that "it would be natural for SCI to take advantage" of its acquisitions of crematoria by steering its business to them: "As prices at SCI's crematoria are generally higher than those of competitors, this would be a clear loss to consumers." Therefore, "SCI should be required to post prices of competing crematoria at every SCI funeral directing branch. . . ."

Finally, there should be an end to SCI's devious ploy of concealing its identity from the purchaser. It should be required "to disclose its ownership of funeral directing businesses prominently in all documentation presented to customers and in all advertisements or other promotional material used in connection with those businesses. We believe it is highly desirable that the disclosure of ultimate ownership of funeral directing branches should be the general practice throughout the UK."*

---

*Action by the government to implement the recommendations of the Monopolies and Mergers Commission (MMC) was delayed for some months by SCI's application for judicial review. When the application was rejected by the High Court, the minister for corporate and consumer affairs was able to announce, on December 18, 1996, that he had accepted "undertakings from SCI which follow closely the MMC's original recommendation," and that they would instruct all its branches throughout the U.K. to disclose SCI's ownership of their premises.

Reverberating throughout SCI's promotional literature, in memoranda from American executives to British staff and in written declarations for public consumption, are the words "dignity," "respect," "tradition." These are repeated as a sort of mantra, meant to reassure everyone of the company's sincere intention of preserving Britain's ingrained funerary customs.

But then—oh dear!—SCI really put its foot in it by producing an illustrated brochure bearing the imprimatur of the staid and ancient British firm of the Kenyon Funerals now owned by SCI. The message: "Disasters cause the greatest public relations challenge any carrier can meet." The *Sunday Telegraph* (May 12, 1996) made hay with this, under the headline OUTRAGE OVER FUNERAL FIRM'S PICTURE BOOK OF DEATH, with examples of the photos captioned "Macabre Marketing: A Montage of Disaster and Death." Vivid scenes from some of Britain's worst disasters: Lockerbie, Zeebrugge, Piper Alpha, and the Scilly Isles helicopter crash. Also featured were gruesome views of corpses being autopsied and the dead pilots hanging from the wreckage.

The families of victims were furious; Pamela Dix, whose brother died in the Lockerbie disaster, told the *Telegraph,* "This is both offensive and completely inappropriate—it strips away the dignity of the dead. A brochure like this shows they have in no way taken into account the emotional needs of survivors. People will feel very hurt." A survivor of Lockerbie said, "It is quite terrible. I don't know why they have to have photographs at all. Everybody in the airlines and emergency services knows what they do. This is insensitive." Philip Lewis, chief executive of Kenyon Funerals in its pre-SCI days, said he was "appalled" by it: "I would not have done it and, frankly, I'm shocked. It is turning tragedy into an advertising slogan and is breaking every code we work under."

Kenyon, founded in 1816, had an exalted past, having buried such dignitaries as Lord Mountbatten and Sir Winston Churchill; it had been undertaker for the Royal Family, but no longer. The Queen withdrew the royal contract when Kenyon was bought out, "preferring to deal with named individuals rather than large conglomerates," according to Keith Leverton, whose firm, Levertons, is presently under contract to the Palace. True to form, SCI has been trying—so far without success—to obtain funeral records of

British monarchs whose funerals were handled by Kenyon. They would doubtless use this information in future publicity, much as they have done with claims to Elvis Presley and U.S. presidents, all of whom died long before SCI acquired the premises that arranged their funerals.

English Country Funerals

In the English countryside, the style and conduct of funerals are, it seems, pretty much unchanged from time immemorial. This may be explained by the fact that the conglomerates have generally satisfied their takeover appetites by swallowing high-volume mortuaries and chains located in urban areas.

J. W. and J. Mettam are undertakers in the small Derbyshire town of Bakewell. Mr. Roger Jepson, managing director, says that their coffins are made on site as of yore, measured to fit in a range of sizes starting at 5 feet 5 inches by 16 inches and going up in 2-inch increments. Small coffins for children are made to order. Materials used are various woods or chipboard.

The Mettams provide a full service, as much or as little as the family wants and is prepared to pay for. Prices range from $1,056 (660 pounds) for the complete basic funeral, with oak veneer coffin, to the top-of-the-line Devonshire, solid oak coffin, for $1,750. Included in the price are collection of the body, obtaining death certificate, making all arrangements with church or crematorium, notices in newspapers, all transportation for accompanying family—they will even arrange for a funeral tea at a suitable hotel if asked. They cater to all denominations and to nonreligious groups such as the British Humanist Association.

In one respect, there has been a departure from the old ways: embalming is on the rise. It is always done if the body is to be sent abroad, or transported any distance within the U.K. It is also usually done if the family is coming to the Chapel of Rest to see the body—unless the family specifically objects. Unlike the mortuaries in the USA—where mortuaries routinely refuse to permit viewing unless the body has been embalmed—families here often view unembalmed bodies. In about 70 percent of cases the family (they often bring children) does ask to see the body, and this is encouraged.

However "viewing"—as the U.S. funeral directors call it—is generally limited to the close family members and is in no way comparable to the American custom of a general spectacle for the neighbors, coworkers, and mere acquaintances.

What about American caskets? They are never used in this way, although Mr. Jepson has heard of them in London. Floral tributes? Less of those—more donations to worthy charities. The coffin, closed, is usually at the front of the church.

A friend described the funeral of a retired farm foreman who bred his own Shire horses. "The tiny church was packed," she said. "It couldn't hold half the people who came, so there was a crowd in the churchyard. It was snowing, and bitterly cold. His family had arranged for a dray drawn by a Shire, all got up super-smart, to carry the coffin to the church. There is a steepish hill and I heard a sound which took me back sixty years—the scrape of the brake on the wheel of the dray. The farm men lined up outside the church and made an arch of pitchforks when the coffin was carried out. Talk about moving to tears—a village funeral is a killer, far worse than a big London affair." It would seem that the Derbyshire countryside is for the moment quite safe from incursions of the American way.

At the other end of England, country funerals are conducted in much the same manner. A friend visited Philip Wakely and his brother Simon, of A. J. Wakely and Sons in Bridport, Dorset. They have two other funeral parlors under the same family name in Beaminister and Lyme Regis, all within a twenty-mile radius. The firm was established in 1897, and holds strongly to long-standing custom.

While they no longer make coffins on the premises, these are all in the traditional coffin shape. Thus far, nobody has asked for an American casket, said Mr. Wakely, "but if people wanted them, we'd have to supply them." As in Derbyshire, "people are tending to ask for charitable contributions, and only the family brings flowers from their own gardens," he said.

Prices range from $1,040 for an oak-veneered coffin with engraved nameplate, removal of the deceased within a twenty-mile radius, hire of a hearse, pallbearers and funeral director's arrangement fee to the "Dorset Burial Funeral," which comes with an oakdene-paneled coffin, for $1,952.

There is no extra charge for embalming, which would come under funeral director's costs and is carried out according to the wishes of the family. "Many families in Dorset still like to view the deceased in their own homes," Mr. Wakely said, "and this is the only time we recommend embalming; but some families do not want embalming even when the body will be in their home for as long as a week. Others prefer to use Wakely's Chapel of Rest for the purpose; again embalming is optional." The Wakelys estimate that fewer than 25 percent of their clients opt for embalming.

So far, SCI's entry into the British funeral industry, as in the case of Mettam's, poses little threat to the Wakelys. Philip Wakely said that although the new American presence is "kind of scary," it "has only affected us from a distress point of view," as people read about SCI in the papers and assume that all funeral directors operate like them.

18

Press and Protest

For as long as anyone now alive can remember, our traditional American way of caring for and remembering the dead has been subjected to criticism.

—*American Funeral Director*, June 1961

To hear the funeral men complain about the bad press they get, one might think they are the target of a huge newspaper and magazine conspiracy to defame and slander them, to tease them and laugh at them, and eventually to ruin them.

Actually, they have not fared too badly. There have been—from time to time—documented exposés of the funeral trade in national magazines of large circulation; occasional short items in *Time, Newsweek, Business Week,* and the like; and a few feature stories in metropolitan newspapers.

Industry leaders spend an enormous amount of time worrying over these articles. Criticism, and how to deal with it; projected magazine articles, and how to get them suppressed; threatened legislation, and how to forestall it—these are their major preoccupations. If all else fails, they snarl at the world from the pages of the funeral trade press, like angry dogs behind a fence unable to get to grips with the enemy.

Two articles, published a decade apart, caused particular consternation and alarm within the industry: "The High Cost of Dying" by Bill Davidson, which appeared in *Collier's* magazine in May 1951, and "Can You Afford to Die?" by Roul Tunley, in the *Saturday Evening Post* of June 17, 1961.

The Davidson piece very nearly triggered a major upset for the funeral industry, at least in California. It was the most comprehensive statement on the industry that had thus far appeared; it was detailed and well documented; and it made some very specific charges: "Even this honest majority [of undertakers] is guilty of accepting a mysterious, nation-wide fixing and raising of prices," and "The burial industry's great lobbying and political strength enables it to cow a significant number of legislators and jurists and do pretty much as it pleases. . . . The lobbying is spearheaded in the state legislatures by associations of funeral directors and cemeteries."

The funeral press reacted, as usual, like a rather inefficient bull confronted with a red flag. In a brave attempt at incisive sarcasm, *Mortuary Management* prefaced an editorial: "Coal is black and dirty. A Collier is 'a vessel for transporting coal'—Webster." The words "shabby handling" and "dirty journalism" reverberated through its pages. Forest Lawn's spokesman Ugene Blalock called it "an invitation to socialism." But what was to follow required a subtler and more sophisticated approach than mere angry denunciation.

Because the article dealt quite fully with funeral industry abuses in California, the legislature of that state launched an official investigation into "Funeral Directors, Embalmers, Morticians and Funeral Establishments." For a while it looked as though real trouble was in store. The resolution creating the investigating committee mentioned a "need for closer regulation" of funeral establishments and "needed revision of laws" relating to the funeral business. The funeral men were thrown into a state of alarm and confusion; should they or shouldn't they answer the questionnaires sent out by the legislative committee? ("Don't be in too big a hurry to complete and send in your questionnaire," counseled *Mortuary Management*.) Should they or should they not cooperate with the committee's investigators?

This consternation in the ranks proved to have been unwarranted, for their interests were being more than adequately protected. The committee's report, when it finally appeared in June 1953, over the signature of Assemblyman Clayton A. Dills, must have been cause for much rejoicing and self-congratulation in funeral circles. What a relief to read, after the months of nagging uncertainty, "The funeral industry of California is unusually well organized for the public interest. . . . Criticisms of retail prices overlook the high operating costs, many of which are mandatory under the public health laws, while others are required under social and religious custom and the stress of emotion. . . . It is the considered opinion of the committee that no further legislative action is needed in this matter."

The report has a strangely familiar ring to anybody versed in the thought processes and literary style of funeral directors. There are phrases that could have come directly out of the proceedings of a National Funeral Directors Association convention: "Embalming is first and foremost an essential public health measure. A concomitant function, which developed with the evolution of embalming and funeral directing as a distinct vocation, is to restore the features of the deceased to a serene and natural appearance. Both functions demand a high degree of professional skill based on specialized education and training." There is mention of the "evolution of the funeral director as a part of the American way of life"; there is praise for the funeral home with its "special features planned and furnished to provide facilities and conveniences to serve the living and reverently prepare the dead for burial." The Association of Better Business Bureaus pamphlet *Facts Every Family Should Know* (itself based on material furnished by the NFDA) is reproduced in its entirety as part of the report.

Was this report really written by a subcommittee of the California State Assembly? Apparently not. A more plausible explanation of how it came to be written is contained in a letter that came into my possession. The letter—dated July 24, 1953—is from J. Wilfred Corr, then executive secretary of the California Funeral Directors Association, and is addressed to Mr. Wilber M. Krieger, head of National Selected Morticians:

Dear Mr. Krieger,

Thank you for your letter dated July 21 congratulating us on the Dills Committee Report and requesting 12 copies. The 12 copies of the report will be mailed to you under separate cover.

I want to correct a possible wrong impression as indicated in the first sentence of your letter. You congratulated us on "the very fine report that you have prepared and presented to the Dills Committee." Although this may be one hundred percent correct, it should be presumed that this is a report of and by the Dills Committee, perhaps with some assistance.

Actually Warwick Carpenter and Don Welch wrote the

report. I engineered the acceptance of the report by Dills and the actual filing of the report, which was interesting. One member of the committee actually read the report. He was the Assemblyman from Glendale, and Forest Lawn naturally wanted the report filed. He approved the report and his approval was acceptable to the others.

Sometime when we are in personal conversation, I would like to tell you more about the actual engineering of this affair. In the meantime, as you realize, the mechanics of this accomplishment should be kept confidential.

Cordially yours,
J. Wilfred Corr

Mr. J. Wilfred Corr later became the executive director of the American Institute of Funeral Directors. He contributed occasional articles to *Mortuary Management* in which he made ringing appeals for ever-higher ethical standards for funeral directors: "Perhaps we will live to see the triumph of ethical practices, born of American competition, fair dealing and common honesty." Mr. Donald Welch was one of California's most prosperous undertakers and the owner of a number of Southern California mortuaries. Mr. Warwick Carpenter was a market analyst who prepared the statistics on funeral costs used in the legislative committee report. According to *Mortuary Management,* the statistics were originally developed by Mr. Carpenter for Mr. Welch, "to illustrate an address he made before a national convention of funeral directors." *Mortuary Management* opines that Mr. Carpenter "performed a very helpful service to funeral directors in California now under investigation." The assemblyman from Glendale who actually read the report was the Honorable H. Allen Smith, who went on to Congress.

The report itself was liberally circulated by the undertakers, who rather naturally saw it as a first-rate public relations aid.

The ten years following the *Collier's* article were relatively tranquil ones for the funeral industry, at least so far as the press was a matter of concern to it. Mr. Merle Welsh, at the time president of the National Funeral Directors Association, was able to report to the 1959 convention: "By our constant vigil there is a lessening of the derogatory and sensational in written matter. Several articles of which we have been apprised have either not been written or were watered down versions of that which they were originally intended."

A year later, *Casket & Sunnyside* made the same point: "For many years only a very few derogatory articles about funeral service have been printed in national publications. . . . Many times the information that an author is planning such an article is leaked to a state association officer or to NFDA, so that the proper and accurate information may be given such writer without his asking for it. In practically all such instances, such proposed articles either never appear or appear without their 'sensational exposé,' entirely different articles than were at first planned."

The funeral men were far from easy in their minds, however, for a new peril was appearing on the horizon. Said Mr. Welsh, "I could speak for hours on the problems and rumors of problems besetting funeral service as a result of the times. . . . There are memorial societies and church groups trying to reform funeral practices. There are promoters telling funeral directors to take on a plan or plans or else. There are writers who would like to reduce the American funeral program to a $150 disposal plan. . . . While it is true we have patches of blue in our sky through which shines the light of professionality, there are also dark clouds involving crusades, promotions, unjustifiable attacks and designs to replace the American funeral program of to each his own with a $150 disposal plan."

There is a semifictional character, who often crops up in lawyers' talk, known as the "man of ordinary prudence." He is a person of common sense, able to look at transactions with a normal degree of sophistication, to put a reasonable interpretation on evidence, to apply rational standards to all sorts of situations. He has, down the ages, often given the undertakers trouble; but never, it would seem, so much trouble as he is giving them in America today. He is, in fact, their worst enemy.

It is he who grins out at the funeral men from the pages of magazines, frowns at them from the probate bench, speaks harshly of them from the pulpit or from the autopsy room. It is he who writes nasty letters to the newspapers about them, and derides them in private conversation. The burden of his criticism has changed little over the years. He thinks showy funerals are in bad taste and are a waste of money. He thinks some undertakers take advantage of the grief-stricken for financial gain. He thinks the poor and uneducated are especially vulnerable to this form of exploitation when a member of the family dies. Lately, he has begun to think that there are important uses to which a dead body could be put for the benefit of the living—medical research, eye banks, tissue banks, and the like. More significant, he is taking some practical measures to provide a rational alternative to the American way of death. Over the years, funeral societies (or memorial associations) have been established in the United States and Canada, devoted to the principle of "simple, dignified funerals at a reasonable cost."

This is, from the undertaker's point of view, a particularly vile form of sedition. the *National Funeral Service Journal* (April 1961) denounced funeral society advocates as "the burial beatniks of contemporary America . . . far more dangerous than the average funeral director realizes, for they are fanatics; they are the paraders for human rights, the picketers of meetings and institutions that displease them, the shouters and hecklers and demonstrators for any number of causes." Whether the mild-mannered clergymen, professors, and social workers who form the backbone of the funeral societies would recognize themselves in this word picture is uncertain, but it is a fairly typical funeral trade reaction to any suggested deviation from their established procedures.

The funeral society people were not the first critics of American funeral practices, nor are they indeed the harshest; they were merely the first to think in terms of an organization through which an alternative to the "standard funeral" might be made available to the public. It is the organizational aspect that terrifies the undertakers, and that gives rise to purple passages in the trade press:

An atomic attack on our Christian funeral customs. . .

———

. . . hang over our heads like the fabled sword of Damocles.

———

The Memorial Associations are like all the other selfish interest groups that infest the American way of life like so many weasels sucking away at the life blood of our basic economy.

———

Those who seek to destroy the very foundation of the American funeral program are making headway.

What do we do about this menace? How do we fight it?

It poses a threat to religion itself.

Those who promote it are in the same class with the demagogue, fadist, and do-gooder who from time to time in history has jumped on his horse and ridden off in different directions.

Some telling blows have been struck directly at the heart of funeral service recently. So far we have been able to roll with the punch. But we must come back championing our heritage. We cannot throw in the towel or fight the way the enemy wants us to. To compromise or do what the opposition does is to lose forever the finest funeral standards in the world.

The very concept of the memorial society is alien to every principle of the American way of life. Therefore, it must be opposed with every ounce of decency we can muster.

What, then, is the "concept of the memorial society" against which these ounces of decency must be mustered? It was originally set forth in a pamphlet issued by the Cooperative League of the USA, entitled *Memorial Associations: What They Are, How They Are Organized:*

> Memorial associations and their members seek modesty, simplicity, and dignity in the final arrangements over which they have control. This concern for spiritual over material values has revealed that a "decent burial" or other arrangement need not be elaborate. . . . Some families wish to avoid funerals and burials altogether. They prefer cremation and a memorial service later, at which the life of the deceased and the spiritual aspects of death are emphasized, without an open casket and too many flowers.
>
> Still others want to will their bodies to a medical school for teaching and research. They also may offer their eyes to an eye bank so the corneas may be transplanted and the blind may see.

Whether it's an unostentatious funeral, a simple burial, cremation, a memorial service, or a concern for medical science, these people want dignified and economical final arrangements. Accordingly they have organized several kinds of memorial associations in more than a dozen states and several Canadian provinces. . . .

Even for the person whose family wants the conventional funeral and burial, membership in a memorial association offers support and counsel in achieving simplicity, dignity, and economy in a service that centers not on public display of the body but on the meaning of death.

Above all, the memorial association provides the opportunity for individuals to have the kind of facilities and services they choose at what is perhaps the most mysterious moment of all.

With these modest objectives, a number of associations flourished by the late fifties. They were organized for the most part by Unitarians, Quakers, and other Protestant church groups; they flourished best in the quiet backwaters of university towns; their recruits came from youngish, middle-income people in the academic and professional world rather than from the lower-income brackets, or, as the *National Funeral Service Journal* put it, "The movement appeals most strongly to the visionary, ivory tower eggheads of the academic fraternity."

Some of the societies function as educational organizations and limit themselves to advocacy of "rationally pre-planned final arrangements." Most, however, have gone a step further and through collective bargaining have secured contracts with one or more funeral establishments to supply the "simple funeral" for members at an agreed-on sum. There is some diversity of outlook in the societies: some emphasize cremation; others are more interested in educational programs advocating bequeathal of bodies to medical schools; still others stress freedom of choice in the matter of burials as their main concern.

All operate as nonprofit organizations, open to everybody, and all are run by unpaid boards of directors. Enrollment fees are modest, usually about $20 for a "life membership"; a few groups collect annual dues. The money is used for administrative expenses, printings, mailings, and the like, and in a few cases for newspaper advertising.

A major objective of all the societies is to smooth the path for the family that prefers to hold a memorial service, without the body present, instead of the "open-casket" funeral—and to guarantee that the family will not have to endure a painful clash with the undertaker in making such arrangements. The memorial service idea is most bitterly fought in the trade. With their usual flair for verbal invective, industry spokesmen have coined a word for the memorial service: "disposal." "Point out that those who know say the disposal-type service without the body present is not good for those who survive," said the president of the National Funeral Directors Association. *Casket & Sunnyside*'s expert on proper reverence wrote, "The increasing support which members of the clergy have been giving to the memorial society movement stems in part from a lack of understanding on the clergy's behalf of what proper reverence for the dead really means to the living. They have little knowledge of the value of sentiment in the therapy of healing."

The idea the funeral industry wants to get across is that a memorial service without the body present is a heartless, cold affair, devoid of meaning for the survivors, in which the corpse has been treated as so much garbage. Actually, the character of a memorial service depends entirely upon the wishes of the family involved. It may be a private affair in a home (or in the chapel of the funeral establishment), or a regular church service conducted according to the custom of the particular denomination. The only distinguishing feature of a memorial service is the absence of the corpse and casket.

The memorial societies might have gone on for years, their rate of growth dependent mainly on word-of-mouth advocacy in very limited circles, had it not been for Roul Tunley's "Can You Afford to Die?" in the June 17, 1961, issue of the *Saturday Evening Post*. This article provided an unlooked-for boost for the tiny memorial associations. With its appearance, the conflict between the funeral industry and the Man of Ordinary Prudence came into the open.

Tunley told the story of the Bay Area Funeral Society, describing its activities in these words: "San Franciscans have lately become witnesses to one of the most bizarre battles in the city's history—a struggle to undermine the funeral directors, or 'bier barons,' and topple the high cost of dying." He concluded that three choices confront the average citizen intent on making a simple, inexpensive exit from the world: "(1) You must make strict arrangements in advance for an austere funeral, a plan which may be upset by your survivors; or (2) You must join a co-operative enterprise like the Bay Area Funeral Society; or (3) You must will your body to some institution. If you do none of these things . . . the final journey will probably be the most expensive ride you've ever taken."

Roul Tunley's article, though milder in tone and less sharply critical of the undertakers than the one in *Collier's,* represented—from the point of view of the industry—a far more potent threat, for it dealt with the kind of practical remedial action which people in any community could take. This put the cat among the pigeons. The "bizarre battle" was about to become positively outlandish.

Pandemonium broke loose in the industry, reflected in headlines which appeared in the trade press: SENTIMENT AND MEMORIAL-IZATION ARE IN GRAVE DANGER!; MISINFORMATION SPREAD AMONG FIFTEEN MILLION AMERICANS!; LORIMER WOULD DIS-OWN IT, OR WE'LL ALL HANG SEPARATELY!; and my favorite, in *Mortuary Management,* THEY CAN AFFORD TO DIE!

There was at first a strong tendency to panic. *Casket & Sunnyside* editorialized:

> There is little doubt that funeral service today, beset by power-ful adversaries, will buckle under the strain unless there is united action in a common cause by all groups of funeral direc-tors. If not, funeral service faces the danger of retrogressing to a point which we do not care to contemplate.

And the *American Funeral Director:*

> Although articles critical of funeral practices have been pub-lished many times before in magazines and newspapers, there are aspects to this one which are especially disturbing. . . . The article is a persuasive sales talk for the memorial societies which today constitute one of the greatest threats to the Amer-ican ideals of memorialization.

And the President of the NFDA:

... part of an organized move to abolish the American funeral program.

From the cacophony of angry voices, a number of distinct viewpoints could be discerned; differences of opinion emerged as to the essential nature of the threat.

The editor of *Mortuary Management* wrote:

> Offhand, it would appear that memorial societies have the one aim of reducing the price of funerals. As you study it, however, you begin to realize that it runs far deeper than price alone. . . . The leaders in these memorial society movements are not necessarily poor folk who cannot afford a standard funeral. Many of them are educated people. Many are both educated and of substantial means. Their objective is only partly to force lower funeral prices. Equally strong is the desire to change established customs. It can be focused on funerals today and on something else tomorrow. The promulgations of these outfits hint at Communism and its brother-in-arms, atheism.

The point that memorial society advocates are not only, or even perhaps primarily, interested in funeral costs was expanded by Mr. Sydney H. Heathwood, a public relations specialist in the funeral field, credited by the *National Funeral Service Journal* with having, years ago, "originated and developed the 'Memory Picture' concept which was adopted by the Joint Business Conference and became familiar to the whole profession." Mr. Heathwood saw "the continuing growth of *clerical* criticism" as the fundamental problem facing the funeral men, and says that as a consequence of it, "the past few months have marked a gathering storm—more dangerous, I believe, in its potential harm to the whole profession than anything before it of the kind."

What he found particularly devastating in the *Post* article was the words of Dr. Josiah Bartlett, Unitarian minister and one of the organizers of the Bay Area Funeral Society: "My people are in increasing rebellion against the pagan atmosphere of the modern funeral. It is not so much the cost as the morbid sentimentality of dwelling on the physical remains," and "[The funeral societies] vowed to work together for simpler and more dignified funerals which are not a vain and wasteful expense and do not emphasize the mortal and material remains rather than the triumph of the human spirit." Mr. Heathwood, in an analysis of the article, concludes: "The criticism of modern funerary refinements is not—in essence—against the costs, as such. Rather, the central part of all the criticism is against the actual goods and services which comprise the modern funeral service." He dismisses as "woolly argument" the charges that "either the critical clergymen are hungry for the funeral director's fees or their criticism shows that they are halfway communists or fellow-travelers."

The *National Funeral Service Journal,* too, was concerned that the memorial societies might become trendsetters in funerary matters: "Unchecked in its early stages, this movement could spread to engulf much of the population, for current funeral customs are based largely on the herd instinct—the doing of a thing because all others do it and because it is the accepted thing to do." And again: "The only thing that will change the custom is for people to become convinced that 'it is the thing to do.' This is what must be guarded against; this is what must be prevented." And again:

The "average" funeral sale is representative of the lowest point or price at which a client can make a selection without feeling cheap in the eyes of relatives or friends. The current average sale . . . could easily be reduced considerably by the Memorial Society Movement, clergy criticism and other types of so-called reform. If others wear silk, you feel conspicuous in anything less costly; if others wear burlap, you would feel superior in gingham.

The cemeterians, watching from the sidelines, had some comments. *Concept* struck a discordant and unkind note:

While it is not necessary to be in agreement with the extremity of their protests, it seems significant that there are so many people who are protesting the costs of funeral services through these societies. Certainly there must be some reason for discontent and these people must feel that there is injustice in funeral prices. It is important that members of the cemetery industry realize this before rushing to the defense of the allied burial industries.

Turning the screw a notch, the writer adds, "The cemetery industry has found its answer to high cost through pre-arrangement."

But has it? Another cemetery writer patiently spelled out for his more complacent colleagues an obvious difficulty for the cemeteries, arising from the tendency of memorial societies to encourage their members to donate their earthly remains to medical science:

What most assuredly results is that the remains are disposed of in a manner other than interment. Consequently, it is axiomatic that these organizations pose a threat to the tradition of earth interment with which our profession is concerned. Memorial associations, therefore, cannot be ignored. I have found, however, that many of my fellow cemeterians are not too concerned over their growth, believing that they may affect others, but never us.

The *American Cemetery* agreed with this appraisal:

Although presently the focal point of their attack is funeral service, the philosophy of the movement is that current American funeral, burial and memorialization practices are largely pagan and wasteful; that they should be greatly simplified; and that regardless of a family's wealth and social position, only modest expenditures should be made for such purposes. If this point of view were to generally prevail, as well it might if not effectively countered, the future of everyone in this field would most certainly be seriously jeopardized.

So did Mr. Frederick Llewellyn, executive vice president of Forest Lawn Memorial-Park, whose speech to the American Cemetery Association was reported in the *American Cemetery*:

In discussing this trend he mentioned funeral services with closed caskets and the "please omit flowers" movement. Although these now only directly affect funeral directors, he said, they will ultimately affect cemeterians as well. Even now, he said, there is a trend toward purchasing fewer large burial estates, less expensive memorials and fewer family mausoleums.

He urged that cemeterians join with funeral directors, florists, and others in the allied memorial fields in educating the general public, including clergymen and newspapermen, regarding the true meaning of memorialization, especially its religious significance.

The debate on how to handle the memorial society problem, what action to take, what stance to assume, reflected some basic differences of approach within the undertaking trade. *Casket & Sunnyside* called repeatedly for united action:

> We firmly believe that there is one best way to meet this threat as well as to counter the mushrooming growth of the memorial societies and the actual or threatened religious encroachments on our concept of funeral service. That is through the efforts of a highly skilled public relations firm to conduct an extensive public relations program on a national basis. Thus, purely unselfishly on our part, we have called on all funeral service and trade organizations to join in this common endeavor.

Mortuary Management advised lying low and saying little:

> We think a serious mistake has been made in parading around over the nation the figures of NFDA's economist, Eugene F. Foran. His average adult funeral service charge has been used for the purpose of telling the public that funerals are not too high. It is fine for the funeral director to possess this information for study but it is dangerous to spread it before the public. . . . Don't make the mistake of engaging in public arguments with memorial society representatives on television or radio to defend the present day American funeral program. That's like shooting craps with the other fellow's dice.

To the extreme annoyance of NFDA officials, the *Post* article was seized on by insurgents within the industry who had found price advertising and solicitation of prearranged funerals to be profitable.

In defiance of NFDA, some of these rushed into print with advertisements substantially agreeing with the *Post* article, offering "dignified funerals" at low costs and prearrangement programs. "Enemies from within!" cried the NFDA leadership, and a convention speaker, flourishing one of the advertisements, said, "The ad says that prearranging a funeral protects the family against sentimental overspending. Yes, there are funeral directors who go further than the most critical writers when they tell the world through their ads and brochures that the family must be protected against itself during the emotionally difficult funeral period."

The NFDA's line was essentially to hold fast, to refuse to have anything to do with the memorial societies, and above all to maintain price levels based on the Foran concept of "overhead per case." There are others who saw it differently. Mr. Wilber Krieger of National Selected Morticians, while yielding to none in his opposition to the funeral societies, thought that the industry had brought this development on itself by its lack of flexibility in "serving people as they wish to be served" and by its failure to meet a growing demand for prearranged and prefinanced funerals. In an address to the selected ones, he said, "Please don't go out and start shouting before the world, 'My cost per funeral is XXX dollars.' Who cares? More funeral directors do more damage in the public mind by talking all the time about this cost-per-funeral fallacy. Who cares about your costs? . . . I am greatly disturbed at what I am seeing across the country. . . ."

If the funeral industry was astir over the *Post* article, no less so were the funeral societies—and particularly the Bay Area Funeral Society. The board members had naturally been pleased that the society was to be the subject of a national magazine article, and had expected there would be some response from readers. But they were completely unprepared for what followed. The headquarters of the society, consisting of a desk and telephone in the building of the Berkeley Consumers Cooperative, was inundated with letters which poured in at the rate of a thousand a week. Volunteer crews were hastily assembled to help with the huge job of answering the letters and processing applications for membership. The editor of *The Saturday Evening Post* reported an equally astonishing flood of letters to the magazine. He commented, "The article seems to have touched a sensitive nerve." The three members of the Bay Area Society who were mentioned by name in the *Post,* Dr. Josiah Bartlett, Professor Griswold Morley, and I, received several hundred letters apiece within the first few weeks; more than a year later, letters were still arriving, sometimes apologetically prefaced, "I only just read 'Can You Afford to Die?' in an old copy of the *Post* at my barber's. . . ."

Even more surprising than the quantity of letters was their quality. Those who are by the nature of their work on the receiving end of letters from the general public—newspaper editors, radio commentators and the like—have told me that a good percentage of the letter writers are crackpots of some kind, that all too seldom does the solid citizen trouble himself to set down his views on paper. The opposite was true of these letters. In tone, they ran the gamut, some bitter, some funny, some reflective; but they were almost without exception intelligent—in many cases deeply thought out—comments on a subject about which the writers obviously felt most strongly. They were indeed evidence of a widespread public revulsion against modern funerary practices, the extent of which even the funeral society advocates had never fully realized. Another extraordinary thing about the hundreds of letters I received was that only one took the side of the funeral industry. It was full of invective, it bore no name, it was signed simply "An American Funeral Director." The Bay Area Funeral Society reported but three hostile letters out of the first eleven hundred.

Some of our correspondents had long since taken matters into their own hands. It seems that a variety of ingenious solutions to the problem were being tried. We learned of the "plain coffin" offered by the St. Leo Shop in Newport, Rhode Island: "For those who would not like to be caught dead in a plush-lined coffin, we offer the traditional plain box of pine, cedar or mahogany, with strong rope handles. Covered with cushions, it doubles as a storage chest and low seat, until needed for its ultimate purpose." And we learned of "the world's first do-it-yourself tombstone kit" offered by a South African inventor—"selling for a sum that is expected to shock traditional monument makers, whose prices generally start at ten times this figure."

We learned of two burial committees connected with Friends Meetings, one in Ohio, the other in Burnsville, North Carolina. When a member dies, the committee supplies a plain plywood box, places the body in it, and delivers it by station wagon to the crematory or medical school. The next of kin pays for the cost of the lumber in the box plus crematory charges and obituary notices. There is no charge for the committee's services, which include making the box. The total expense is generally under $250. The committee arranges for "help with the children or with food, a lift with the housework, hospitality for visiting relatives—a rallying of friends in a quiet coordinated way." A memorial service is generally held three or four days after death.

In the wake of the *Post* article, several other publications took up the subject of disposal of the dead, evoking in each instance spirited response from the funeral industry. The *Reader's Digest* of August 1961 ran an article, "Let the Dead Teach the Living," which pointed to a critical shortage of cadavers for anatomical study in medical schools. Said the *Reader's Digest*, "Every individual who bequeaths his remains to a medical school makes an important contribution to the advance of human knowledge."

Medical Economics, a national physicians' journal, carried a piece describing the participation of doctors in the funeral society movement. A Kentucky pediatrician is quoted as saying, "We should encourage people to use educational, health, or welfare funds as a memorial to the dead rather than throw a lot of money into a barbaric funeral ceremony complete with gussied-up bodies, expensive caskets, parades, and regalia." Said Mr. Howard C. Raether in a speech delivered to the NFDA convention: "The ultimate of all these programs is to give the entire body to medical science. With no body there is no funeral. If there are no funerals, there are no funeral directors. A word to the wise should be sufficient." Said the *National Funeral Service Journal,* "This is a practice that cannot openly be opposed without branding the funeral directors as being indifferent to the health and welfare of mankind. . . . The loss of a casket sale will create a financial blow in those cases where the body is contributed to a medical school. Fortunately, such cases are infrequent at the present time; unfortunately, they may become more frequent in the future."

After Words

Now again the funeral folk are gazing hopefully into a clouded crystal ball. By 1996 more bodies, not fewer, were being donated for medical research, leading those in the trade once more to spread untruths. Thomas Lynch, a Michigan undertaker, wrote in *The Undertaking: Life Studies from the Dismal Trade* (Norton, 1997): "The supply of cadavers for medical and dental schools in this land of plenty [has been] shamefully but abundantly provided for by the homeless and helpless, who were, for the most part, more 'fit' than Russ." Russ—after being discouraged from body donation—fit quite nicely in one of Mr. Lynch's caskets, the author was pleased to report. A quick check with the three medical schools in Michigan indicated that Wayne State and the University of Michigan at Ann Arbor have an "urgent need" for body donors; Michigan State University has a moderate need: "We can always use people."

Once the FTC Funeral Rule was passed in 1984, publicity and protest quieted down. Cremation was more readily obtained, and prices were available over the phone. The spirit of social activism that spurred the memorial societies lost its steam, and membership began to dwindle. In some areas, societies died out altogether. In other areas—where a favorable price had been negotiated with cooperating mortuaries—they flourished quietly.

News stories popped up occasionally when a cemetery or funeral establishment went out of business, the proprietor having absconded with the funds. Lisa Carlson's *Caring for Your Own Dead*—a state-by-state manual for those living in one of the forty-two states where it is legal to bypass the funeral industry entirely—was published by a small press and garnered good reviews, but it was not readily available in bookstores. The funeral industry continued to thrive with relatively little attention.

When the Funeral Rule was reopened for amendments in 1988, the media ignored the hearings. No one was there to hear the stories of continued consumer abuse at the hands of an industry that ignored the rule. No one was there to hear the pleas for bringing cemeteries under the rule. All seemed well for the industry.

But in the eighties—with AIDS deaths a near epidemic—a much younger generation was becoming involved with the final arrangements, and many didn't like what they found.

One of those was Karen Leonard. Her first foray into the realm of death care was as co-owner of a casket-and-urn "gallery" in San Francisco—Ghia—where one could purchase a work of art for the final resting place. Carlson thought that if people were going to purchase their own caskets, they might want a do-it-yourself guide for the rest of the funeral, and rushed off a carton of *Caring* for Ghia to display.

The gallery struggled and only a few books sold, but Leonard found herself surrounded by people with "new" ideas for the dying. Without exception, each had "horror stories" of unpleasant funeral experiences and were looking for more meaningful ways of "celebrating" a life once lived. It wasn't long before Leonard was introduced to the memorial society folks and began her funeral education in earnest.

Carlson began passing along the occasional media inquiry to Leonard. One was from a producer for "20/20." Undercover and with hidden camera, she was able to provide television audiences with a clear look at some of the less-than-ethical practices of the funeral trade.

The industry cried foul, saying that the portrayals were isolated incidents, but it was clearly stung.

The press began to take notice. In 1996 the magazine of the American Association of Retired Persons (AARP), *Modern Maturity*—which had avoided anything "downbeat" for years—finally ran a story on funeral planning. Kiplinger's *Personal Finance* and *Money Magazine* followed suit the next year.

The mood in the Dismal Trade grew nervous. The NFDA opened a Washington, D.C., office where its liaison spends time trotting around Capitol Hill—to win friends and influence people, in preparation for a possible reopening of the Funeral Rule.

A June 1997 editorial in *The Director* might have been written thirty-five years ago but for its let's-all-buck-up tone; President Maurice Newnam offers this fatherly counsel: "The importance of the memory picture created by the properly embalmed and restored loved one is something we must never lose sight of and never be ashamed to ask permission to do. . . . Hold your head high, take care in the work you do and be proud to be an embalmer."

Ron Hast (*Mortuary Management*, February 1997) is more candid: "Think about how the public must perceive funeral service as we caress our solid copper caskets, and extol the virtues of embalming and extended preservation. Our critics are gaining attention, and more and more client families come to us with skepticism. In fact, some clients seeking death care service don't come to us at all."

19

Pay Now—Die Poorer

"In the Depression years, every community had a form of pre-need," mused North Dakota funeral director Tom Fisher in a poolside chat with the author in 1995. "In my own community we had the Farmers Union Burial Cooperative Society."

The early funeral and memorial societies—most of them urban—expressed divergent views on the subject of paying for a funeral in advance. Many societies actively promoted "peace of mind by planning ahead," negotiating for fixed prices with cooperating mortuaries. Not all were willing to part with their money, however. The societies' *Bulletin* warned: "It always pays to plan ahead. It rarely pays to pay ahead."

Today, the need to shelter assets for Medicaid eligibility is another reason people pay for their funeral in advance. There are now no federal guidelines limiting the amount that may be set aside for a funeral. Many states—exercising their options as administrators of Medicaid—have set their own limits. Connecticut has set its limit at $4,800; California, $10,000. In New Jersey, the sky's the limit, and it need hardly be said that this is well known by the vendors of funeral services in that state. A hidden-camera "20/20" investigation captured an undertaker offering to accept $20,000 for a future funeral, assuring the client that any "extra" would be returned to the family.

Funeral directors have a strong motivation to sell ahead of time. Each funeral they have under wraps is one less that will go to a competitor. "A well-run, aggressive preneed program will increase a firm's market share," writes Thomas Barnard in the NFDA journal *The Director.* Given a nationwide proliferation of funeral homes, market share is a driving concern. According to the Funeral and

Memorial Societies of America, "If people died Monday through Friday with two weeks off for the mortician's vacation, the death rate in the U.S. could support 9,288 full-time funeral homes. Yet there are more than 22,000 mortuaries in this country. Many get only one or two funerals a week."

Do people spend more or less when they plan ahead? Prearranged funerals tend to be much less expensive than those arranged by sorrowing survivors, according to some reports. Howard C. Raether took note of this fact long ago at a National Funeral Directors Association convention. He was discussing an analysis of funeral sales: "If it were possible to tabulate all the prearranged funeral services on record, how do you suppose the average of all of them would compare with the average adult figure shown here?" (Average adult figure means average price of an adult's funeral.) "Are you ready, willing and able to become part of a program that is going to lower the quality of the average funeral service selected to the point where you will find it difficult if not impossible to stay in business rendering the service you now give?" He added, "It is good for those who survive to have the right and duty to make the funeral arrangements. Making such arrangements, having such responsibilities, is essential. It is part of the grief syndrome, part of the therapy of mourning. It is a positive hook upon which the hat of funeral service is hung. Why should we tear it down by saying the funeral is for the deceased, therefore he or she should make the arrangements? . . . If funeral directors insist on soliciting pre-need funerals, they are in fact prearranging the funeral of their profession."

More recent developments in the techniques of pre-need selling, a matter of prime importance to the trade, have proved Mr. Raether's dour prediction wrong. According to Ron Hast, that knowledgeable sage of the industry, people tend to be more gullible when seated comfortably in their own living rooms. "Pictures of beautifully displayed caskets are far less intimidating when shown to the prospect while sitting on the sofa than when they are presented in a mortuary's casket selection room. . . . They start to think of them as quality furniture. They will spend *more,* not less, on a prearranged casket."

In any case, those gloom and doom predictions on the impact of prearrangement have long since fallen on deaf ears. By 1995 no less than $20 billion was, according to *Consumers Digest* senior editor

John Wasik, tied down in prepaid funeral and cemetery plans. That estimate, outsized as it seems, is surely on the low side, because SCI alone today lays claim to holdings of $3.2 billion in prepayments.

Today, it is the corporate chains that are doing some of the most aggressive selling. What do they know that the public does not? And what can be wrong with paying in advance to guarantee prices?

Inflation is the bugbear that is used most effectively by the sellers of prepayment plans. In recent years, however, while inflation has been raising the cost of living generally by 2 to 3 percent annually, funeral costs have been increasing by 6 to 7 percent—which is more than the interest the mortuary is pocketing on your prepaid funeral contract. As the numbers pile up, funeral providers are becoming wary of the trap of the guaranteed price. The Midwestern owner of several funeral homes is quoted in the NFDA organ *The Director* as predicting: "Ninety-nine percent of the guaranteed preneeds will be performed at a loss." Likewise aware of the problem, *Funeral Service Insider* advises against guaranteeing prices on future contracts, suggesting the following disclaimer: "If the death benefits are less than the current retail price at the time of death, an additional amount of funds will be due." With an escape clause like that, you—the consumer—have saved no money with a pre-need arrangement. All you've done is paid part of the money in advance, and committed your survivors to pay the funeral director whatever he's charging at the time of death—eliminating the chance that your nearest and dearest will be free to shop around for a better deal.

If you have already purchased a guaranteed-price plan—which leaves you with the feeling that you've got a great deal because the local funeral home will take care of everything—then what?

It's a situation that invites abuse. The daughter of one Vermont woman, who a few years earlier had paid $3,000 for her funeral, was billed for an additional $1,000 service charge by the funeral home's new owner.

How else can the undertaker make up for funeral inflation on a prepaid contract? "Cash Advance" items—cost of the obituary (if there is a fee), the death certificate, flowers, or cemetery expenses—will not have been included in your funeral package. An SCI-owned funeral home charged a Denver husband $200 to fax four copies of his wife's obituary to area newspapers—where the obits ran for free.

A New York widow was told, "We'll take care of everything." The mortician charged her $175 to have her husband's date of death inscribed on the existing family monument. Actual cost of the inscription? $75.

Among the creative ideas currently favored by the industry, none is more profitable, nor more subject to abuse, than its appropriation of the legal fiction of "constructive delivery." Prepayment laws in most states require that prepaid funds be placed in trust. California, for example, requires 100 percent trusting, but, like many states, has a loophole wide enough to accommodate a Cadillac hearse. It exempts from the trust requirement monies paid in advance for the prepurchase of goods such as burial plots, vaults, markers, and so on—the bulk of the cost of burial—provided that the prepurchased items are stored or warehoused for the customer's future use. Constructive delivery is in reality no delivery, and it is the rare consumer who will have the wit to even try to ascertain whether or where the prepaid goods are being stored, let alone have the persistence to demand a glimpse of the items he or she presumably owns.

Neptune Society provides an instructive example of the invitation to large-scale fraud afforded by constructive delivery. A recent release by the California Department of Consumer Affairs announced that three of Neptune's eleven locations (San Pedro, Burbank, and Santa Barbara) were charged with "unprofessional conduct" for allegedly failing to place $12.6 million into a trust fund "or to maintain sufficient merchandise to match purchases." For this egregious fraud, Neptune must have been delighted to receive no more than the customary slap on the wrist in the form of three years' probation, during which they were permitted to remain in business. There is also an order to pay $55,000 to reimburse the department for costs, but nothing is said about reimbursing the consumer $12.6 million for the apparently misappropriated boodle.

Of the $12.6 million, $9 million was allegedly for the sale of caskets and urns. This is odd, because Neptune, numero uno in the for-profit cremation business, well knew that caskets are not required, nor are urns. Karen Leonard, however, has the videotape of a "Dateline NBC" program in which she participated, on which one of Neptune's top salespeople explained, in an expansive mood, that the law requires a casket (cost: $400), while in practice bodies are cremated in a shroud. This avid seller likewise explained that an urn is required by law (cost: $75), whereas a $2 cardboard box is used.

One of the biggest problems—and greatest opportunities for mischief—may be the choice of casket. Like automobiles, casket styles change often, sometimes as frequently as every six months. If your pre-need agreement specifies the "Tuscany H66813D" and the Tuscany H66813D is no longer available, your survivors may be asked, for an added fee, to select a different box.

A legal action now pending in Louisiana suggests that there may be far more serious problems in obtaining the benefits of a pre-need plan.

E. J. Ourso sold his fifteen funeral homes and funeral insurance company, Security Industrial, to Loewen in 1996 for a reported $180 million. One can only speculate on how the value of these properties was broken down in the negotiations over price, but it seems reasonable to guess that the funeral homes were worth no more than $3 million apiece, on average, or $45 million total. Given that assumption, Loewen paid about $135 million for the funeral insurance company.

Why would Loewen pay that much money to take over liability for funeral insurance policies—many of which were sold decades ago for $300 or less—guaranteeing to provide a funeral which today would cost many times that amount? Wouldn't they expect to lose a lot of money when people cash in the policies? Are these people saints? One can only guess, but it seems likely that Loewen expects to sell a lot of "extras" to the survivors.

At this writing, a class action has been filed. Undoubtedly, many versions of the "facts" will be argued before it is resolved. In the meantime, Peggy Porter of Baton Rouge—whose father is a claimant in the suit—wrote a lengthy letter to her state representative, describing the ordeals her family went through with an insurance policy that had promised to fully cover her mother's funeral. The letter is quoted in abridged form below:

Dear Mr. Dardenne,

Please accept this letter as a formal request to personally meet with you to discuss a matter of great importance to the elderly and the "baby boomers" of Louisiana. . . .

Hopefully, you won't send me a form letter telling me that another department handles such matters. I have tried them all. Earlier, I wrote to the La. State Insurance Commission, La. State Board of Embalmers and Funeral Directors, La. State Attorney General's Office, Jefferson Parish Attorney General's Office, New Orleans Better Business Bureau, Funeral Service Consumer Assistance Program and the Federal Trade Commission. . . .

The La. State Insurance Commission, although they are investigating my complaint, say that they do not have jurisdiction over such matters. They say the La. Board of Embalmers and Funeral Directors has control. This involves an insurance policy which should be under the control of the insurance commission. Pam Williams has said that because there have been so many complaints, there has been a task force set up to investigate these matters. This has been happening for more than 20 years. How long and how many complaints does it take to get action and restitution? Mr. and Mrs. Schwartz and my father are in their eighties. Time is running out.

The La. Board of Embalmers and Funeral Directors replied to my complaint by saying, in a "unanimous decision they found no apparent violation of the statutes, rules and/or regulations under which the board is empowered to operate." They also stated that the Board has no jurisdiction over "insurance" policies. I wasn't given the opportunity to appear and speak before this board made this decision. The La. Board of Embalmers and Funeral Directors is a farce. According to its Rules and Regulations, this board is made up of seven members appointed by the Governor. Six of those members are either embalmers or funeral directors and one is a consumer that must be at least 65 years old. A consumer doesn't have a chance. . . .

The Attorney General's Office says they are without jurisdiction over this matter, that all insurance matters are subject to regulation by the La. Insurance Commission and that these transactions are specifically exempted from the Unfair Trade Practices Act and Consumer Protection Law. How can such matters, which will at some time in their life affect almost every consumer, be exempt from the Unfair Trade Practices Act and Consumer Protection Law?

. . . In June 1942, my father purchased a funeral policy from Tharp-Sontheimer Life Insurance Company for my mother, Liberty Lemoine Feldheim, as well as one for himself. Later, in 1943 & 1945, he purchased one for each of his three daughters at a cost of approximately $218 per policy. Two hundred eighteen dollars does not seem like much, but in the 1940s, when your annual salary was approximately $3,000, it was quite a lot. As you can see, the policy included just about everything needed for a complete funeral. This policy was not purchased through a fast-talking salesman but from my grandfather, his father. I feel confident that my grandfather would not have sold these policies to family members and friends if he had known that it was a scam or fraudulent.

On April 15, 1996, my mother died. On April 16, 1996, my father and two sisters met with David Rogers with Tharp-Sontheimer, 1600 N. Causeway Boulevard, Metairie, La. In going over the arrangements they were shown one casket that he said was included in the policy. It looked as if it was covered in a felt material that resembled carpet padding (bits and pieces glued together) and that it might fall apart from the weight of a body. My father asked if he could pay extra for a better casket. They refused and said ANY changes in the casket voided the policy, but they would give a credit of $300 toward the cost of a more expensive funeral. This seems like the old "Bait and Switch" scam so widely used to swindle people.

My father then said he would take the original casket with the services offered in the policy and donate the casket to someone's family who couldn't afford one and purchase an additional casket. Again they refused. They stated that under a Federal Trade Commission ruling they were not allowed to substitute or upgrade a casket or even separate a casket from the services. (In a recent conversation with the FTC, I have been told there is no such ruling.)

Please note on the enclosed price list of caskets available, there are no Embossed Grey Tharson or Grey Analea Cloth

Covered Caskets, as specified on the policy. Since they were not listed, they were not available. Why were they only shown one casket when the policy specifically lists two caskets? How do we know that the one casket offered was one of the two specified in the policy? When asked which one it was, the Tharson or the Analea, they simply say it is the one that goes with the policy. Could it be Tharp-Sontheimer had already made their own substitutions in the caskets when they said they were not allowed to? What gives them the right to make their own substitutions without notification and/or approval of the policyholder?

. . . After several futile requests were made to have them allow us to pay for a better casket without voiding the rest of the services offered in the policy, my father and sisters, feeling both emotionally and physically drained, did what the funeral homes rely on them to do. They chose a different casket and the services they wished to have and in the end were given an invoice in the amount of $7,916.84 after the $300 credit. The cost of the chosen casket alone was $3,595.00 plus tax. From there they went to see David Rogers' supervisor and Chairman of the Board, Stephen Sontheimer, at the 4127 S. Claiborne Avenue, New Orleans office to plead their case. Having to deal with my mother's sudden death combined with five days of little to no sleep while at the hospital, we were all in emotional turmoil. At a time when compassion and understanding were most definitely needed, they found Mr. Sontheimer to be very arrogant, disrespectful and degrading. Mr. Sontheimer refused their repeated request and led them to believe that there was absolutely nothing he could do. Why would the insurance company and/or funeral home not allow you to purchase a different casket without voiding the rest of the benefits of the policy if it were not meant to be a scam of "Bait & Switch" or "Insurance Fraud." What harm could it do? We are aware of at least one New Orleans funeral home that has allowed such changes.

Enclosed is a copy of the invoice for my mother's funeral. As you can see, $7,916.84 is a far cry from the $218 he originally paid. There was no credit given for inflation, unless you want to consider the $82 difference in the amount paid and the face value. Do you honestly think that people would have purchased these policies if they would have known that they would be offered inferior merchandise or that all they would have been given was a $300 credit? They could have invested the original $218 in a regular savings account with a minimal interest rate and would have had several thousand dollars after 50 years. If you add the figures for the services originally offered in the policy and their respective costs today, from the Security Funeral Homes price lists and the invoice, the credit figure should have been more like $5,067.00.

My father bought these policies 50 years ago to protect himself and his family from having to face the high costs of funerals and possibly not having the funds to cover them. He did what he thought was right, he bought through an honest agent (his father) and from what he thought was a reputable and trustworthy company, Tharp-Sontheimer. In our extended family alone there are at least eight more of these policies yet to be used.

. . . Since the purchase of these policies in the '40s, Tharp-Sontheimer was bought out by Delta Life Insurance, Security Industrial Insurance Company and most recently The Loewen Group for $180 million. It proves that there was and still is definitely a lot of unsuspecting people of Louisiana being swindled out of money. This is very upsetting. Just recently *The Advocate* and the *Times-Picayune* praised E. J. Ourso, who owned Security Industrial Insurance, for his $15 million donation to an LSU Business School to be named in his honor. In one article he was quoted as saying, "I'm not up here through ambition, drive and persistence—two things got me here: her (Marjory's) fertility and compound interest." The truth is he was running a scam: Selling preneed burial policies, collecting people's nickels, dimes or quarters each week and, by his own admission, receiving interest on these monies, sometimes for as long as 50 years. When the time of "need" came there was usually some excuse or reason (usually involving the quality of the casket) which prevented the policy holder or his family from receiving the full benefits of the policy. All he did was pay the $300 or so and just pocketed all the interest. . . .

There was a recent suit between Tessier and Rabenhorst Funeral Home and Insurance where the appeals court ruled in favor of Tessier in a matter very similar to ours. There are also two other families I am aware of that are filing suits. Not everyone has the funds to file civil suits nor the stamina to follow through on their complaints when all they get are reply letters or people telling them that "it's not my job." Everyone keeps passing the "Buck." Most of the complaints have fallen through the cracks of Louisiana politics. When is this going to stop? When are Louisiana politicians going to stop their crooked ways and stand up for the people of Louisiana?

I hope you will use your resources and do a thorough investigation into this matter. You might be surprised how widespread this problem is in Louisiana. It is going to take new state laws governing the insurance and funeral industry to protect the people of Louisiana from these fraudulent activities. Teresa Fox, who lives in Kenner and also has a similar complaint, has been trying to get help for the past two years and has contacted her representative, Glenn Ansardi. Maybe if we all work together, it won't take another 20 years before changes can be made. . . .

Sincerely yours,
Peggy F. Porter
Enclosures

This situation in Louisiana may serve as an example of problems elsewhere. Lee Norrgard, consumer affairs analyst for AARP, has been monitoring the problems of prepaid funerals. In *Final Choices: Making End-of-Life Decisions* (ABC-CLIO, 1992) he writes: "Is there adequate consumer protection for buyers of preneed plans? At this point, the answer is no. Regulations, investigations, and auditing are minimal in most states. In at least one instance, some of the worst abuses surfaced as a result of private legal actions rather than state enforcement activities. . . . Buyer beware!"

The *Consumers Digest* article reports that "about $50 million in preneed funds was stolen or reported missing nationwide." As of 1997 only seven states had some sort of guarantee fund to protect consumers against such default: Florida, Indiana, Iowa, Missouri, Oregon, Vermont, and West Virginia.

Anyone who has paid for a funeral—or is thinking about it—should ask, "Where is the money invested and is it safe?" There are several ways to handle funeral financing in advance, some safer than others.

When you make out a check to the mortuary to pay for a pre-need funeral, there is *no* guarantee that the money will find its way to safe-keeping. One funeral director complained that he hadn't had a funeral in thirteen weeks and was worried about how to meet business obligations. When "Mildred" prepaid for her funeral, he used the money for his mortgage payments, despite the fact that the state required that 100 percent of the funds be placed in a federally insured institution. It's likely that he had every intention of taking care of Mildred when she died, but when the state finally put him out of business for other misdeeds, officials discovered that $150,000 in prepaid funeral money—including Mildred's—had vanished.

Few states require that all prepayments be placed in trust. Fewer still do any auditing. This is particularly true of cemetery prepayment and perpetual-care funds. The cemetery owners generally have unrestricted access, which accounts for the scandalously high incidence of misappropriation of endowment care funds. Without conscientious auditing, there can be no assurance that prepaid funds are safe. California, which is one of the few states that require 100 percent trusting of funeral prepayments, also leads the nation in the incidence and the magnitude of the thievery.

Perhaps most at risk are those in small towns—where everyone knows everyone—who place great trust in the local funeral director. In 1977, after receiving an estimate of $587 for the simple funeral she wanted, Annie Patterson sent a note to the man she thought of as "her" funeral director:

I will be sending a little each month as I am living on Social Security.

Annie told her children that "it was all taken care of," and—because she was a meticulous and responsible person—no one doubted her.

When Annie died almost twenty years later, "her" funeral director had already passed away. A son had taken over the business, but Annie's family felt comfortable calling the small-town funeral home she had trusted for her final care. The first sign of trouble came when they were told, "You know it will be more than $587, don't you?" When a final funeral bill was presented for $3,695, there was no mention of the $587 that had been prepaid, let alone any interest that might have accumulated. The family was shocked. A simple cremation and graveside service was all they had arranged. A scramble through Annie's shoe box of important papers turned up no receipts. Annie had never used checks; she always paid in cash.

Insurance policies generate a relatively low rate of appreciation. The seller gets a commission, and the insurance company pays itself to invest the funds. "Insurance-funded preneed arrangements are the fastest growing preneed product on the market," says Lee Norrgard. A number of funeral-related companies are getting into the funeral insurance business. "Forethought"—which is sold through funeral homes—is managed by the Batesville Casket Company and guarantees to "freeze" the wholesale price of the casket to your funeral home. But the low rate of growth on the policy—estimated at 3.63 percent—doesn't match overall funeral inflation. "I can handle that," said one undertaker, "because my prices are where they should be" (high, one would find) "and I don't mind guaranteeing the funeral price." Unless the funeral home chooses to make such a commitment, survivors may be hit with additional costs.

Master trusts set up by morticians' associations exist in thirty-two states. Only some of your prepaid funeral money may end up in the trust, depending on state law. Colorado, for example, requires a deposit of only 75 percent, allowing the funeral director or other sales agent to pocket a 25 percent commission. State associations that promote these trusts are paid a quarterly fee based on total investment—a strong motivation to push them. Commingled funds can be invested at a high rate of return which allows your account to grow at more than 5 percent on average while still covering the various fees. Some contracts use this growth to guarantee funeral goods and services; some do not. A few states permit a funeral home to withdraw an annual administrative fee, but most mortuaries leave it in the trust to grow, according to Nancy Gorchoff at the Access Financial Group, which manages such accounts for several states. The trust fund group takes care of reporting the interest. How much you get back if you were to cancel your arrangements would vary from state to state. Even the states that require 100 percent trusting permit the undertaker to claim an administrative fee.

A pay-on-death trust account at your local bank will give you the most control and flexibility. Sometimes called a "Totten Trust," it can be moved easily if you do; it's as safe as the bank it's in. Pennsylvania attorney David Morrison, who specializes in elder law, recommends that you name yourself, or a close friend or next of kin—not the mortuary—as the beneficiary.

Whether you choose an irrevocable funeral plan or not will depend on whether you need to shelter assets prior to applying for SSI or Medicaid. Morticians are always eager to sell an irrevocable funeral contract, especially if you have arranged for a rather elaborate exit. Most people think that when it's "irrevocable," the body is all but in the hearse, and some funeral directors may use the "irrevocable" ploy to keep the arrangements fixed.

When her father died at a very old age, P.F. decided to opt for an immediate cremation rather than the funeral with viewing for which he had already paid. All her father's friends had died, and the few scattered relatives would not be able to attend. When the funeral home refused to honor her request to change the plans, she walked out, then transferred the body—and the funeral funds—to another mortuary.

Mrs. S., after hearing a social worker at the senior center advise about protecting funeral money before ending up in a nursing home, promptly visited the local funeral director to make arrangements. She wanted to be embalmed before she was cremated, she said—just to make sure she was dead. The funeral director started adding various other charges to the list on his yellow legal pad (urn, urn vault, tent at the cemetery) until the total was over $3,200. Mrs. S., eager to protect her children from any worry or expense, wrote a check on the spot, made out to the local bank where her trust account would be held. But after a few weeks, she was troubled. She had selected cremation because she wanted to keep the cost down. A bill of $3,200 seemed like too much, so she wrote to the state Funeral Board. There was nothing the board could do, she was told—her plan was "irrevocable." Only after the intervention of the local memorial society—which pointed out numerous FTC violations in the transaction—and the help of an interested employee in the Department of Banking and Insurance did the funeral home agree to refund her money.

Irrevocable plans can almost always be transferred from one funeral home to another, but few morticians will offer this information. When Mrs. H. moved in, the nursing home insisted that funeral arrangements be made without delay. Her daughter—without any consultation—arranged for a $4,000-plus funeral at the only funeral home in town, written up in an irrevocable funeral contract and paid for from Mrs. H.'s own checking account. It had been difficult for Mrs. H. to manage her affairs—arthritis had taken away her sense of independence and control, and she'd depended on her daughter to write her checks, among other things. But she knew that the $4,000 funeral was not to her liking. With the help of a Senior Law Project attorney, she was able to transfer her "irrevocable" funeral plan to another funeral home. After writing up an irrevocable agreement for a $695 cremation, the new funeral director instructed the bank to refund the difference.

In short, an "irrevocable" trust does not require you to give up all rights to control your investment. If a funeral director attempts to take undue advantage of your situation, you may have legal recourse.

In most cases, shielding assets in order to qualify for government benefits is the only sound reason for paying for a funeral in advance. The only way to do that is with an irrevocable trust. But keep in mind that even though your trust account is irrevocable, you will be responsible for declaring the interest income because it will ultimately be used for your benefit. Mrs. M., in South Carolina, was irate: "The funeral home sent me a statement showing how much interest I'm supposed to declare on my income tax return. I don't have that money anymore, and when I die the funeral home will get it all. Why should I have to pay taxes?"

20

New Hope for the Dead

A t the June 1996 Nashville gathering of nonprofit funeral and memorial societies, Lisa Carlson—the executive director of the Funeral and Memorial Societies of America (FAMSA)—issued a call for social activism:

> If every mortuary in the country offered fair prices and a wide range of options, did not indulge in manipulation of the grieving, did not hide the low-cost caskets, did not dominate the funeral boards with self-serving regulations, did not limit the options for caring for your own dead in certain states or who can sell caskets, there would be no reason for our societies. We are the only national group monitoring the funeral industry for consumers. We have an obligation to protect the public at large, not just our members, especially given the high rate of noncompliance with the Funeral Rule.

The following year—with the cooperation of other consumer groups including AARP and the Consumer Federation of America—FAMSA petitioned the FTC to reopen the Funeral Rule for new amendments. Key objectives will be: to outlaw the nondeclinable fee, to legitimize private viewing of unembalmed bodies, to specify costs in connection with body donation, and to bring cemeteries under the coverage of the Funeral Rule. The situation will demand close attention from consumers, given the predictable response from the industry—which is happy, indeed, with the rule as it stands.

Who are these meddlesome do-gooders willing to take on a well-heeled and powerful industry? "Unitarians, Quakers, eggheads, and old farts who are nothing more than a middleman for the industry and a cheap funeral," was one glib characterization. Carlson cheer-fully acknowledged that she qualifies for "at least three of those four."

The practice of group planning for funeral arrangements started early in the century in the Farm Grange organization in the Northwestern United States. From there the idea spread to the cities, mainly under church leadership. The People's Memorial Association of Seattle, organized in 1939 by a Unitarian minister, was the first urban group. Organizations spread gradually along the coast, then eastward across the United States, and again northward into Canada. Vancouver boasts the largest such society today, with over 100,000 members.

By 1963 the societies had become a continent-wide movement, and the Cooperative League of the USA called a meeting in Chicago, where Canadian and American societies together formed the Continental Association of Funeral and Memorial Societies. Canadian societies later dropped out, and the name was changed to the "Funeral and Memorial Societies of America" in 1996.

Funeral planning and memorial societies generated public pressure that resulted in the 1984 Funeral Rule. But once members were convinced that consumers had what they needed, social activism waned. Only a few of the societies continued to conduct annual price surveys of area mortuaries. Many had negotiated discounts for members with cooperating establishments; as a cooperative buyer's club they had been very successful, and their memberships grew without fanfare. Smaller societies, staffed by volunteers, were still struggling; others went out of existence altogether.

John Blake, who lived in Egg Harbor, Wisconsin, knew nothing about memorial societies in 1986. That year, when his mother died in Bremerton, Washington, Blake flew out to arrange for her cremation. "The funeral director was going to burn a $150 box," Blake said. "My mother won't get into that," he told the funeral director with a chuckle. "She was a very frugal woman." So Blake and his son-in-law and two grandchildren built "a nice little box" with $20 worth of lumber. Only after her death did they discover that she had been a member of the People's Memorial Association. Had they known, the cost would have been even less.

Blake soon became involved in the Wisconsin societies. But the personal satisfaction of family participation remained a strong force in his life. When Lisa Carlson's *Caring for Your Own Dead* was published the next year, he felt that disseminating it through the societies was a matter of importance. It was on his urging that Carlson became involved in the society movement.

A new option had become available—handling all funeral arrangements without an undertaker, as had been the custom a century ago. The first edition of *Caring for Your Own Dead* sold 10,000 copies.

Karen Leonard—seduced into casket sales for the "fun" of it— soon found herself the director of the Redwood Funeral Society in Northern California. Taking a page from the funeral industry's own indispensable Grief Therapy mantra, she perceived the therapeutic benefits of caring for one's own dead. Jerri Lyons and others, with Leonard's support, started the Natural Death Care Project in 1996. They assisted families in handling nearly fifty deaths the very first year. Members from their group expect to establish similar projects in other states.

The option of caring for your own dead, if it takes hold, will mark a break with the trend towards ever-more-costly and -mechanically impersonal journeys to the grave. Which direction will the American public choose? On the one hand, there can be a return to funerals in the true American tradition, where friends and family do everything necessary without the intervention of so-called professionals; or, on the other, a further abdication of personal responsibility, where we accept the best and most costly merchandise the trade has to offer, not excluding absurdities such as Batesville's Burping Casket.*

---

*So-called protective caskets, having been heavily merchandised over the years, now outsell all other burial receptacles combined. Ask a funeral director why someone already dead will need protection, and he will, if he follows the manufacturer's script, reply with severity, "To prevent alien and foreign objects from reaching your loved one." There is one Southern mortician who, following his own drummer, has reduced the explanation to: "To keep bugs and critters out." But as with any lucrative idea that has not been thought through, the casket manufacturers and the undertakers who serve as their exclusive distributors soon had to face up to the consequences. Protective caskets, which command substantially higher prices than those that are "unprotected," achieve protection by using an impermeable, inexpensive rubber gasket as a sealing device. This causes a buildup of methane gas, a byproduct of the metabolism of anaerobic bacteria, which, thriving in an airless environment, have a high old time with the contents of the sealed casket. Exploding-casket episodes occurred with sufficient frequency to induce Batesville, the acknowledged leader in the field, to design a new line of protective caskets to deal with the crisis. A "permeable" seal is used, which lets the accumulated gases leak—or "burp"—out, to prevent the buildup of gas that causes the lids to blow off (and the appalled relatives to go to court).

On the East Coast, after months of persistence by Byron Blanchard of the Boston-based Memorial Society, the Public Health Department conceded, in the summer of 1996, that consumers had a legal right to care for their own dead. A regulation promulgated by the Funeral Board—requiring a funeral director to obtain the disposition permit—had been declared illegal in 1909 but had nonetheless remained on the books.

FAMSA has taken on the daunting task of monitoring funeral laws countrywide. Aware that not everyone will opt to handle all funeral arrangements without a mortician, they stand ready to assume the cause of the consumer's right to choose meaningful and affordable funerals. At Carlson's prodding, societies are doing more price surveys and checking for FTC compliance. The FAMSA office serves as a clearinghouse for consumer complaints and maintains a Web site with a wide range of funeral information: www.funerals.org/famsa.

That spirit of social activism has attracted new resources. Lamar Hankins, a Texas lawyer with a history of contributing pro bono time to social issues, is typical. He is working to build an endowment for a legal fund to assist consumers—those with few other options, or residents of states where issues have national implications. Individual societies—many of which had been somnolent for the last decade—are responding with enthusiasm to the renewed spirit of activism, and new societies are emerging.

By 1997—with more and more commercial cremation businesses calling themselves "Societies"—the nonprofit societies felt they were undergoing an identity crisis. The "Ohio Cremation and Memorial Society," for example, was attracting customers who thought it represented the well-respected nonprofit consumer group. As a result, FAMSA is encouraging member societies to change their names to "Funeral Consumer Information Society of ———."

The name change also reflects a broader base of interest. Those who join are not just those choosing immediate burial or cremation with a memorial service; even those planning a funeral with the casket present are avoiding funeral excess by seeking society help. Larry Burkett, founder of Christian Financial Concepts, admonishes his following to live without debt; that includes funeral debt. On a weekly show syndicated to more than six hundred stations, Burkett—a member of the Atlanta, Georgia, society—has commended the societies. After a half-hour interview with Carlson in January 1997, the FAMSA phones were flooded with inquiries about how to contact a local society.

Men and women who support legislative changes and see the need for an ongoing watch of the funeral industry will want to get involved in society activities. For those seeking alternatives to a costly funeral, a onetime lifetime membership in one of the nonprofit societies will offer up-to-date local price information.

What is to be done if at the time of crisis you are unable to reach a memorial or funeral society? Send a friend to two or more mortuaries to obtain their general price lists and casket prices. Ask for the cost of direct cremation, including transportation costs and crematory fees. Likewise, for the cost of immediate burial. Pay no money in advance. If death has not yet occurred and you wish to pay in installments, do so by setting up a Totten Trust, naming yourself or a relative or close friend as beneficiary. Remember, above all, that many funeral homes have a "no-walk" policy, which means simply that if and when you start to walk out, the price will come down, down, down until a level acceptable to you is reached.

Directory of Not-for-Profit
Funeral and Memorial Societies

Memorial and funeral planning societies do area price surveys and may have negotiated a discount for members. Request a brochure for affordable funeral options. Most societies are run by volunteers. Consequently, the phone numbers in this directory may change from time to time. If you have difficulty contacting a society, you may call the FAMSA office at 1-800-765-0107. If there is no society nearby, you may join Friends of FAMSA and receive benefits until a new society is launched.

In the United States

Alabama

Call the FAMSA office

Alaska

Anchorage   Cook Inlet Memorial   907-566-3732
  P.O. Box 102414, 99510

Arizona

Phoenix   Valley Memorial Society   602-929-9659
  P.O. Box 0423, Chandler, 85244-0423

Prescott   Memorial Society of Prescott   520-778-3000
  P.O. Box 1090, 86302-1090

Tucson   Memorial Society of Southern Arizona   520-721-0230
  P.O. Box 12661, 85732-2661

Arkansas

Fayetteville   NW Arkansas Memorial Society   501-443-1404
  P.O. Box 3055, 72702-3055

California

Arcata   Humboldt Funeral Society   707-822-8599
  P.O. Box 856, 95518

Bakersfield   Kern Memorial Society   805-854-5689
  P.O. Box 1202, 93302-1202   805-366-7266

Berkeley   Bay Area Funeral Society   510-841-6653
  P.O. Box 264, 94701-0284

Fresno   Valley Memorial Society
  P.O. Box 101, 93707-0101

Los Angeles   Los Angeles Funeral Society   818-683-3545
  P.O. Box 92313, Pasadena, CA 91109-2313   818-683-3752

Modesto   Stanislaus Memorial Society   209-521-7690
  P.O. Box 4252, 95352-4252

Palo Alto   Funeral and Memorial Planning
  Society   650-321-2109
  P.O. Box 60448, 94306-0448   888-775-5553

Sacramento   Sacramento Valley Memorial
  Society   916-451-4641
  P.O. Box 161688, 95816-1688

San Diego   San Diego Memorial Society   619-293-0926
  P.O. Box 16336, 92176

San Luis Obispo   Central Coast Memorial
  Society   805-543-6133
  P.O. Box 679, 93406-0679

Santa Barbara   Channel Cities Memorial
  Society   805-640-0109
  P.O. Box 1778, Ojai, CA 93024-1778   800-520-PLAN

Santa Cruz   Funeral and Memorial Society of
  Monterey Bay   408-426-3308
  P.O. Box 2900, 95063-2900

Sebastopol   Redwood Funeral Society   707-824-8360
  7735 Bodega Ave., #4, 95473

Stockton   San Joaquin Memorial Society   209-465-2741
  P.O. Box 4832, 95204-4832

Colorado

Denver   Rocky Mountain Memorial Society   303-759-2800
  4101 E. Hampden Ave., 80222

Connecticut

Bridgewater   Funeral Consumer Information
  Society of Connecticut   860-350-4921
  P.O. Box 34, 06752

Delaware

Served by Memorial Society of Maryland

District of Columbia

Washington   Memorial Society of Metropolitan
Washington   202-234-7777
1500 Harvard St. NW, 20009

Florida

Cocoa Funeral and Memorial Society of Brevard County	407-453-4109
P.O. Box 276, 32923-0276	407-636-3363
DeBary Funeral Society of Mid-Florida	904-789-1682
P.O. Box 392, 32713-0392	407-668-6822
Ft. Myers Funeral and Memorial Society of Southwest Florida	941-743-0109
P.O. Box 7756, 33911-7756	
Gainesville Memorial Society of Alachua County	352-378-3432
P.O. Box 14662, 32604-4662	
Orlando Memorial and Funeral Society of Greater Orlando	407-677-5009
P.O. Box 953, Goldenrod, FL 32733-0953	
Palm Beach Gardens Palm Beach Funeral Society	561-659-4881
P.O. Box 31982, 33420	
Pensacola and Fort Walton Beach Funeral and Memorial Society of Pensacola and West Florida	904-477-8431
7804 Northpointe Blvd., 32514	
Sarasota Memorial Society of Sarasota	941-953-3740
P.O. Box 15833, 34277-5833	
St. Petersburg Suncoast-Tampa Bay Memorial Society	813-898-3294
719 Arlington Ave. North, 33701	
Tallahassee Funeral and Memorial Society of Leon County	850-224-2082
1006 Buena Vista Dr., 32304	

Tampa   Memorial Society of Tampa Bay
45 Katherine Blvd., #307, Palm Harbor, 34684-3648

Georgia

Atlanta   Memorial Society of Georgia   404-634-2896
1911 Cliff Valley Way NE, 30329   800-840-4339

Macon   Middle Georgia Chapter   912-477-1691
4825 Brittany Dr., 31210

Hawaii

Honolulu   Memorial Society of Hawaii   808-946-6822
2510 Bingham St., Room A, 96826

Idaho

Boise   Idaho Memorial Association   208-343-4581
P.O. Box 1919, 83701-1919

Illinois

Chicago   Chicago Memorial Association
P.O. Box 2923, 60690-2923

Urbana   Champaign County Memorial Society
309 West Green St., 61801

Indiana

Bloomington   Bloomington Memorial Society   812-332-3695
2120 North Fee Lane, 47408

Indianapolis   Indianapolis Memorial Society
5805 East 56th St., 46226

Valparaiso   Memorial Society of Northwest
Indiana   219-464-3024
P.O. Box 329, 46384-0329

Iowa

Iowa City   Memorial Society of Iowa River
Valley   319-338-2637
120 North Dubuque St., 52245

For all other areas, call the FAMSA office

Kansas

Check Missouri or call the FAMSA office

Kentucky

Louisville   Memorial Society of Greater Louisville
  P.O. Box 5326, 40255-5326

Louisiana

Baton Rouge   Memorial Society of Greater Baton Rouge
  8470 Goodwood Ave., 70806

For other areas, call the FAMSA office

Maine

Auburn   Memorial Society of Maine   207-786-4323
  P.O. Box 3122, 04212-3122

Maryland

Bethesda   Memorial Society of Maryland   800-564-0017
  9601 Cedar Lane, 20814

Massachusetts

Boston   The Memorial Society   617-859-7990
  66 Marlborough St., 02116

East Orleans   Memorial Society of Cape Cod   508-862-2522
  P.O. Box 1375, 02643-1375   800-976-9552

New Bedford   Memorial Society of SE Mass.   508-994-9686
  71 Eighth St., 02740

Springfield   Memorial Society of Western Mass.   413-783-7987
  P.O. Box 2821, 01101-2821

Michigan

Ann Arbor   Memorial Advisory and Planning
  Society   313-665-9516
  2030 Chaucer Dr., 48103

Detroit   Greater Detroit Memorial Society   313-886-0998
  P.O. Box 24054, 48224-4054

Flint   Memorial Society of Flint   810-239-2596
  P.O. Box 4315, 48504-4315

For all other areas, call the FAMSA office

Minnesota

St. Cloud   Minnesota Funeral and Memorial
  Society   320-252-7540
  717 Riverside Dr. SE, 56304

Mississippi

Call the FAMSA office

Missouri

Kansas City　Funeral and Memorial Society of
　　Greater Kansas City　　　　　　　　　　816-561-6322
　　4500 Warwick Blvd., 64111

St. Louis　Memorial and Planned Funeral
　　Society　　　　　　　　　　　　　　　314-997-9819
　　216 East Argonne Ave., 63122-4310

Montana

Billings　Memorial Society of Montana　　406-252-5065
　　1024 Princeton Ave., 59102

Malta　Funeral Consumer Information Society
　　of Montana　　　　　　　　　　　　　406-654-2158
　　P.O. Box 377, 59538

Missoula　Five Valleys Burial Memorial
　　Association　　　　　　　　　　　　　406-543-6952
　　405 University Ave., 59801

Nebraska

Call the FAMSA office

Nevada

Reno　Memorial Society of Western Nevada　702-329-7705
　　P.O. Box 8413, University Station, 89507-8413

New Hampshire

Epping　Memorial Society of New Hampshire　603-679-5721
　　P.O. Box 941, 03042-0941

New Jersey

Cherry Hill　Memorial Society of South Jersey
　　401 Kings Highway North, 08034

East Brunswick　Raritan Valley Memorial
　　Society　　　　　　　　　　　　　　　732-572-1470
　　176 Tices Lane, 08816

Lincroft　Memorial Association of Monmouth
　　County　　　　　　　　　　　　　　　732-842-2251
　　1475 West Front St., 07738

Madison   Morris Memorial Society   973-540-9140
  P.O. Box 509, 07940-0509

Montclair   Memorial Society of Essex   973-783-1145
  P.O. Box 1327, 07042-1327

Paramus   Central Memorial Society   201-843-4168
  156 Forest, 07652

Plainfield   Memorial Society of Plainfield   908-889-5377
  520 William St., Scotch Plaines, 07076-1910

Princeton   Princeton Memorial Association   609-924-5525
  48 Roper Road, 08540   609-924-1604

New Mexico

Albuquerque   Funeral Consumer Information
Society of Northern New Mexico
9701 Admiral Dewey NE, 87111

Las Cruces   Memorial and Funeral Society of
Southern New Mexico   505-526-7761
P.O. Box 6531, 88006-6531

New York

Albany   Memorial Society of Hudson-Mohawk
Region   518-465-9664
405 Washington Ave., 12206-2604

Binghamton   Southern Tier Memorial Society
183 Riverside Dr., 13905

Buffalo   Greater Buffalo Memorial Society   716-885-2136
695 Elmwood Ave., 14222-1601   716-837-8636

Corning   Memorial Society of Greater Corning   607-962-7132
P.O. Box 23, Painted Post, 14870-0023   607-936-6563

Farmingdale   Memorial Society of Long Island   516-541-6587
P.O. Box 3495, 11735-0694

Ithaca   Ithaca Memorial Society   607-273-8316
P.O. Box 134, 14851-0134

New Hartford   Mohawk Valley Memorial
Society   315-797-2396
P.O. Box 322, 13413-0322   315-735-6268

New York   Memorial Society of Riverside
Church   212-870-6785
490 Riverside Dr., 10027

New York   Community Church of New York
   Funeral Society   212-683-4988
   40 East 35th St., 10016

Poughkeepsie   Mid-Hudson Memorial Society   914-229-0241
   249 Hooker Ave., 12603

Rochester   Rochester Memorial Society   716-461-1620
   220 Winton Road South, 14610

Syracuse   Syracuse Memorial Society   315-446-0557
   P.O. Box 67, De Witt, 13214-0067

White Plains   Westchester Funeral Planning
   Association   914-946-1660
   Rosedale Ave. and Sycamore Lane, 10605

North Carolina

Asheville   Blue Ridge Memorial Society   704-669-2587
   P.O. Box 2601, 28802-2601

Chapel Hill   Memorial Society of the Triangle   919-942-6695
   P.O. Box 1223, 27514-1223

Greensboro   Piedmont Memorial and Funeral
   Society   910-674-5501
   5137 Charleston Road, Pleasant Garden, 27313

Wilmington   Memorial Society of the Lower
   Cape Fear
   P.O. Box 4262, 28406-4262

North Dakota
See South Dakota

Ohio

Akron   Memorial Society of Akron-Canton
   Area   330-836-4418
   3300 Morewood Road, 44333   330-849-1030

Cincinnati   Memorial Society of Greater
   Cincinnati   513-281-1564
   536 Linton St., 45219

Cleveland   Cleveland Memorial Society   216-751-5515
   21600 Shaker Blvd., Shaker Heights, 44122

Columbus   Memorial Society of the Columbus
   Area   614-436-8911
   P.O. Box 14835, 43214-4835

Toledo   Memorial Society of Northwest Ohio   419-475-1429
2210 Collingwood Blvd., 43620-1147

Oklahoma

All Oklahoma cities call 1-800-371-2221

Oregon

Madras   Oregon Memorial Association   541-475-5520
P.O. Box 649, 97741 (Cities in Oregon)   888-475-5520

Pennsylvania

Erie   Memorial Society of Erie   814-456-4433
P.O. Box 3495, 16508-3495

Harrisburg   Memorial Society of Greater
Harrisburg   717-564-8507
1280 Clover Lane, 17113

Philadelphia   Memorial Society of Greater
Philadelphia   215-567-1065
2125 Chestnut St., 19103

Pittsburgh   Pittsburgh Memorial Society   412-621-4740
605 Morewood Ave., 15213

State College   Memorial Society of Central
Pennsylvania   814-237-7605
780 Waupelani Dr. Ext., 16801

Rhode Island

East Greenwich   Memorial Society of Rhode
Island
119 Kenyon Ave., 02818

South Carolina

Columbia   Memorial Society of the Midlands   803-772-7054
1716 Ashford Lane, 29210

South Dakota

Lemmon   Funeral Consumer Information
Society of the Dakotas   605-374-5336
HCR 66, Box 10, Lemmon, 57638

Tennessee

Chattanooga   Memorial Society of Chattanooga   423-624-2985
3224 Navajo Dr., 37411

Knoxville   East Tennessee Memorial Society
  P.O. Box 10507, 37939

Nashville   Middle Tennessee Memorial Society   615-329-0823
  1808 Woodmont Blvd., 37215   888-254-3872

Texas

Austin   Austin Memorial and Burial
  Information Society   512-480-0555
  P.O. Box 4382, 78765-4382

Corpus Christi   Memorial Society of Southern
  Texas   1-800-371-2221
  3125 Horne Road, 78415

Dallas, Denton, Fort Worth, Lubbock, Tyler, Wichita Falls
  Memorial Society of North Texas   214-528-6006
  4015 Normandy, Dallas, 75205   (TX/OK) 800-371-2221

Houston   Houston Area Memorial Society   713-526-4267
  5200 Fannin St., 77004-5899

San Antonio   San Antonio Memorial Society   210-341-2213
  7150 Interstate 10 West, 78213

Waco   Memorial Society of Northern Texas,
  Central Texas Chapter
  4209 North 27th St., 76708-1509   (TX/OK) 1-800-371-2221

Utah

Call the FAMSA office

Vermont

Chester   Southeast Branch, Vermont
  Memorial Society   802-875-3192

Hinesburg   P.O. Box 457, 05461   (VT) 800-805-0007

Sheffield   Northeast Branch, Vermont
  Memorial Society   802-626-8123

Virginia

Arlington   Memorial Society of Northern
  Virginia   703-271-9240
  4444 Arlington Blvd., 22204

Charlottesville   Memorial Planning Society of
  Piedmont   804-293-8179
  717 Rugby Road, 22903

Glen Allen   Funeral Consumer Information
 Society of Virginia   804-745-3682
 P.O. Box 3712, 23058-3712

Virginia Beach   Memorial Society of Tidewater   757-428-6900
 P.O. Box 4621, 23454-4621

Washington

Seattle   People's Memorial Association   206-325-0489
 2366 Eastlake Ave. East, #409, 98102

Spokane   Spokane Memorial Association   509-924-8400
 P.O. Box 13613, 99213-3613

Yakima   Funeral Association of Central
 Washington   509-248-4533
 1916 North Fourth St., 98901

West Virginia

Northeast area served by the Maryland Society

Wisconsin

Egg Harbor   Memorial Societies of Wisconsin   920-868-3136OA
 6900 Lost Lake Road, 54209-9231   (WI) 800-374-1109

Milwaukee   Funeral Consumer Information
 Society of Greater Milwaukee
 13001 West North Ave., Brookfield, 53005   414-782-3535

Wyoming

Call the FAMSA office

In Canada

Alberta

Calgary   Calgary Co-op Memorial Society   403-248-2044
 216 Marpole Bay NE, T2A 4W9

Edmonton   Memorial Society of Edmonton and
 District   403-944-0196
 10242-105th St., T5J 3L5

Red Deer   Memorial Society of Red Deer and
 District   403-340-1021
 Box 817, T4N 5H2

British Columbia

Vancouver Area   Memorial Society of British
  Columbia   604-527-1012
  #212 - 624 Sixth St., New Westminster, V3L 3C4

Manitoba

Winnipeg   Funeral Planning/Memorial Society
  of Manitoba   204-452-7999
  661 Jubilee Ave., R3L 1P5

New Brunswick

Fredericton   Memorial Society of New
  Brunswick
  P.O. Box 622, E3B 5A6

Ontario

Belleville   Memorial Society of Quinta   613-968-7640
  16 Linton Park Road, K8N 4K9

Guelph   Memorial Society of Guelph   519-822-7430
  P.O. Box 1784, N1H 7A1

Hamilton   Funeral Advisory Society of
  Hamilton District   905-389-8240
  P.O. Box 89026, L8S 4R5

Kingston   Memorial Society of Kingston   613-531-8948
  c/o Burdsall, 960 Killarney Cr., K7M 8C6

Kitchener   Memorial Society of Kitchener-
  Waterloo   519-579-3800
  P.O. Box 113, N2G 3W9   (Cambridge) 519-653-5705

London   Memorial Society of London   519-472-0670
  P.O. Box 1729, N6A 5H9

Niagara   Niagara Peninsula Memorial Society 905-358-5060
  P.O. Box 21021, L2E 6Z2

Ottawa   Ottawa Memorial Society   613-828-4926
  1903-1025 Richmond Road, K2B 8G8

Peterborough   Funeral Planning Association 705-742-0550
  P.O. Box 1795, K9J 7X6

Sudbury   Memorial Society of Northern
  Ontario   705-673-5532
  c/o Maitland, 384 Van Horne St., P3B 1J3

Thunder Bay   Memorial Society of Thunder Bay   801-683-3051
P.O. Box 501, P7C 4W4

Toronto Area   Funeral Advisory and Memorial
Society   416-241-6274
55 Saint Phillips St., Etobicoke, M9P 2N8

Windsor   Memorial Society of Windsor District   519-969-6767
P.O. Box 481, N9A 6M6   519-966-1064

Quebec

Montreal   L'Association Commemorative
Funeraire de Montreal   514-485-8527
P.O. Box 881, NDG Sub N, H4A 3S3

Saskatchewan

Lloydminster   Lloydminster-Vermilion Memorial
Society   306-825-3769
4805 47th St., S9V 0K2

Saskatoon   Memorial Society of Saskatchewan   306-374-5190
P.O. Box 1846, S7K 3S2

Index

Index

Index